Women and the Mathematical Mystique

Volumes based on the annual Hyman Blumberg Symposia
on Research in Early Childhood Education
Julian C. Stanley, general series editor

Women and the Mathematical Mystique

PROCEEDINGS OF THE EIGHTH ANNUAL
HYMAN BLUMBERG SYMPOSIUM
ON RESEARCH IN EARLY CHILDHOOD EDUCATION

EXPANDED VERSION OF A SYMPOSIUM
OF THE AMERICAN ASSOCIATION FOR THE
ADVANCEMENT OF SCIENCE ENTITLED "WOMEN
AND MATHEMATICS"

EDITED BY LYNN H. FOX, LINDA BRODY, AND DIANNE TOBIN

THE JOHNS HOPKINS UNIVERSITY PRESS
BALTIMORE AND LONDON

The Johns Hopkins University Press, Baltimore, Maryland 21218
The Johns Hopkins Press Ltd., London

Library of Congress Cataloging in Publication Data

Hyman Blumberg Symposium on Research in Early Childhood Education, 8th, Johns Hopkins
    University, 1976.
    Women and the mathematical mystique.

    (Studies of intellectual precocity; no. 5)
    "Expanded version of a symposium of the American Association for the Advancement of
Science entitled 'Women and mathematics.'"
    Includes index.
    1. Women in mathematics—Congresses. 2. Women mathematicians—Congresses. 3. Sex
differences in education—Congresses. 4. Mathematics—Study and teaching—Congresses.
I. Fox, Lynn H., 1944- II. Brody, Linda. III. Tobin, Dianne. IV. American Association for the
Advancement of Science. V. Title. VI. Series.
QA27.5.H95 1976   370.15'6   79-3655
ISBN 0-8018-2341-2
ISBN 0-8018-2361-7 pbk.

CONTENTS

TABLES

FIGURES

CONTRIBUTORS

Linda Brody is a project associate of the Intellectually Gifted Child Study Group at The Johns Hopkins University, Baltimore, Maryland 21218.

Patricia Lund Casserly is a research associate in the Developmental Research Division of the Educational Testing Service, Princeton, New Jersey 08540.

Sanford J. Cohn is an instructor of special education at Arizona State University, Tempe, Arizona 85281.

John Ernest is a professor of mathematics at the University of California, Santa Barbara, California 93106.

Elizabeth Fennema is an associate professor of education at the University of Wisconsin, Madison, Wisconsin 53706.

Lynn H. Fox is an associate professor of education and coordinator of the Intellectually Gifted Child Study Group at The Johns Hopkins University, Baltimore, Maryland 21218.

Ravenna Helson is an associate research psychologist at the Institute for Personality Assessment, University of California, Berkeley, California, 94720.

Abraham S. Luchins is a professor of psychology at the State University of New York, Albany, New York 12222.

Edith H. Luchins is a professor of mathematical sciences at Rensselaer Polytechnic Institute, Troy, New York 12181.

Carolyn T. MacDonald is Advanced Institutional Development Program coordinator at Rockhurst College, Kansas City, Missouri 64110.

Lucy W. Sells is a National Science Foundation-funded public-service science resident, Math/Science Network, Berkeley, California 94708.

Dianne Tobin is a project associate of the Intellectually Gifted Child Study Group at The Johns Hopkins University, Baltimore, Maryland 21218.

Throughout this book the support and encouragement of significant others is mentioned as an important factor in the lives of young women. The editors of this volume would like to dedicate this book to our own supportive parents:

Gertrude and Harry Hussey
Ruth and William Erdmann
Ruth and Solomon Hodas

PREFACE

This is the eighth volume in the series based on the annual Hyman Blumberg Symposium on Research in Early Childhood Education and the fifth one concerned with intellectual talent, in this case sex differences in mathematical talent and achievement. Thus, it is the fifth volume in the Studies of Intellectual Precocity series. This volume is based substantially on revised and updated versions of papers presented at the Hyman Blumberg Symposium, cosponsored by the American Association for the Advancement of Science in Boston in February 1976. That symposium was organized and chaired by Lynn H. Fox.

We are greatly indebted to the Amalgamated Clothing Workers of America for a sizable endowment to The Johns Hopkins University, the income from which helped finance this symposium. We would also like to acknowledge the support of the Spencer Foundation, which has funded research by the Study of Mathematically Precocious Youth and the Intellectually Gifted Child Study Group (IGCSG) at The Johns Hopkins University. The Robert Sterling Clark Foundation also supported intervention work by the IGCSG described in this volume. Several chapters report data from research funded by the National Science Foundation.

We would like to thank Ilse Harrop, former secretary to the IGCSG, for her careful attention to detail and consistency in the preparation of the manuscript. We have also benefited greatly from the encouragement and comments of Julian C. Stanley, general editor of the Blumberg series.

INTRODUCTION

Lynn H. Fox

In those languages that assign gender to words, the word *mathematics* is feminine, but *mathematician,* meaning the studier or doer of mathematics, is masculine. Herein lies the crux of the mathematical mystique. Is the world of mathematicians truly a masculine domain, into which women must venture with caution and trepidation? Are women who have entered it more "masculine" than other women? In what ways do females differ from males with respect to mathematical achievement and ability? To what extent can these differences be attributed to the self-fulfilling prophecy and socialization experiences at home and in school that reinforce the mathematical mystique? What research evidence suggests ways to remediate the results of or prevent the avoidance of the study of mathematics and careers in which high-level mathematical skills are required?

In recent years there has been a growing interest in sex differences in abilities, interests, and achievement among children, adolescents, and adults. At meetings of the American Psychological Association, the American Educational Research Association, the Association for Women in Mathematics, and the National Council of Teachers of Mathematics the issue of sex differences in mathematical talent and achievement has been discussed more than once. The purpose of this volume is to bring together the opinions and data collected by mathematicians, mathematics educators, psychologists, and sociologists on the topic of women and mathematics. It is hoped that the combined research of scholars with different perspectives will clarify the issues and lead to better future research, as well as generate ideas for change.

A well-known psychologist once said to a graduate student, "I like to see women psychologists doing research on sex differences—that leaves all the important research for the men." Is research on sex differences really unimportant or of interest only to feminists? The chapters in this volume seem to suggest otherwise. Research on sex differences can serve two important functions. First, it may improve the productivity and satisfaction with life of at least half the world's population—women. Second, research on sex differences can contribute insight into other theoretical and applied questions being researched in the fields of mathematics education; sociology; and developmental, social, cognitive, educational, and personality psychology. Indeed, to seek the reasons why men and women may differ with respect to interest in the study of and the pursuit of careers related to mathematics is to study a vast number of interesting and important questions about human behavior.

The text that follows is divided into four sections. The first, entitled "Female Mathematicians," includes two studies that focus on adult mathematicians. In chapter 2 Edith and Abraham Luchins delve into characteristics, development, and problems of women who pursue careers as mathematicians. In chapter 3 Ravenna Helson explores the personality profiles of creative women mathematicians and compares them with their male peer group and other, less creative women in their field. Together, these chapters provide the reader with insight into how difficult the road to professional success in mathematics can be. The study reported by Luchins and Luchins was funded by the National Science Foundation, and Helson's work was conducted at the Institute for Personality Assessment Research, University of California at Berkeley.

The second section, entitled "Sex Differences in Mathematics Achievement and Course-taking," explores the question of the nature, extent, and possible causes of sex differences in mathematics achievement. In chapter 4, John Ernest views the problem from his perspective as a male mathematician and college professor who became curious as to the whys and hows of differences in mathematical interest and attainment at all educational levels. In chapter 5, sociologist Lucy Sells examines the parallels between women and minorities with respect to course-taking in high school and subsequent barriers to career access. In chapter 6, Elizabeth Fennema reviews the literature on sex differences, particularly studies dealing with large populations, such as Project Talent. She relates these studies to her own efforts to identify affective correlates to differential course-taking and achievement among junior- and senior-high-school students in Madison, Wisconsin. This study was funded by the National Science Foundation. The last chapter of this section, chapter 7, written by me and Sanford Cohn, reports the sex differences found among mathematically precocious youths in the eight years of research conducted by the Study of Mathematically Precocious Youth, under the direction of Julian C. Stanley, at The Johns Hopkins University and funded by grants from the Spencer Foundation.

The third section, entitled "Facilitating Women's Achievements in Mathematics," highlights efforts to remediate or intervene to prevent or reverse the effects of the mathematical mystique. Chapter 8, by Carolyn MacDonald, describes a successful remediation approach at the college level. Chapter 9, Patricia Casserly's more naturalistic study, identifies key behavioral features of a school and its teachers in programs in which young women successfully pursue mathematics at advanced levels. The studies by MacDonald and Casserly were funded by the National Science Foundation. In chapter 10, Linda Brody and I describe a longitudinal comparison of gifted girls who participated in an accelerative program with equally able but nonaccelerated peers. And in chapter 11, Dianne Tobin and I report on a career awareness approach for gifted adolescent girls. These latter two studies were funded by grants to the Intellectually Gifted Child Study Group at The Johns Hopkins University from the Spencer Foundation and the Robert Sterling Clark Foundation, respectively.

The final section contains a summary chapter in which I attempt to integrate the common themes and research findings from all the previous chapters. The implications of these studies for the design of future research and the development of programs of remediation, intervention, and prevention are explored.

With the exception of chapter 6, which deals with studies of large populations of students from all ability groups, the chapters in this volume are concerned primarily with sex differences in achievement, course-taking, and career attainment among students with above-average to very high levels of intellectual ability for whom the study of advanced mathematics in high school and college and the pursuit of professional careers are appropriate and realistic.

It is hoped that this volume will stimulate other researchers, provide useful information and ideas for mathematics teachers at all levels, and serve parents, counselors, and all others who seek to understand the educational and intellectual needs of girls and young women.

I

Female Mathematicians

2

FEMALE MATHEMATICIANS: A CONTEMPORARY APPRAISAL

Edith H. Luchins and Abraham S. Luchins

ABSTRACT

In 1975 a questionnaire was sent to members of the Association for Women in Mathematics. The replies from 350 female members (40 percent of the membership) provide a picture of contemporary women in mathematics and of what has encouraged and/or discouraged them in their studies and careers. The responses were compared with those of a small sample of male mathematicians who answered the questionnaire. Interviews were also conducted with mathematicians and college mathematics majors. Based on the response patterns, recommendations are offered for ways in which to dispel the mystique about women in mathematics. In addition, a multiplicity of approaches is suggested for removing educational and career barriers to women in the mathematical sciences.

In the spring of 1975 a questionnaire was sent to the members of the Association for Women in Mathematics (AWM) to discover why there are relatively few women in mathematics, what factors have encouraged or discouraged contemporary female mathematicians, and what can be done to attract more women to the mathematical sciences (Luchins 1976). Additional information was obtained through personal interviews with mathematicians at mathematics meetings and through questionnaires administered to graduate and undergraduate students majoring in mathematics and related disciplines. It was hoped that data collected from a large sample of female mathematicians, supplemented with data from the male mathematicians sampled, would shed light on specific factors that encourage or discourage the choice of a career in mathematics.

AWM RESPONDENTS

The questionnaire sent to the AWM membership was open-ended to allow for greater flexibility in responding (even though answering and scoring therefore required more time). Of the approximately one thousand AWM members sent questionnaires, about 40 percent (350 women and 52 men) responded. This sample was not intended to be representative of female and male mathematicians in the United States. Relatively few male mathematicians and not all female mathematicians belong to the AWM. Those men who belong may have exceptionally favorable attitudes toward women; others may belong for administrative reasons. The AWM was chosen because it provided access to a large sample of female mathematicians.

Virtually all of the respondents had graduate training; half of the women and one fifth of the men had received their highest degree within the past five years. Sixty-eight percent of the women and significantly more of the men—98 percent—held their doctorate. About 70 percent of the women and 90 percent of the men held academic positions; the men tended to hold higher-level or administrative positions. The women had considered more careers besides mathematics and had held a greater variety of nonmathematics positions. Women averaged ten years of employment in mathematics, while men averaged seventeen. Some of the above career data are summarized in table 2.1. The respondents ranged in age from about twenty to seventy. Four fifths were between thirty and fifty years of age. The mean age of the women was thirty-seven, and of the men, forty-two.

It is of interest that fewer of our respondents were single or divorced than in some other studies of scientists (for example, Centra 1974; Cuca 1976). About two thirds of the female respondents and four fifths of the males were married; over 70 percent of those who were or had been married had children. Thus the average respondent—female or male—was married and had children, which provides a picture that is quite different from the usual conception of a mathematician (E. F. Keller 1944; Morawetz 1973).

The spouses of both female and male respondents were mainly in professional occupations; 36 percent of each group were in the academic world. The spouses of 30 percent of the women and 6 percent of the men were mathematicians. About 18 percent of the female respondents mentioned that their career had been interrupted because of family responsibilities, and 15 percent indicated that the location of their employment was determined by their spouse's career. Only 7 percent of the women said they had difficulties in combining job and family responsibilities. A similar proportion noted that they took an academic job in order to have time for their families or because of its flexible time schedule.

TABLE 2.1. Summary of career and marital data for AWM respondents

	Respondents	
	Women (N = 350)	Men (N = 52)
Career data		
Mean age	37	42
Mean years math employment	10	17
Percentage having academic employment	71%	88%
Percentage with Ph.D.	68%	98%
Marital status (%)		
Single	26%	12%
Married	63%	83%
Divorced	9%	6%
	Single Women (N = 92)	Married Women (N = 221)
Career data		
Mean age	37	37
Mean years math employment	10	10
Highest degree (%)		
Bachelor's	3%	3%
Master's	27%	32%
Doctorate	69%	66%

Most respondents thought that mathematics was a good career for women and that it could be fairly easily combined with marriage and family, especially with the help of an understanding spouse. Some thought that a career in mathematics was easier in this respect than a career in other sciences, since mathematics does not usually require a laboratory or special equipment and thus can be done at home. One male mathematician with young children who was married to a biologist claimed that his wife's return to work, which necessitated being in the laboratory, was much harder than it would have been had she been a mathematician.

No differences were noted between the career progress of single female respondents and that of married respondents. Career data, summarized in table 2.1, show no statistically significant differences in mean age, percentage with doctorate, or mean number of years employed as a mathematician. Nor are there significant differences in the proportion of single and married women at various academic ranks. In each group about one tenth are instructors; about one third, assistant professors; half as many, associate professors; and one tenth, full professors. (In contrast, none of the male respondents was an instructor, one quarter were associate professors, and one half were full professors.) Comparison was also made of ninety-three women whose highest degree was a master's degree with 239 women who held a doctorate (most but not all doctorates of philosophy). Relatively more of the former were instructors (18 percent, as compared with 8 percent of the latter), and fewer were associate professors (11 percent, as compared with 17 percent) or full professors (4 percent, as compared with 12 percent). In general, our data reveal more women at the lowest academic ranks and fewer at the highest ranks than the 1972 survey of female mathematicians with the Ph.D. degree (Morawetz 1973).

The women listed a greater variety of mathematical specialties than the men, and there were also differences in frequency of preference. The top listings are given in table 2.2. Algebra, listed most often by the women, ranked third for the men. Analysis, the women's second choice, was first for the men. Topology was the men's second choice. It is interesting to speculate whether their choices were related to sex differences in verbal skill and spacial perception, possibly due to cortical differences (see Maccoby and Jacklin 1974; Sperry 1975). Algebra probably has more verbal content and requires less ability in spatial perception than do analysis and topology. It is also interesting to speculate why mathematics education was tied for third rank by the women but was not mentioned by the men.

Initial Interest in Mathematics and Career Decisions

When were respondents first attracted to mathematics and why? Early interest, that is, by the age of six or before starting to school, was reported by 13 percent of the women and by 17 percent of the men. One third of the women and half of the men were interested in mathematics by age eleven or in elementary school. Most of the others became interested early in secondary school, usually in algebra and geometry courses. Less than 2 percent report that they were first attracted by calculus, and less than 1 percent by trigonometry.

Why were they attracted to mathematics? Reasons relating to the respondents' enjoyment of mathematics were cited most often (by half the women and three quarters of the men). Mathematics came naturally to them, they were good at it, they liked it, they were fascinated by its problem-solving or puzzle-solving aspects and, later, by its logical, axiomatic, and theorem-proving features. Next in frequency was the mention of inspiring teachers.

Table 2.3 gives the ages at which subjects reported their initial interest in mathematics, as well as the age at which they first decided on a career in mathematics. About a third of each group decided on a career in mathematics by the time they were in high school. About half of each group made the career decision in undergraduate school. Of the remainder, more of the men decided to become mathematicians while in graduate school or by age twenty-five, while more of the women decided after that. Twice as many women as men said that they chose mathematics because of the job opportunities it offered or because they wanted to teach. About a quarter of each group mentioned that they preferred it to other disciplines — ten percent of the women and 23 percent of the men chose it over an

TABLE 2.2. Mathematical specialties listed most frequently by AWM respondents

Specialty	Women		Men	
	Percentage	Rank	Percentage	Rank
Algebra	23	1	13	3
Analysis	13	2	39	1
Computer science	7	5	4	7
Geometry	0	7	6	6
Mathematics education	11	3	0	8
Number theory	5	6	12	4
Probability and statistics	9	4	8	5
Topology	11	3	23	2

TABLE 2.3. Age of first interest and of math-career decision for AWM respondents

Age or school level	Women	Men
First interest in math		
Before 6 or preschool	13%	17%
7-11 or elementary school	22	29
12-17 or secondary school	53	40
18-21 or undergraduate school	6	12
Math-career decision		
7-11 or elementary school	3	6
12-17 or secondary school	33	25
18-21 or undergraduate school	43	46
21-25 or graduate school	7	17
After 25 or after graduate school	9	4

experimental science. The applications of mathematics to other fields was infrequently mentioned as a reason for career choices; however women mentioned it somewhat more often than men.

Encouragement and Discouragement

What factors or people encouraged or discouraged respondents in their mathematical studies and careers? People were mentioned more frequently than other factors. The percentages of those who cited various people as encouraging or discouraging their decision to become mathematicians are shown in table 2.4.

Surprisingly, more women than men recall being encouraged by their families and friends, and parents, fathers, and husbands were mentioned most frequently. About two thirds of each group recall being encouraged by a teacher. The encouragement was uneven, especially for women. At the graduate level only one fifth as many women were encouraged by teachers as at previous levels.

TABLE 2.4. Encouragement or discouragement reported by AWM respondents

	Women	Men
Encouraged by		
Family and/or friends	38%	27%
Teachers	64	69
Pre-college	29	14
Undergraduate	31	39
Graduate	6	15
Advisers	9	8
Colleagues	6	6
Any person or persons	78	81
Discouraged by		
Family and/or friends	17	14
Teachers	21	8
Pre-college	4	2
Undergraduate	8	4
Graduate	11	2
Advisers	11	4
Colleagues	6	0
Any person or persons	47	27

Female teachers were specifically mentioned by some female and male respondents; for example, one woman wrote that she was most encouraged by "my one woman college math professor—not that the others weren't encouraging but . . . her influence meant more."

Discouragement by one or more persons was reported by half of the women and by one quarter of the men. These differences are statistically significant, but it is also significant that *any* of these people—and some are now eminent mathematicians—encountered discouragement as a mathematics student or professional.

Reports of discouragement by parents were about equal for females and males. Three times as many women as men, however, mentioned being discouraged by teachers or advisors, the most marked difference being at the graduate level. Sexist reasons for discouragement were offered by one fifth of the women but by none of the men.

Encouraging factors other than people were cited by about one third of the women and by one quarter of the men. Most frequently cited were the respondents' ability and liking for mathematics (by 15 percent of the women and 10 percent of the men) and fellowships, scholarships, and other aid (6 percent and 4 percent, respectively). Respondents were encouraged by their high performances and grades on mathematics tests and courses and by being accelerated in mathematics or allowed to take special courses.

Different Treatment

Even more striking results were obtained when the respondents were asked, Were you treated differently because of being female (or male) as a

TABLE 2.5. AWM affirmative responses in percents to question,
Were you treated differently as math students or professionals
because of sex?

Level	Women (N = 350)	Men (N = 52)
Pre-college	23%	6%
Undergraduate	26	8
Graduate	43	8
Professional	54	4
Any	80	9

TABLE 2.6. Frequency of reports of being treated
differently because of being female

Age group	N	Percentage
20-30	100	72
31-35	100	86
36-45	75	60
46-70	70	71

mathematics student or as a mathematics professional? Eighty percent of
the women but only 9 percent of the men answered yes. Moreover, such
reports increased for the women as their training progressed, while they
remained low for the men (see table 2.5). Furthermore, the frequency of
complaints was about as great or greater for the younger women as for the
older ones (see table 2.6).

Some women said that at the pre-college level their peers treated them
as though they were strange. They were told that boys do not like or are
afraid of smart girls, especially mathematics whizzes. Their teachers paid
more attention to the boys or expected less of the girls, and they were
advised to consider more traditional careers. At the undergraduate level,
and even more at the graduate level, some of their teachers and advisers
questioned their competence or did not take seriously their interest in
mathematics; they had to prove themselves more than the men. Some of
them were confronted with the assertion that a woman would get married
and have children and either not finish the degree or not pursue a career in
mathematics. At the professional level, some reported denial of employment, a lower salary, or less advancement potential than equally or less
qualified males.

According to our respondents' reports and perceptions, affirmative
action has not yet been effective. The younger women mentioned that they
were frequently interviewed for positions but seldom offered them. In
some cases there seemed to be a kind of backlash—for example, a fear that
if in the future a woman's contract was not renewed or she was not granted
tenure, then the university would be accused of having discriminated against
her. On the other hand, a few women who were appointed—as the token

woman in the department—felt that it was mainly because the department had to comply with affirmative-action requirements. Some said that they were given temporary positions and were expected to teach only lower-level courses and to take care of such traditionally female responsibilities as school social functions. Others complained that they felt isolated from their male colleagues or that their male colleagues seemed restrained or uncomfortable around them. Interviews with male mathematicians suggested that there may be some basis for this feeling, since a few of them admitted that they would feel uncomfortable with a female colleague or even female graduate students. One male mathematician claimed that because of the close relationship between doctoral adviser and advisee, he would not want to have a female doctoral student (and even if he wanted to, his wife would not want him to). Moreover, because of deep-rooted social mores, he could feel protective or patronizing toward a female mathematician but not at ease with her. He pointed out that it would take time to change such attitudes. The majority who were interviewed, however, said that they would welcome mathematically talented female students and colleagues.

Awareness of Female Mathematicians in the Past

Although there have been a number of famous female mathematicians throughout history, students of mathematics sometimes are unable to name any. For example, when twenty-six mathematics majors in a junior-senior-level algebra class were asked to name famous female mathematicians, twenty-four gave none, two listed Emmy Noether, and one of the latter also listed Wolkaneski (for Kovalevsky). In contrast, when they were subsequently asked to name three to five famous (male or female) mathematicians, twenty-two students answered, listing an average of four (male) mathematicians. History-of-mathematics books tend to pay scant attention to female mathematicians (see Luchins 1979). Yet there are some source materials (for example, Dubreil-Jacotin 1971; Osen 1974; and Reid 1970). These should be made more widely available, and there should be more emphasis in future publications on female mathematicians, past and present.

Awareness of Contemporary Female Mathematicians

Mathematicians at various meetings were asked to list five outstanding contemporary mathematicians; a woman's name was seldom given. The major complaint was that it was difficult to choose only five from so many outstanding (male) mathematicians. However, when they were asked to list five outstanding contemporary women, many claimed that they did not know five, and some named none. The choices of those who did name some women tended to reflect a familiarity with a given specialty or literature. For example, at an algebra convention more algebraists were named; at an applied-mathematics convention more women in applied mathematics or in analysis or partial differential equations were named; and at an international convention a few limited themselves to mathematicians from their own country.

To simplify the task, on the AWM questionnaire respondents were asked to name the three most outstanding contemporary female mathematicians. Fifty percent of the women and 21 percent of the men gave no name at all. In part this may reflect resentment of the question. About 22 percent of the women and 4 percent of the men said that they did not know any outstanding contemporary female mathematicians. Those who gave reasons usually mentioned their own lack of acquaintance with research literature and/or the insufficient visibility of female mathematicians.

About half of the respondents listed one or more names. There was more agreement among the men than among the women. The top three choices for the men were selected by 29, 23, and 23 percent of them, respectively, whereas the top three choices for the women were selected by 17, 12, and 9 percent, respectively. There were some striking differences between the two groups; for example, the fourth choice of the men (a Russian analyst), who was named by 19 percent of them, was only the ninth choice for the women and received only slightly more than 2 percent of their votes.

Nonetheless, there was some consensus among the women and men. They agreed on the top three names, although not in the same order. These women were, in alphabetical order, Julie Robinson, Mary Ellen Ruder, and Olga Taussky-Todd—who have made significant contributions to algebra, logic and number theory, and topology. Moreover, there were twenty-five names common to the two lists. Most of them were American. Their number and the quality of their work and recognition apparently give the lie to the statement—which is attributed to unknown mathematicians (by Lester 1974; cf. Boring 1975)—that only one or two female mathematicians in the whole country qualified to hold a tenured position in a major university. Several women on the list hold such positions, and others are qualified to do so. While women are certainly underrepresented at the major universities, it is not solely because of a lack of qualified candidates.

Greater visibility of female mathematicians is needed, and it will result from their research, publications, and professional activities. Articles, brochures, books, slides, and movies about some of the women should be prepared and widely distributed. Moreover, there is a need for some change in attitudes of female mathematicians toward themselves and their work. We found that they tended to be less confident about themselves, their abilities, and their contributions than men. Interviews with thirty recent Ph.D.'s (1973-75), eighteen of them women, revealed that fewer women than men thought that their doctoral theses were significant contributions or worthy of publication or that they could do worthwhile independent research. In some cases the women's theses and research were judged by more experienced mathematicians (including their advisers) as significant and worthy of publication. (It is possible that in line with social standards, the men were more reluctant than the women to reveal a lack of self-confidence, especially to a female interviewer, but that they might do so when talking to their male advisers.) Female mathematicians need to become more confident of their own abilities and less dependent on the encouragement of others. Encouragement, however, should be available when needed. And nowhere is this more important than for the girls who can go on to become mathematicians.

CONCLUSIONS AND RECOMMENDATIONS

In order for women to overcome barriers in the mathematical sciences, it seems essential to dispel the mystique concerning women and mathematics. This requires changing attitudes of mathematicians themselves, as well as those of teachers, advisers, and counselors. It requires reaching students, parents, and the general public. The difficulty of the task is compounded by the traditional isolation of the research mathematician. People see mathematicians as being unable to communicate with anyone but other mathematicians (and indeed this has been posited as one reason for the high rate of intramarriage among mathematicians). One mathematician (Steen 1975) claims that there is no other discipline of which there is so little public understanding.

When AWM respondents were asked why there are—and have been —relatively few female mathematicians, three quarters of them stressed the social conception of mathematics as masculine, not feminine. They point out that women are not encouraged to think in terms of mathematical careers and that they are treated differently. They did *not* give some of the explanations offered by male mathematicians whom we interviewed: for example, that women are not interested in mathematics or do not think as well mathematically as do men.

When asked what changes should be made if women are to be encouraged to consider careers in mathematics, less than 2 percent of the respondents thought that no changes were necessary. The women and men agreed on the nature of the changes. For the pre-collegiate level, for example, they included the following:

1. Increase the emphasis on mathematics education; advise girls to take four years of high-school mathematics.
2. Encourage women; don't discourage them.
3. Strive for more equal treatment of women and men.

4. Provide more female role models.

5. Make teachers and advisers more aware of career opportunities in mathematics.

6. Change attitudes toward, and social conceptions of, mathematics as a masculine domain.

There is a close tie-in between the last two recommended changes: The notion of mathematics as a masculine domain may be weakened if teachers and advisers are made more aware of career opportunities in mathematics for both men and women. This was strikingly evident on visits to high schools where counselors admitted discouraging girls from pursuing mathematics because they did not think it offered opportunities for them. Moreover, students and parents also need to be made more aware of these opportunities. Of the students we questioned who had changed their minds about being math majors, a common reason for the switch was that they did not know what to do with mathematics except to teach it. Clearly more information has to be spread about the varied career options that training in mathematics opens up.

Eighty-one percent of the female respondents and 75 percent of the males agreed that more women should be encouraged to study mathematics. Those who disagreed did so mainly because they thought that jobs were not available now for either sex or that only those who are highly talented should be encouraged.

Recommendations for Expanding Professional Opportunities

Several recommendations, from various sources, for expanding professional opportunities referred to the need for more fellowships for those not affiliated with a university or institute, special fellowships and scholarships for women, and child-care provisions in fellowships. Some respondents thought that universities should broaden their conception of community service to include raising a family. They noted that tenure provisions need reevaluation, in particular the up-or-out notion and the stipulation of a specific number of years in which to make certain professional progress. Tenure for part-time work was suggested (it is already in effect in a few universities, such as the University of Waterloo). Written and unwritten antinepotism laws are particularly difficult for mathematicians because of the high rate of intermarriage. Most chairmen whom we interviewed frowned on hiring a husband and wife for positions with tenure or leading to tenure. Some would do so only if both were the "best" available for the given positions. The question was raised, Can a mathematician do his best work when he has to commute a long distance or be separated from his spouse during the week in order that both be employed in mathematical positions? While some departments go out of their way not to hire a competent woman because she is married to a member of the department, others consider that it is no worse than hiring an uncle and a nephew or two close friends. In recent years more departments include spouses both of whom have tenure. We interviewed several such husband-wife teams, as well as their colleagues, and they did not report any special problems. Also mentioned as possibilities were shared teaching and more part-time positions.

Recommendations for Expanding Career Opportunities

We saw that interest in mathematics tended to be manifested at an early age and that career decisions were made relatively early. These findings point to the importance of early home and school influence. Mathematical talent should be recognized early and nurtured, not wasted. Parents *and* schools spend time and money developing musical talent; mathematical talent should be regarded as equally precious, and it should be looked for in both women and men.

Above all, it is important not to discourage. Who knows how many sensitive people—women and men—are lost to mathematics because of discouragement? Usually people gifted in mathematics have other talents too, so they can turn to other interests, but at what costs to themselves and to mathematics?

Discouragement may be more disastrous for women than for men, since our society gives women more latitude for failure to achieve academic and career goals. It is permissible, and in some cases expected, for a woman to stop school if she marries or has a child or if her husband's job location changes, but none of these factors by itself is an acceptable excuse for a man. Given the difficulties of mathematics and the social pressures, it may take only a small amount of discouragement to tip the scales in favor of quitting the pursuit of a mathematics career.

Encouragement alone is not enough. One male mathematician mentioned four women who started doctoral work with him and whom he viewed as every bit as good as his best male doctoral students: Not one finished the doctorate, despite his encouragement, which they readily acknowledge. Some stopped because they got married or their husbands changed jobs or because they shifted to music or another area, in some cases math-related. We need to create an environment in which a talented female mathematics student is more likely to complete her training and pursue a mathematics career than exists at present.

Teachers, advisers, and counselors seemed to have the impression that there were few career opportunities in mathematics for women, which may explain some of the discouragement and different treatment that young women received. Students also voiced this opinion and gave it as a reason for not majoring in mathematics. For example, one first-year, female college student wrote: "If I thought that I could get a job using math, I would change my major to math right now." While the employment picture is not bright for either women or men, it is not as dismal nor as narrow as they paint it. Positions are available in some areas of mathematics and in disciplines related to mathematics, such as operations research, computer science, and such interdisciplinary areas as mathematical biology, mathematical psychology, and mathematical sociology.

Our respondents recommended that women (and men) be encouraged to study mathematics, as well as an area to which they could apply it—psychology, sociology, anthropology, architecture, physics, mechanics, engineering. This would not only broaden their knowledge but it would increase their job possibilities. These recommendations are in line with those of the Council of the American Mathematical Society, as written in a letter of 17 November 1975 by the council's president, Lipman Bers, to chairmen of mathematics departments.

If more women can be interested in studying mathematics, more teachers will be needed. Good teachers should be in demand after the public outcry about the drop in Scholastic Aptitude Test scores. The demand should be even greater after the recent (September 1979) report by the National Assessment of Educational Progress of a decline in the mathematical achievement of nine-, thirteen-, and seventeen-year-olds, as compared with performances by the same age groups in 1973. New positions can be created; for example, female mathematicians could be roving counselors, visiting different schools to talk to students, teachers, and guidance personnel. Other positions were also mentioned, including consultants to the various media—for example, to correct the inept job now being done in the converting from the Fahrenheit to the Celsius scales and to help in the metric conversion.

The need for public understanding of mathematics calls for communication and linguistic skills, which some female mathematicians possess to a high degree. Female mathematicians should be able to use their writing and speaking skills to help bridge the gap between mathematicians and the public. Information should be collated and widely disseminated about what women have done in mathematics, what they are doing now, and what they can do in the future.

Recommendations for Instructional Changes

There are ways of presenting mathematical material that enhance flexibility and perceptual restructuring. One way is to combine the problem-solving approach of Georg Polya (1957) with the Gestalt psychological approach of Max Wertheimer (1945). Good results were obtained by using the combined approach to teach boys and girls in the elementary grades how to find the area of regular polygons and the volume of regular solids (Luchins and Luchins 1947, 1970). When this approach was used in teaching high-school geometry to two groups of about fifteen girls each who had failed the New York State geometry regent examination, they then passed the exam with an average grade in the 80s. It is now being applied to selected topics in calculus, and there are hopes for expanded use of this approach. Also being planned is the creation of material suitable for students and teachers based on the historical development of calculus.

The educational pendulum has swung from rote learning by drill to teaching of abstract structures and set theoretical terminology. These may be central to foundations of mathematics but not to concrete mathematical problems. Problem-solving approaches that enable the learner to obtain insights into the particular structure of a particular problem and to become more adept at recentering so as to arrive at a possible solution are necessary. Such approaches can be combined with learning by drill or learning to make certain skills habitual. Mechanization has a place in learning mathematics (Luchins 1942). It is also necessary to distinguish between a good guess and a bad guess, a good error and a bad error (Luchins and Luchins 1970; Wertheimer 1945).

Flexibility-rigidity tests have been used and show somewhat less flexibility for women, perhaps as a result of attitudinal factors. Gestalt spatial tasks that called for finding areas by restructuring figures showed that female mathematics majors were better than other women, and that while women were not quite as good as men at solving the problems initially, they were better at using verbal hints than men not majoring in mathematics (Luchins and Luchins 1979). The findings may be related to differences in rigidity, spatial perception, verbal ability, and ego orientation. What is required is to find methods that can teach students to become more flexible and more adept at restructuring and problem solving. This will not necessarily cause girls to win national mathematics contests, but it may enable more girls (and more boys) to learn how to approach mathematical problems and how to enjoy them.

A historical-cultural approach is desirable, one which emphasizes the people who discovered or created mathematics and the times in which they did so. Concern with the humanistic aspects of mathematics may make the study of mathematics more appealing to both women and men (see Bell 1937; Courant and Robbins 1943; and Kline 1964).

The roles of mathematics in our society should also be dealt with so that students have some idea of what mathematicians do. Consideration should be given to a course on the senior-high-school or first-year-college level that acquaints students with various options that could be followed for further study, such as applied mathematics, operations research, and computer science (Luchins 1976).

There should be a concern with intuitive-recreational mathematics, from the lower grades to the adult-education level. The respondents in this study were often attracted to mathematics because it was fun; stress on the fun and puzzle-solving aspects of mathematics may help to dispel some of the fear of the subject. Mathematical skills and routines would still have to be learned and even made habitual so they would be available for problem solving and puzzle solving and for the many ways in which mathematics is used by citizens of a scientific society. Theorem proving should be stressed in courses such as geometry, which also attracted many of the respondents. There is a need for improvement in the teaching of mathematics (Kline 1977). Better teaching by enthusiastic, inspired, and inspiring teachers can encourage more women to study mathematics and to pursue mathematics careers.

REFERENCES

Bell, E. T. 1937. *Men of mathematics.* New York: Simon and Schuster.
Boring, P. Z. 1975. Antibias regulations of universities: A biased view? *AAUP Bulletin* 61 (3): 252-55.
Centra, J. A. 1974. *Women, men, and the doctorate.* Princeton: Educational Testing Service.
Courant, R., and Robbins, H. 1943. *What is mathematics?* New York: Oxford University Press.
Cuca, J. 1976. Women psychologists and marriage: A bad match? *APA Monitor* 7 (1): 13.
Dubreil-Jacotin, M.-L. 1971. Women mathematicians. In *Great currents of mathematical thought,* ed. F. LeLionnais, trans. Howard G. Bergman, vol. 1, pp. 268-80. New York: Dover.
Keller, E. F. 1974. Women in science: An analysis of a social problem. *Harvard Magazine* 77 (2): 14-19.
Kline, M. 1964. *Mathematics in western culture.* New York: Oxford University Press.
————. 1977. *Why the professor can't teach: Mathematics and the dilemma of university education.* New York: St. Martin's Press.
Lester, R. A. 1974. *Antibias regulations of universities: Faculty problems and their solutions.* New York: McGraw-Hill.
Luchins, A. S. 1942. Mechanization in problem solving: The effect of Einstellung. *Psychological Monographs* 54 (6): 1-95.
Luchins, A. S., and Luchins, E. H. 1947. A structural approach to the teaching of the concept of area in intuitive geometry. *Journal of Educational Research* 40 (7): 528-33.
————. 1970. *Wertheimer's seminars revisited: Problem solving and thinking.* 3 vols. Albany: Faculty Student Association, State University of New York at Albany.
————. 1979. Geometric problem solving related to differences in sex and mathematical interests. *Journal of Genetic Psychology* 134: 255-69.
Luchins, E. H. 1976. Women in mathematics: Problems of orientation and reorientation. National Science Foundation Final Report.
————. 1979. Sex differences in mathematics: How not to deal with them. *American Mathematical Monthly* 86 (3): 161-68.

Maccoby, E. E., and Jacklin, C. N. 1974. *The psychology of sex differences.* Stanford: Stanford University Press.

Morawetz, C. S. 1973. Women in mathematics. *Notices of the American Mathematical Society* 20 (3): 131-32.

Osen, L. M. 1974. *Women in mathematics.* Cambridge, Mass.: M.I.T. Press.

Polya, G. 1957. *How to solve it.* Garden City, N.Y.: Doubleday.

Reid, C. 1970. *Hilbert.* New York: Springer-Verlag.

————. 1976. *Courant in Göttingen and New York: The story of an improbable mathematician.* New York: Springer-Verlag.

Sperry, R. W. 1975. Left-brain, right-brain. *Saturday Review* 9: 30-33.

Steen, L. A. 1975. Public understanding of mathematics. *Notices of the American Mathematical Society* 23 (7): 363-64.

Wertheimer, M. 1959. *Productive thinking,* Enlarged edition edited by Michael Wertheimer. New York: Harper.

3

THE CREATIVE WOMAN MATHEMATICIAN

Ravenna Helson

ABSTRACT

Research contributions of forty-four female Ph.D.'s in mathematics were rated on creativity by peers in appropriate fields of specialization. Women whose work was rated as more creative than the average research paper in mathematical journals were compared with the other members of the sample. Their personality characteristics and research style were further studied in comparisons of female with male mathematicians and of mathematicians of both sexes with writers of both sexes. Results show that the creative women mathematicians were flexible, individualistic, and introverted and had strong symbolic interests. Like creative writers, however, they lacked the social confidence and discipline that creative men mathematicians possessed (and which seems advantageous for academic success). This difference in personality between creative men and women mathematicians seems attributable in part to their very different life circumstances. Subgroups of women mathematicians, constituted on the basis of research style, are shown to have differed markedly in personality, cognitive abilities, characteristics of parents, ethnicity and social integration of the family, and situational conditions at the time of assessment. Hypotheses are offered to explain these findings, and case studies illustrate how interest in mathematics developed in members of the different subgroups. One subgroup of creative women showed the "confident inventiveness" characteristic of creative men in mathematics; comparisons among women point to social-developmental sources of this feature of research style. The fact that there were three subgroups about equal in creativity shows that women with a variety of personality traits can do creative work in mathematics.

In the mid 1950s the Institute of Personality Assessment and Research (IPAR) began a series of investigations of eminent creative individuals (Barron 1969; MacKinnon 1962). Were there personality characteristics associated with creative achievement? Was there a "creative personality" common to workers in different fields? And why were there so few creative women? Did women lack originality, aggressiveness, the ability to think abstractly, the courage of their convictions? Or were social barriers responsible? People had asked these question before, but IPAR now had better methods for studying them.

There were several reasons for choosing mathematics as an area in which to study creativity in women. The very fact that there were only a few creative women mathematicians seemed advantegeous. It might be possible to study not just a sample but virtually all of them. Perhaps these women would show particularly clearly the essential traits of the creative person, of either sex, and surely such an investigation would contribute to the appraisal of creativity in women and of women's potential for scientific accomplishment. A felicitous development was that Richard Crutchfield, who was also at IPAR, undertook a study of male mathematicians, so comparisons of men and women became possible.

The procedure at IPAR was to invite subjects, in groups of about ten, for a weekend at the institute. There was a full schedule of tests of various kinds, interviews, group discussions, even charades. The staff of psychologists mixed socially with the subjects, observed the group procedures, and afterwards described each person by means of ratings and check lists. The descriptions by different staff members were averaged and provided a powerful tool for the assessment of personality. As it turned out, some of the male mathematicians were studied by Crutchfield at the Institute for Advanced Study at Princeton, and the rest were sent packets of tests by mail. The women, however, participated in the weekend assessments, so there is a rich body of data available about them.

DESIGN OF THE STUDY OF WOMEN MATHEMATICIANS

Sample and Criterion of Creativity

In the period of planning the study it soon became evident that creative women mathematicians did not always have a regular position at a university and that it would not be possible to constitute an adequate sample by simply drawing up a list of women from the directories of institutions of higher education. Instead, names of women who had attended graduate school and obtained the Ph.D. degree in mathematics between 1950 and 1960 were requested from a sample of institutions (Helson 1971). Mathematicians at these and other universities provided additional names, particularly of women they considered creative.

Of fifty-three invitations extended, forty-four (83 percent) were accepted. Three women were tested later than the others and are not included in all analyses. Three wives of faculty members at the University of California at Berkeley were asked to provide data only about their research style. The number of subjects thus varies between forty-one and forty-seven.

The appropriate criterion of creativity for these women seemed to be the *quality* of the individual's research. Number of publications or general reputation and influence, though easier to measure, would be less suitable as a criterion for a group so marginal in the profession. Therefore, ratings for each mathematician were obtained from a group of specialists in her own area of mathematics. A seven-point scale was used, a rating of 4.0 signifying that the subject was about as creative as the author of an average research paper in a mathematical journal. The ratings were highly reliable. Subjects rated above 5.0 were classified as "creative."

The subjects ranged in age from twenty-four to sixty-four, the average age being forty-one. Two thirds were married. One third had Jewish parents, and most of the rest were from a Protestant background. Creative and comparison women did not differ in these respects, nor in the quality of their graduate school. As in the sample of male mathematicians, foreign cultural influence was strong. Half of the creative women were born in Europe or Canada, and almost half of the native-born subjects had at least one parent born in Europe. The difference in the number of foreign births in the creative and comparison groups is significant at the 10-percent level. However, foreign-born and native-born creative women do not differ in the characteristics that will be reported as significantly differentiating creative from comparison subjects.

Measures

A great many tests and measures were obtained during the assessment weekend. The following discussion will emphasize several measures of personality and one measure of self-reported mathematical style.

One category of measures for assessing personality consists of two paper-and-pencil inventories, the California Psychological Inventory (Gough 1957) and the Adjective Check List (Gough and Heilbrun 1980). A second category of measures is observations of the assessment staff, recorded in various ways. For example, the hundred-item Clinical Q Sort (Block 1961) comprises statements about personality that are sorted in a prescribed normal distribution according to how characteristic or uncharacteristic of the person being described each item is. A third source of information about personality is the personal-history questionnaire and interview. The questionnaire was answered by the subject. The interview was unstructured, but afterwards the interviewer made ratings, commented on various questions, and wrote a personality sketch.[1]

Mathematical style was assessed by the Mathematicians Q Sort, consisting of fifty-six items about work attitudes and research habits that the mathematicians sorted to describe themselves (Helson 1967). Considerable

[1] The personal history interviewers were Frank Barron, John D. Black, Peter Madison, Harold R. Renaud, Silvan S. Tomkins, George S. Welsh, and Charles Wenar.

effort went into the development of this instrument. Items that pretest subjects found unclear or unimportant were discarded, and suggestions for additional items were solicited. In its final form, the Q Sort seemed to interest the mathematicians, and most of them found that they could describe themselves satisfactorily.

These measures of personality and mathematical style will be utilized repeatedly in this paper. Measures of intelligence, interests, esthetic ability, and other aspects of personality or life history that receive mention are described more fully elsewhere (Helson 1971).

WOMEN MATHEMATICIANS
AND THE CREATIVE PERSONALITY

Introductory Overview of the Sample

The California Psychological Inventory (CPI) yields scores on eighteen scales, which are intended to give a comprehensive picture of the inter-personal and intellectual characteristics of the individual. The scores for an individual or group may be plotted as a personality profile. On the profile sheet, scales to the left have to do with social poise and ascendancy; those in the center, with regulation of impulse; and those to the right, with modes of intellectual functioning. Examples will be given later in this paper. Harrison Gough, the author of the CPI, has provided this interpretation of the group profile of the women mathematicians: "Two implications stand out at once. The first has to do with superior intellectual functioning, an unusual combination of perseverance, adaptiveness, and sensitivity to the new and unforeseen. The second has to do with temperament, which in this case appears to be moderate and even subdued, and yet without loss of individuality or spark. The basic portrait is of a perceptive, cognitively open, highly intelligent individual, reflective and reserved, yet capable of responding creatively to her personal world."[2]

Another group portrait of the women mathematicians comes from the items from the Clinical Q Sort that the assessment staff placed as most salient in their personalities: "Genuinely values intellectual and cognitive matters"; "appears to have a high degree of intellectual capacity"; "values own independence and autonomy"; "is a genuinely dependable and re-sponsible person"; "prides self on being objective and rational."

Differences between Creative and Comparison Women

The subjects whose work was rated above average in creativity were compared with other women mathematicians. The findings reported are significant beyond the .05 level of confidence.

---

[2] Personal communication from Harrison Gough.

Validation of the criterion ratings. Findings from the professional-history data bank supported the validity of the criterion ratings in showing that the women classified as creative had been performing at a level superior to that of the comparison women. They received the Ph.D. at an earlier age, submitted their first paper for publication before the Ph.D. rather than after, published more papers, and received more grants and fellowships after graduate school (Helson 1971).

Personality characteristics. On the CPI, the creative subjects scored higher than the comparison subjects on the flexibility scale and lower on the communality and the achievement-via-conformance scales. In combination with other features of their profiles, these findings indicate that the creative subjects were strongly motivated to create their own forms and to express and validate their own ideas but did not enjoy routine duties or working within a highly structured framework.

Welsh (1975) has developed measures of two personality traits, labeled "origence" and "intellectence," that he postulates to be fundamental in creative personality. Scales can now be scored from the revised Adjective Check List (ACL) (Gough and Heilbrun 1980) to assess personality characteristics associated with the various conjoint relationships of these variables. Peak scores for almost two thirds of the comparison women were on the scale for low origence combined with high intellectence; but, as Welsh would predict, peak scores for almost two thirds of the creative women were on the scale for high origence combined with high intellectence. Standard scores for the two groups differ significantly on these two scales, indicating that the comparison women described themselves as rational, astute, and self-disciplined, whereas the creative women perceived themselves as more self-preoccupied, autonomous, unorthodox, and temperamental.

These findings based on the subjects' self-descriptions on personality inventories are supported by the IPAR staff observations. The staff observers did not know the women's creativity ratings, but analyses show that they judged the following Clinical Q Sort items to be more descriptive of the creative subjects than of the comparison subjects: "Thinks and associates to ideas in unusual ways"; "has unconventional thought processes"; "is an interesting, arresting person"; "tends to be rebellious and nonconforming"; "genuinely values intellectual and cognitive matters"; "appears to have a high degree of intellectual ability"; "is self-dramatizing, histrionic"; "has fluctuating moods." The statements judged to be more descriptive of the comparison women were : "Judges self and others in conventional terms like 'popularity,' 'the correct thing to do,' social pressures, etc."; "is a genuinely dependable and responsible person"; "behaves in a sympathetic or considerate manner"; "favors conservative values in a variety of areas"; "is moralistic."

Mathematical style. The creative subjects described themselves as more involved in research than the comparison women did, and they seemed to employ less fully conscious cognitive processes ("must exert effort to express a mathematical train of thoughts in words"; "solution to a problem often comes from an unexpected direction"). They also describe themselves, however, as inventive and ingenious. Comparison women were more interested in teaching, salary, and understanding the ideas of others; and they described themselves as more organized and efficient in their work style (Helson 1971).

Interests. The creative women expressed strong interest in leisure activities that were primarily intellectual in nature: attending concerts, listening to classical records, going to plays, reading classics, and hiking. The comparison subjects were more heterogeneous in their strong interests and had a larger number of moderate interests than the creative subjects. The creative women seem to have simplified their lives to a few things about which they cared very much. They spent most of their time in research and homemaking; they spent less time than the comparison subjects in teaching, administration, community activities, and politics.

Esthetic sensitivity. The creative and the comparison women were asked to make mosaic designs. The designs made by the creative subjects were judged by a panel of experts as having more artistic merit and as more pleasing than those of the comparison subjects.

Intelligence and cognitive abilities. The creative and the comparison women appear not to have differed on the Wechsler Intelligence Scale, though only part of the sample was tested (MacKinnon and Hall 1973). On the Concept Mastery Test, developed by Terman to assess high intelligence as it has been utilized and enriched in adult cultural experience, the creative subjects did somewhat better than the comparison subjects ($p < .10$). Their average score of 144 is higher than that of the Stanford Gifted subjects (137), industrial research scientists (118), and military officers (60) and essentially the same as that of the creative male mathematicians (148). It has been suggested that sex differences in the understanding of physical and mechanical relationships contribute to the disinclination of women for mathematics and the sciences. Thus, creative women might show an unusual facility in this area. Creative and comparison subjects, however, did not differ on the Bennett Mechanical Comprehension Test. Both groups did well in comparison with most women but less well than men (Helson 1971).

Childhood background. More creative women had fathers who were professional men, and in the opinion of the personal-history interviewers, they were more identified with their fathers than the comparison women. Although the women mathematicians as a whole came disproportionately from families of girls, the creatives, unless they came from very large families, were particularly likely not to have brothers. A number of the women mathematicians seem to have been adopted as the "son" of an intellectual father.

Summary

The outstanding finding of this study is the striking difference in personality between the creative and comparison women. The creatives differ from the comparison women in a strong intellectual orientation more than in "raw intelligence." On a variety of measures and in a variety of areas, they show strong symbolic interests, introversion, independence, and lack of constriction. These characteristics have all been attributed to the "creative personality," and the creative women mathematicians actually demonstrate them more clearly than the men (Helson and Crutchfield 1970). Perhaps social pressures make it so difficult for a woman to be a creative mathematician that only those who persist are introverted individualists with a deep inner motivation.

DIFFERENCES BETWEEN MEN AND WOMEN MATHEMATICIANS

Although the creative women clearly have more of a "creative personality" than less creative women, the important comparison in real life is usually with creative men. The male mathematicians did not participate in the assessments, but their scores on measures such as the CPI and the Mathematicians Q Sort can be compared with those of the women.

On the CPI, the comparison men and women are quite similar in personality (see figure 3.1), but the creative men score significantly higher than the creative women on several measures of social ascendancy and on intellectual efficiency (see figure 3.2).

On the Mathematicians Q Sort both the creative men and the creative women had a pattern of characteristics that differentiates them from all other mathematicians. The creative men described themselves as having confidence, initiative, ambition, impact on the environment, and intellectual balance and soundness. In contrast, the creative women described themselves as nonadventurous and inner-focused. In the work style of the creative women the self is totally committed, unconscious as well as conscious processes are involved in the creative effort, and emphasis is directed toward developing what is within rather than toward exploring or mastering the environment (Helson 1967). Comparison men and women differed very little in the way they described their work style.

What are we to make of the fact that the creative men and women differ from each other more than the comparison men and women do and how are we to understand their distinctive styles, particularly that of the

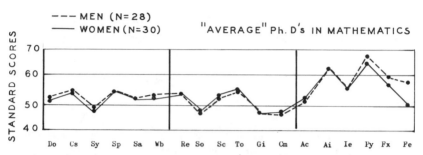

FIGURE 3.1. Profiles of men and women mathematicians on the CPI: comparison subjects

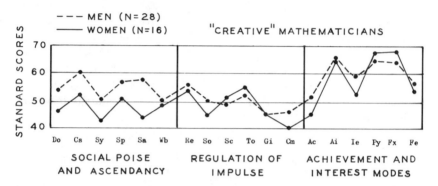

FIGURE 3.2. Profiles of men and women mathematicians on the CPI: creative subjects

KEY: Do (dominance); Cs (capacity stat.); Sy (sociability); Sp (social pres.); Sa (self-accept.); Wb (well-being); Re (responsibility); So (socialization); Sc (self-control); To (tolerance); Gi (good impress.); Cm (communality); AC (achiev. via conformance); Ai (achiev. via independence); Ie (intellectual efficiency); Py (psychological-mindedness); Fx (flexibility); Fe (femininity); EM (empathy)

women? It is surely relevant that although the creative men and women had careers that were quite similar though graduate school, their lives at the time of testing were very different. The men had published more papers and held important positions at prestigious places. Only two or three of the women taught graduate students, and one third, including some of the most highly rated, had no regular position at all. Most of the married women were married to mathematicians, and nepotism was a frequent problem. Also, half of the creative women had young children.

One could argue that the inner-focused, emotional, low assertive style of the creative women was a strategic adaptation to a life situation in which they worked in relative isolation, often distracted by their responsibilities as homemakers and mothers (Helson 1975). If so, one might see the style of the creative men as also a strategic adaptation to their life situation, in which they occupied positions that rewarded them and put heavy demands on them for competitive exertion and intellectual leadership. The men and women comparison subjects could be seen as adopting strategies that sacrificed creativity for the more tangible, immediate, or congenial necessities of teaching and earning a living.

There are, however, other factors to consider. As suggested earlier, creative women who persevere in mathematics may be more introverted, unconventional, and less adaptable than the creative men, or there may be sex differences in the creative personality not confined to mathematics that are not attributable to one's job situation. In order to weigh these various factors, it would be helpful to know something about sex differences in a field that imposes less divergent conditions of life on its creative men and women than mathematics does.

SEX DIFFERENCES AMONG MATHEMATICIANS AND WRITERS

Unlike mathematics, literary fantasy for children is a field to which men and women have contributed in about equal numbers. Also, institutional organization is minimal. Writers usually work at home. Like mathematics, however, writing attracts highly creative individuals.

Criterion ratings of creativity, the CPI, and a Writers Q Sort were available for fifty-seven authors of literary fantasy for children (Helson 1977). These men and women were compared with the men and women mathematicians.

Personality Characteristics and Work Style

An analysis of variance on CPI scales was conducted to find out whether the two groups of creative women and the two groups of creative men differed in similar ways from their respective comparison groups. Other analyses investigated the similarity between the creative men and women writers and between the creative men and women mathematicians (Helson 1978).

The results are clear. The two groups of creative women have the most in common. Both appear to be somewhat stubbornly unconventional and individualistic and tend not to be social leaders but to have an original and engrossing inner life.

The two groups of creative men scored similarly on only one scale (self-control). Both groups scored low and thus appear to have more access to anger and negative emotion than comparison men.

The two groups of creative writers, men and women, have much in common, including the same core of traits that characterized the creative women. On the other hand, the two groups of creative mathematicians, men and women, scored similarly on only one scale (flexibility). On three scales (sociability, self-acceptance, and achievement via conformance) the creative men and women mathematicians scored significantly *differently* in relation to their comparison groups.

The set of findings, then, informs us that the creative male mathematicians are different from the other groups. They have a personality in which there is relatively more social assurance and assertiveness and less conflict with conventional channels of expression and achievement.

By examining comparable items from the Mathematicians Q Sort and the Writers Q Sort, it can be shown that the creative writers of both sexes describe their work style in a way that resembles that of the creative women mathematicians more than it does that of the creative men mathematicians (Helson 1978). That is, there is more emphasis on emotional involvement and participation of the unconscious than on initiative and mastery.

There is, however, one area in which the two samples of creative men differ from other subjects in one way, while the creative women differ in another way. Creative men emphasize their ambition to do great things, whereas creative women convey the strength of their motivation by their willingness to set aside other things for their work (see table 3.1).

Summary

These comparisons of writers and mathematicians show us that the creative style of the women mathematicians is not peculiar to them; they share it with creative writers. And yet, is it an appropriate style for mathematics? Why are the creative women in mathematics different from the creative men? We still do not know to what extent the inner-focused, low assertive style is a function of life situation and to what extent it is rooted in basic personality characteristics. A useful approach at this juncture would seem to be to study individual differences among the mathematicians and factors associated with differences among subgroups.

SUBGROUPS OF WOMEN MATHEMATICIANS

Designation of Subgroups

There are many ways of differentiating among people. In this study it seemed desirable to form subgroups that would have some relation to mathematical performance. Also it would be advantageous to be able to compare subgroups across the lines of sex. Thus the Mathematicians Q Sort was chosen to provide a basis for the identification of subgroups.

A cluster analysis (Tryon and Bailey 1970) of the data from the entire sample of 109 men and women produced four clusters (Helson 1967). The

TABLE 3.1. Placement of Q Sort items about ambition and commitment by men and women mathematicians and writers

	Mathematicians (N = 111)			Writers (N = 54)		
	Creative Mean	Comparison Mean	t	Creative Mean	Comparison Mean	t
"Has an earnest desire to make a mark in mathematics" ("has a keen desire for fame and immortality in literature").						
Women	2.83	3.00	-.56	3.00	2.73	.58
Men	3.94	3.03	4.25***	3.75	2.73	2.43*
t	-4.58***	—		-1.93	—	
"Subordinates other things to research (literary) goals; puts these values before others."						
Women	3.44	2.43	3.24**	3.67	2.27	3.89***
Men	3.03	2.65	1.28	2.92	2.67	.54
t	1.24	—		1.60	—	

*p < .05.
**p < .01.
***p < .001.

33

TABLE 3.2. Clusters of the mathematicians Q Sort for men and women mathematicians
(N = 109)

Characteristics	Oblique factor coefficient
Cluster 1	
Is neat and orderly in his habits and manner of work.	.85
Enjoys the freedom of working in a messy terrain.	−.49
Has an active, efficient, well-organized mind.	.48
Prefers to get miscellaneous chores out of the way before settling down to research.	.47
Feels emotionally tense when a result becomes imminent.	−.38
Cluster 2	
Work is characterized by inventiveness and ingenuity.	.75
Lacks confidence; is afraid to strike out in new directions.	−.71
Is flexible and adaptable in his thinking, able to shift and restructure easily.	.49
Does not work on problems known to be very difficult.	−.48
Reacts quickly to research problems; immediately generates a great number of ideas.	.42
Research interests lie within a rather narrow range.	−.40
Research problem is likely to originate in attempt to extend known proofs or results rather than in attempt to clarify a nebulous area.	−.39
Work is characterized by intuitive power.	.37
Easily distracted; tries to secure optimum conditions for concentration.	−.35

first two clusters—which were all that were readily manageable—are shown in table 3.2. The first cluster contrasts orderliness with a free, messy, and emotional attitude toward mathematics. The second cluster contrasts an inventive, confident, ambitious, and intellectually flexible attitude with its opposite—cautious, inner-oriented, shy, and settled.

These cluster dimensions would seem to represent two antitheses that are of general importance for creativity in mathematics, and probably in science generally. There is an "essential tension" (Kuhn 1963) between the scientist's need to respect the order of the past, to uphold it and build upon it, and the need to destroy this order or to live in chaos until a new synthesis is created. There is a second antithesis between inner contemplation and outer mastery. Mathematicians are known to be introverted (Campbell 1974; Helson and Crutchfield 1970), and there is a general negative relationship between interest in science and leadership (Holland 1973). And yet, original contributions usually require an element of risk-taking and initiative in the outer world.

In the present sample of men and women mathematicians, creative subjects score lower than comparison subjects on cluster 1, and men, especially creative men, score higher than women on cluster 2. In fact, the emergence of these two clusters in the cluster analysis is probably attributable to the fact that creativity and sex were major variables in the sample. But of

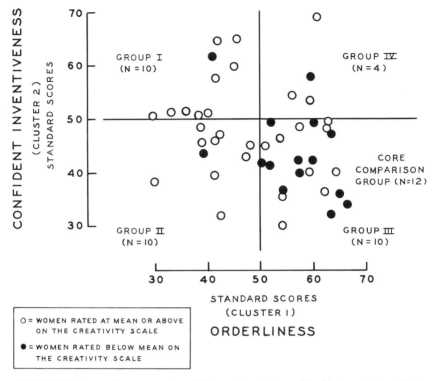

FIGURE 3.3. Scores of women mathematicians on two clusters of the Mathematicians Q Sort

course they are very important variables. All in all, it seems worthwhile to explore the possibility that different patterns of scores on these two cluster dimensions will identify an important and revealing set of subgroups of mathematicians.

Figure 3.3 plots the scores of the women mathematicians on the two dimensions. Each person can be assigned to one of four quadrants. One notes right away that there are very few women in the upper right quadrant, high on both orderliness and confident inventiveness. A similar plot for the male mathematicians would show few men in the lower left quadrant, low on both dimensions. In the case of both men and women, most subjects who were rated below the mean on creativity fall in the lower right quadrant, high on orderliness and low on confident inventiveness.

Let us distinguish four groups of women: those in the upper left quadrant; those the lower left quadrant; those in the lower right quadrant who were rated average or above in creativity; and those in the lower right quadrant who were rated below average in creativity. These groups will be designated Group I, Group II, Group III, and Group C (or core comparison group), respectively. There will also be a small Group IV, consisting of women who scored high on both dimensions, but it will be disregarded for

TABLE 3.3. Characteristic features of work style for subgroups of women

Characteristics rated highest	Mean placement (5-point scale)
By group I	
Feels emotionally tense when a result seems imminent.	4.2
Enjoys the freedom of working in a messy terrain.	3.9**
Has a lively sense of mathematical curiosity and inquiringness; a desire to know and understand.	3.8
By group II	
Research interests lie within a rather narrow range.	4.7**
Finds it difficult to read the works of others and prefers to spend her energies on own work.	4.4**
Feels emotionally tense when a result seems imminent.	4.0
Is somewhat deficient in command of basic sources and technical literature in the field.	4.0
Takes an esthetic view; is sensitive to matters of form and elegance in research problems.	3.9
Lacks confidence; is reluctant to strike out in new directions.	3.8
By group III	
Prefers to work on problems that lend themselves to elegant and exact solutions.	4.2
Research interests lie within a rather narrow range.	4.1
Has a lively sense of mathematical curiosity and inquiringness; a desire to know and understand.	4.0
By group C	
Has a need to teach; enjoys instructing and working with students.	4.4
Takes an esthetic view; is sensitive to matters of form and elegance in research problems.	3.8
Research problem is likely to originate in an attempt to extend known proof or results rather than in an attempt to clarify a nebulous area.	3.8
Prefers to get miscellaneous chores out of the way before settling down to research.	3.8
Can imagine enjoying work other than mathematics.	3.8

**$p < .01$ (t test for difference between group indicated and Group C).

the present. Groups I, II, and III were about equal in creativity, although it should be noted that the criterion of creativity has, in effect, been changed: Women rated as average in creativity are now included with those rated above average. Only in this way can enough subjects be mustered to make comparisons of "creative" subgroups.

Work Styles

As one might anticipate, the several groups emphasized different items from the Mathematicians Q Sort in describing their work styles (see table 3.3). Group I emphasized excitement, curiosity, and pleasure in working in a "messy terrain." Members of Group II described themselves as emotionally

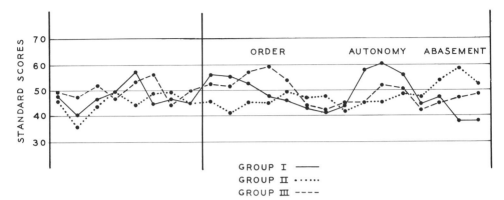

FIGURE 3.4. Profiles of three subgroups of women mathematicians on the Adjective Check List

involved with their own work and uncomfortable or inadequate in relation to the outside world. Group III expressed a preference for elegant and exact solutions. They had narrow research interests but a lively mathematical curiosity. The core comparison group had less interest in research than the other groups.

Personality Characteristics

The personality characteristics of the groups are consistent with their mathematical styles. Figure 3.4 shows the distinctive profiles of the three creative groups on the Gough-Heilbrun "need" scales of the Adjective Check List. The peak score for Group I is on the autonomy scale; for Group II it is on the abasement scale; and for Group III, on the order scale. The profile of Group C is not shown, but it is very similar to Group III's, except exaggerated—the peak on order is much higher, and scores for heterosexuality, affiliation, and change are much lower.

The ACL manual says that those who score high on autonomy are independent, assertive, and self-willed, heedless of the preferences of others when they themselves wish to act. In contrast, those with high scores on abasement are self-effacing and may have problems with self-acceptance. They face the world with anxiety and foreboding, and their behavior is often self-punishing, perhaps in the hope of forestalling criticism and rejection from without. Those who score high on order·seek objectivity and rationality and are firm in controlling impulse. These remarks are not offered as descriptions of the subgroups of women mathematicians (because their peak score on the ACL is not all there is to know about them) but as a designation of some important dimensions of difference in their personalities.

Differences in the way the groups describe themselves were borne out and elaborated by differences in the way the IPAR staff saw them. For example, results from the Clinical Q Sort showed that the IPAR staff described members of Group I—more than the other women—as having a clear-cut and internally consistent personality, being relatively free of self-concern, initiating and responding to humor, being productive, having insight into their own motives, expressing hostility directly, and characteristically pushing and trying to stretch limits. They behaved in a less feminine manner.

Characteristics seen as more salient in Group II than in other women included a propensity to fantasy and daydreams, unpredictability and fluctuating moods, a brittle ego-defense system, and an interesting, arresting personality. They were seen as less cheerful than the other women.

Group III was seen as genuinely valuing intellectual and cognitive matters and as enjoying sensuous experiences (including touch, taste, and smell).

Group C was described as uncomfortable with uncertainty; judging self and others in conventional terms; favoring conservative values; alert to differences between self and others; genuinely dependable and responsible; priding self on objectivity and rationality; moralistic; fastidious; and over-controlled. They were seen as less intellectual and as having less intellectual capacity.

The subgroups also differed significantly on cognitive tasks. Group I scored highest on the Unusual Uses test of originality; Group II scored highest on the Terman Concept Mastery and the Gottschaldt Figures, a measure of ability to break configural set; Group III scored lowest on Unusual Uses and the Gottschaldt Figures; and Group C scored lowest on the Terman Concept Mastery and on a perceptual-cognitive test designed to measure ability to change figure-ground relationships. These results showed that the groups who described themselves as low in orderliness tended to score higher on measures of originality and cognitive flexibility than groups who described themselves as high in orderliness.

It would be very interesting to be able to show that the subgroups differed in mathematical speciality. The only difference that has been established is that Groups I and II were less often specialists in algebra or analysis than Groups III and C. Group I led in applied interest, and Group II led in logic, but these differences did not reach significance.

Some Background Findings

The work of Datta (1973), Lesser (1976), Rosenberg (1965), Sarason (1973), and others suggests the importance of ethnic background for the development of cognitive style and self-esteem. In this study, religious background of parents is one of several demographic variables that distinguish among the subgroups of women mathematicians. Groups I, IV, and C were predominantly Protestant, and Groups II and III were predominantly non-Protestant (see table 3.4). Thus, Protestants who were rated at least average in creativity were generally high in confidence and inventiveness, while non-Protestants with comparable ratings on creativity were generally more cautious and inner-oriented. Also, most subjects low in creativity were Protestants.

Another characteristic that co-varied with religious background in this sample of mathematicians was education of father. Fathers of Groups II and III, the non-Protestant groups, were the most highly educated. Group I fathers were intermediate, and Groups IV and C had fathers with the least education (see table 3.4). As one might expect, the highly educated fathers were professional men, so that Groups II and III abounded in women whose fathers were professors, engineers, or physicians. Fathers of members of the other groups were usually in business, large or small, the lesser professions, or perhaps skilled trades or farming. Another variable related to education of the father was the difference in education between father and mother. Groups II and III came from homes in which the father was almost always better educated than the mother; the other groups came from homes in which the parents usually had the same education.

Finally, there is some evidence that more families of Groups II and III were "incomplete" or considered "foreign" in their communities. Four of five women in whose homes there was death or divorce in the subject's childhood were from Groups II and III. Although Groups I, II, and III do not differ in the number of foreign-born, more members of groups II and III moved with their families from their native country when they were children or adolescents.

Some Hypotheses

It seemed puzzling that there should be such striking demographic differences among the subgroups. Three hypotheses will be advanced to explain the relationships, but it should be emphasized that they are crude and should be regarded as tools for exploration.

The first hypothesis is that clusters 1 and 2 reflect dispositions acquired in early stages of development. Cluster 1 assesses alternative attitudes toward authority and toward feelings of shame and self-doubt (Erikson 1963) that are associated with the parents' attempt to control the young child's bowels, bodily exploration, and locomotor activity. Cluster 2 taps introversion versus extraversion and masculinity versus femininity, but along with these it assesses a confidence and initiative in dealing with the outside world that may be interpreted in a developmental context. In Erikson's version of psychoanalytic theory, to gain this initiative the child must surmount "Oedipal" conflicts. His or her success in doing so depends in part on the severity of conflictful and guilty feelings toward parents but also on the degree to which these conflicts can be transferred, transformed,

TABLE 3.4. Some background characteristics distinguishing groups I, IV, and C from groups II and III

Groups	Religious background[a]		Father's education[b]		Difference in parents' education[c]	
	Protestant	Non-Protestant	College	Noncollege	Father more educated	Father not more educated
I, IV, and C	19	6	8	16	4	20
II and III	7	13	15	4	15	3

a $\chi^2 = 7.81$, p < .01.
b $\chi^2 = 8.87$, p < .005.
c $\chi^2 = 16.68$, p < .001.

and worked out in school and in other areas of the world outside the family.

A second hypothesis is that the predominantly Protestant groups developed vulnerabilities in the course of their socialization that were different from those developed by Groups II and III and that important factors in the socialization experience were (1) Protestant or non-Protestant values and (2) the degree of integration of the family into the wider society. Briefly, it is hypothesized that Groups I and C experienced more vulnerability in the area of order versus disorder, because of Protestant emphases on cleanliness, independence, and emotional control, and that Groups II and III experienced more vulnerability in the area of initiative and confidence, because the barrier between the family and the outer world reduced opportunities for working out attitudes toward parents and siblings by means of identifications and interests outside the family. Especially for bright and introverted little girls, the combination of the barrier between family and outer world and the superior education and status of the father would have intensified Oedipal conflicts.

It would be a mistake to construe the main variables too narrowly in terms of religious background. Some of the women who are atypical of their quadrant in ethnicity seem to have had psychological experiences similar to those of their fellows. For example, one of the Protestants in Group II grew up in an enclave within a Catholic culture. Another Protestant in Group II had no father in the home to help her separate from her loving but moody mother, a factor likely to create difficulties in the development of initiative and management of guilt.

The third hypothesis is that differences between groups with similar socialization pressures may be understood in terms of their having reacted to these pressures in different ways. Members of Group I rebelled against adult control, at least inwardly, and reacted counteractively to shame and self-doubt; they emphasized their autonomy and the value of their own productions. Group C internalized parental dictates and tried to obtain approval by strict control and good behavior. Because of the Protestant emphasis on independent achievement and the social integration of their families in the community, members of Group I were likely to show initiative and confidence in competition at school. On the other hand, Group C found their initiative restricted by dutifulness, self-doubt, and ambivalence toward parental figures.

It has been hypothesized that both Groups II and III were handicapped in the development of initiative by guilt feelings toward parents. As Group II tends to undercontrol and Group III to overcontrol (low vs. high scores on cluster 2), perhaps the difference was that members of Group II remained outwardly dependent in many ways but sought to work out their dilemmas by developing the fantasy and imagination that is characteristic of the period of initiative vs. guilt (Erikson 1963). Groups III became at least superficially self-sufficient by suppressing personal feelings or subjecting them to strict control.

Parents and Early Development

Several kinds of information were analyzed to discover their consistency with the above hypotheses. One of these was the subjects' descriptions of their parents on dimensions of a semantic differential (Osgood, Suci, and Tannenbaum 1957). Three dimensions each were chosen to assess (1) Protestant values and/or social integration (strong-weak, stable-unstable, clean-unclean) and (2) personal qualities not closely related to Protestant values and social integration (deep-shallow, pleasant-unpleasant, warm-cold). One dimension (safe-dangerous) was chosen on the grounds that it might relate to Oedipal problems common to the period of initiative versus guilt. Hypotheses were that parents of Groups I and C would have modeled the first set of values more strongly than parents of Groups II and III, that there would be no difference or less difference on the second set, and that Groups II and III would perceive their parents as having been less "safe."

As table 3.5 shows, Groups I and C described their parents as stronger, safer, and somewhat more stable than did Groups II and III.[3] Differences on the other dimensions were not significant. The only contradiction to the hypotheses occurred on the clean-unclean dimension. Although Group II differed significantly from the other groups, describing their parents as somewhat less than perfectly clean, Group III described theirs as the cleanest of all.

Another source of information relevant to the hypotheses was the personal-history interviewers' ratings of the most likely childhood precursors of interest in mathematics. The items rated were a set of defense mechanisms from the psychoanalytic repertoire. "Reaction-formation to primitive body expressiveness" and "need for autonomy in fantasy" were items that seemed to represent (alternative) methods of coping with the problem of autonomy versus shame and self-doubt. The predominantly Protestant groups (I and C) would be expected to receive significantly more high ratings on this pair of items. "Sublimation of sexual curiosity or curiosity about the body and its functioning," "sublimation of hostility," and "redoing" seemed more appropriate for problems of initiative versus guilt. The predominately non-Protestant groups (II and III) would be expected to receive high ratings on these. No prediction was made about a sixth item, "withdrawal."

Results showed that Groups I and C did have more high ratings on the predicted items, and Groups II and III received more high ratings than Groups I and C on "sublimation of hostility" and "redoing." The addition of "sublimation of sexual curiosity," however, reduced the discrimination.

The third hypothesis asserts that Group I differed from Group C, and Group II from Group III, in their ways of dealing with similar problems (shame and self-doubt in the first case, guilt and dependence in the second). Because of the small size of the sample, to test this hypothesis, each group

---

[3] In these analyses, members of Group IV have been assigned to other groups on the basis of creativity and ethnic background: two to Group I, two to Group III, and one to Group C.

TABLE 3.5. Descriptions of parents on selected dimensions of the semantic differential

Dimension	Mean scores				Groups I and C vs. II and III ($df=37$)	
	Group I	Group C	Group II	Group III	t	p
Strong-weak	2.0	2.7	2.8	3.9a	2.45	.02
Stable-unstable	2.1	2.6	3.1	3.2	1.78	.10
Clean-unclean	1.7	2.0	2.4b	1.4	—	
Safe-dangerous	1.8	2.2	3.2	3.0	2.94	.01
Pleasant-unpleasant	1.8	2.1	2.6	2.6	—	
Warm-cold	2.3	3.0	3.4	3.6	—	
Deep-shallow	2.6	3.0	2.5	2.8	—	

aParents described as weaker by group III than by all other subjects ($t=3.21$; p < .005).
bParents described as less clean by group II than by all other subjects ($t=2.50$; p < .02).

was compared with all other subjects, and the best pair of differentiating items was determined. For Group I this pair was "need for autonomy" and "sublimation of sexual curiosity." For Group C, it was "reaction-formation to primitive expressiveness" and "withdrawal." For Group III, the best pair of items was "sublimation of hostility" and "redoing." Group II could not be differentiated from the other women at the 5-percent level of significance. However, when Group II was combined with Group I, the two groups together received more high ratings on "sublimation of sexual curiosity."

Finally, the groups were compared on two Transactional Analysis scales (Williams and Williams, in press) that can now be scored on the ACL. The free-child and the adapted-child scales are considered to assess ego states carried over from childhood. Persons in the ego state of the "free child" are ebullient and not inclined to hold themselves in check or postpone gratification. Low scorers on the free-child scale are conservative, self-denying, and lacking in zest. A person in the state of the adapted-child has difficulty in overcoming dependent role behaviors, dislikes confronting contemporary reality, and seeks satisfaction in dreams and fantasy. Low scorers on the adapted-child scale have achieved more independence, apparently by suppressing their feelings or developing an insensitivity to those of others (Gough and Heilbrun 1980).

It was hypothesized that Group I would score higher than Group C on the free-child scale and that Group II would score higher than Group III on the adapted-child scale. Table 3.6 shows that these hypotheses were confirmed and that the designated groups have the extreme scores on each scale.

Summary. These findings from three different sources—the subjects' descriptions of parents, the life-history interviewers' inferences about developmental patterns, and scales developed to assess ego-states carried over from childhood—tend to support the hypotheses. The hypotheses, however, are oversimplified, and the evidence for them is indirect. The topic has seemed worth pursuing because there has been very little investigation of how the family's values and cultural integration affect a daughter's conflicts and coping techniques and how these in turn affect both the style and the success of her professional development.

Current Conditions of Life

The preceding material pertains to the hypothesis that patterns of mathematical style reflect influences from the past. To what extent may factors of the present be influencing research style?

Two important ways in which the groups differed were with respect to age and responsibility for child-rearing. The extremes are represented by Group C, whose mean age was 44 and of whom 75 percent were childless,

TABLE 3.6. Comparisons of subgroups on free-child and adapted-child ego state (ACL)

Scale	Group I	Group II	Group III	Group C	t
Free-child	54.1	44.8	46.0	38.2	3.12[a]
Adapted-child	51.0	60.3	46.7	50.7	3.09[b]

[a] $p < .01$, Group I versus Group C.
[b] $p < .01$, Group II versus Group III.

and Group II, whose mean age was 34 and of whom 70 percent had children. Though 60 percent of Groups I and III had children, Group II had *more* children, *younger* children, and included more single young women than the rest of the sample. It is evident that these facts of life situations must have contributed to the lack of confidence and initiative in Group II (even though the personality characteristics of Group II may also have made them vulnerable to role conflicts).

Four Lives: Childhood to Young Adult Years

Individual histories are helpful in bringing findings to life. Cases have been selected on the basis of their showing many of the empirically demonstrated characteristics of their subgroup. In the interest of preserving anonymity, each story will end at about the time of the individual's first professional position. That this shortening of the life history will emphasize past over contemporaneous factors is in some ways regrettable. However, the cases illustrate very well the different contexts in which interest in mathematics develops. Teachers of mathematics will see that young women of different types respond very differently to educational techniques and interventions.

Ann A— — (Group C). The parents of Ann A— — were teachers. As was customary before World War II, the mother had stopped working when she became pregnant with the first child. Not only was the father's salary modest, but he lost the savings he tried to invest. Ann remembers him as a strict disciplinarian, emphasizing perfect schoolwork and complete obedience. The mother felt abused, was impatient and excitable, and Ann dreaded the scenes that often took place. Sometimes the family played bridge together, but usually "everyone was buried in a separate book." The mother, who was "often in a state of worry about matters I could do nothing about," confided particularly in Ann. Ann considers herself more like her mother than like her father but adds, "my mother identified herself with me."

Achievement at school was "not encouraged; it was expected." Ann did well, but she had no real sense of accomplishment because other children called her a teacher's pet and made fun of her clothes, which were hand-me-downs. Mrs. A— — taught her children arithmetic and algebra at home on various occasions "to keep them occupied." But then Ann was bored at school and was even reprimanded because "she wasn't supposed to have learned that yet." For a short period in high school she worked ahead of the class and spent class time helping other students and correcting papers. Then she was put in a private school, where such activities were not encouraged. (There seems to have been little realization that Ann was a child of stellar intelligence. Her score on the Concept Mastery Test was 170, some 30 points above Terman's average "genius.")

Even in college Ann seldom thought about a career. It did occur to her that she did *not* want to teach. But what else did women do? She took math only after a persuasive talk from the dean, who had seen her good grades in physics. She then enjoyed her math courses and majored in mathematics. "I didn't work very hard," she says, "but I was reasonably thorough and conscientious. I think my professors thought my work good, but none of them mentioned graduate school to me."

After college Ann took a position in industry, but women were not allowed in the training courses that would have qualified her for a position in engineering mathematics, so she quit and went to graduate school. There at last she found her fellow students rather congenial. She tended to work in spurts, for pleasure rather than competitively or with thoughts for the future. Her chief liability was that she became extremely nervous and tense about examinations and giving talks. She thought of herself as a future teacher of mathematics rather than as a mathematician.

The rest of Ann's career proceeded in much the same way. Her motivation was ambivalent or lukewarm; she thought little about the future, elicited only occasional encouragement, and overcame few obstacles. From the beginning, says her interviewer, mathematics for her was a way of gaining approval through compliance. "Mathematics enabled me to convince myself I had done what was expected of me," she told him. "When I was done I knew it was done. I like things conclusive."

Her greatest satisfaction now is in teaching students to think in an orderly, clear, logical fashion. According to the interviewer, teaching permits her to comply through teaching others to comply; it also permits her to have "children," to whom she can be kinder than her parents were to her. She has never had an intimate relationship with anyone, male or female. Real children she finds "frightening"—as though they were untamed id impulses, the interviewer commented. He added: "When one combines a lack of warmth with heavy-handedness in the parents, it is not too surprising that the product is as in this case an individual who cannot express strong positive affect toward people or activities lest they appear libidinal or rebellious."

Barbara B— — (Group I). Barbara B— —'s parents also had little money, but they were active in church and civic affairs, and the family entered into many activities as a group. The father was a tradesman. The mother had a strong sense of duty and did not take a subordinate position in the household. Standards were strict, emphasizing "honesty and kindliness." Barbara seems to have been closer to her father than to her mother, of whom she was somewhat afraid. With her father there was the bond of an illness, inherited through his side of the family, which marked her life. She wept many bitter tears over the frustration of being shut in, as she often was, and of being prevented from doing things she wanted to do.

In high school Barbara specialized in science. It was an unusual thing for a girl to do at that time and place. In contrast to the experience of Ann, Barbara's teachers offered much encouragement, even though they did reprimand her for "always daydreaming in class." Calculus was not offered in the high school, but both mathematics and science teachers encouraged her to read it on her own. "The science teacher, once he got used to having a girl underfoot, also gave me a good grounding in dynamics and electrical theory, and in my last year he allowed me to run loose in his own private laboratory."

At the university, she found the teachers "inspiring." She collected scholarships and prizes, and her professors "took for granted" that she would take graduate study. "It sounds heavy," she says, thinking of herself as a rather shy and work-oriented introvert, "but I was quite active in student affairs and on the whole rather popular." Her graduate-school experience was similar.

Like Ann, Barbara had problems fitting into the "real world." Desirable teaching positions were scarce. Her first job was in industry, where she found in the research branch a discouraging prejudice against women. But the work was challenging, and "I enjoyed showing what a woman could do."

This last statement of hers—"I enjoyed showing what a woman could do"—reflects an important aspect of her motivation to do mathematics. Dr. B——'s interviewer believed that her interest began as a counteractive response to the effect of *shame* (interviewer's emphasis). In fact, the need to counteract shame was still active, he thought, because she remarked to him that some of the assessment procedures had made her feel "so big," with a gesture to indicate two inches tall. He attributed the importance of the shame to various sources (perhaps puritanical child-rearing practices, being the youngest child in a family with wonderful older brothers, and so forth), but particularly to the handicap that frequently made her a "shut-in." She is fascinated by mathematics because "there is something surprisingly perfect about how it comes out if you can get it to come out." She enjoys "being able to use what I know to solve a problem that somebody else is finding intractable."

Carolyn C—— (Group II). Again, the family was poor. They did everything together. The parents, both apostates, were members of no social or religious group, and relationships with the outside were reduced to a minimum. For example, the children did not go to school until they were eight, and they skipped grades whenever possible. Family values centered around "being different." The father was "a thinker, a talker, an aggressive, argumentative underdog, a magnetic personality, a man of unfulfilled potentialities. As a father he was kind, intrusive, and completely devoted." He appeared very sure of himself, so his ideas appeared to be the only right ones. Among them was the conviction that the outside world was hostile and the family had to stick together against it. Carolyn was his favorite child. The mother was "gentle, maternal, discretely intelligent, a weaker personality but ethically sound and introspective."

"We were all great and curious readers, hobbyists, and music lovers. ... Our parents were sincere intellectuals and encouraged us to aspirations of mental and cultural development." Carolyn's chief loves were literature and the cello. At school she did well in all subjects, but although "plane geometry showed a glimmer of its greatness to come . . . algebra was a terrible bore. The teachers were lovely people but not mathematicians and had themselves—and gave their students—no inkling of the real nature of the subject. I took the minimum."

Carolyn had planned to get a secretarial job after high school because she knew her family couldn't afford to send her to college. A teacher heard of this and insisted that she apply for a scholarship. College was "a tremendous experience." Carolyn came to mathematics as a requirement for physics, after a series of intellectual devotions to other subjects. "The mathematics department urged me to take advanced courses. The further I went the better grew my understanding of the real nature of the subject, and the greater my feeling of revelation and astonishment."

After much soul-searching, she went to graduate school. There she had her first experience in teaching, which gave her much pleasure. She was obsessed with mathematics. "I morally believed that every problem *had* to be solved." Her advisor suggested a problem; then she disappeared for a year and returned with her thesis essentially done.

Like the other women whose early careers we have discussed, Dr. C— — now had problems, though hers seem somewhat different. In her first position after the Ph.D., her work did not go particularly well. Perhaps she lacked an interested mentor. Perhaps her introversion prevented her from broadening her outlook at a time when it would have been advisable to do so. Certainly the domination of her father had finally to be dealt with. One of his views—which she had accepted—was that marriage was not good for women. But now she did get married, and she also had children. Although she was happy in these developments, the problems of the dual-career family arose, and, most distressing, her intellectual confidence and morale sank to almost zero.

Dr. C— — writes the following sketch of herself as a mathematician:

> Too much given to working alone with its hazards and assets: prefer devising an original approach to digging around in existing literature for preliminary groundwork. Prefer to have my ideas tested and proved before exposing them

to anyone else for criticism or collaboration. Characteristic approach: I must have a specific problem—not just be fooling around waiting to see what may evolve. Then I tackle it with infinite patience and attention to detail. First, empty space; then structurization step by step; finally the mystic moment of insight.

Dr. C— —'s interviewer thought her attraction to mathematics contained in it a desire to worship her father as a god but also a desire to escape his human domination and to increase her own initiative in the relationship. "The primary lure was communion with the father and the penetration of the primal scene or the holy of holies."

Dorothy D— — (Group III). Dorothy grew up in a well-to-do home in which the mother stressed education, good manners, and general cultural interests and the father, a successful and highly rational professional man, did not express his views at all. Although "there were no overt manifestations," Dorothy felt "a lack of harmony between my parents." Her father was extremely quiet, read most of the time, and had occasional outbursts of violent anger for trivial reasons. Dorothy "knew he loved me," but she was afraid of him. On the other hand, her mother "gave herself airs." Dorothy resented her rigidity and constant supervision. "My mother encouraged intellectual achievement only in the sense that she disapproved of anything but the best schoolwork." A thoughtful child, Dorothy saw a great gulf between what adults did and what was comfortable. She wanted no part of adult life, though she felt herself capable of anything she decided she wanted to do.

The family made several moves during Dorothy's childhood. Her teachers always held her in high esteem and were an important source of encouragement. She recalls "some geometry instruction which I loved. It consisted of being given three parts of a triangle and being asked to make a plan for constructing it (and to do the actual construction as homework). I was extremely quick at seeing how to do that. . . . I absolutely refused to learn processes the reasons for which I did not quite understand. My manipulations were generally correct but not fast. I liked deducing, generalizing, etc., but rather disliked applying mathematics to 'real life' situations as proposed in some problems."

Dorothy's interest in mathematics in high school was part of a general outlook that she describes as follows: "I was interested in figuring out a way in which people could live reasonably and justly and I admired everything rational, displaying contempt for everything emotional, sentimental, and even lyrical." She goes on to say that she "experienced some strange emotions (partly fear, partly some inexplicable surge of emotion) when I was among people who, as a group, expressed some worship of a hero or an ideal. I felt perhaps 'too bad I cannot sincerely join them.'"

At college Dorothy made some important friendships and got married. Later, hearing of interesting job opportunities, she went to graduate school to study mathematics. While as a school child "there was an almost purely esthetic pleasure in listening to a piece of deductive reasoning, step by step," and later in doing short pieces of deductive reasoning herself, in graduate school she became aware of the role that guessing, inductive thinking, and bold courage play in creative mathematics. She became more discriminating, demanding that deductive reasoning lead where she wanted to go.

Dr. D— — considers her basic asset to be her insistence on understanding a subject from the bottom up. She impresses people as charming, competent, and effective, which she is, but she often feels unsure of herself and wants to be led rather than to lead. Her interviewer considered the active-passive conflict to be an important one in her personality.

SUMMARY AND DISCUSSION

The outstanding finding of the first study was the striking difference in personality between women mathematicians rated high in creativity and other women mathematicians. The creative women had strong symbolic interests and were introverted, originai, and independent. The comparison subjects were much more orderly and conventional. Differences in intelligence and specific cognitive abilities were less evident than the differences in personality.

Comparisons of men and women mathematicians showed that the less creative men and women were more similar in personality than the creative men and women. Whereas the creative men had more initiative and assertiveness in their research style than other subjects did, the creative women were inner-oriented and low in assertiveness. Comparisons of creative mathematicians and writers, relative to comparison groups, showed that the personality and style of the creative women mathematicians resembled that of creative writers of both sexes. The creative women mathematicians were not complete mavericks, then. But why were the sex differences in creative style greater among mathematicians than among writers? The creative male mathematicians had responsible, prestigious positions at high-pressure institutions, while few of the creative women had contact with graduate students, one third had no regular job, and half had young children to take care of. Many of the men and women writers worked at home, so their life styles tended to be less dissimilar than those of men and women mathematicians.

On the other hand, such facts did not refute the hypothesis that there are two primary creative styles, one high in ego-assertiveness and the other low, and that although some men incline to the first and others to the second, most women show the low-assertive style (Helson 1967, 1968, 1978). If the low-assertive style is not appropriate for mathematics, then as long as such sex differences exist, are creative women doomed to a low level of accomplishment in this field?

A next step in the exploration of this issue was to study factors associated with the adoption of different research styles within each sex. Two main dimensions of variation in research style were (1) orderliness versus an emotional, disorderly attitude and (2) confident inventiveness versus constriction and inner focus. Creative mathematicians of both sexes scored lower on the first dimension, and men, especially creative men, scored higher on the second. A graph of scores on the two dimensions shows that most subjects (of either sex) who were rated low on creativity scored high on order and low on confident inventiveness. Few women scored high on both dimensions, and few men scored low on both.

Among women, four subgroups were identified in three of these quadrants (the sparsely populated quadrant of scores high on both dimensions being disregarded). Three of the subgroups were about equal in creativity, and the fourth consisted entirely of women rated below average in creativity. Comparisons of subgroups showed that they differed in personality, cognitive performance, and background. For example, the three creative groups each had peaks on different scales of the ACL: autonomy, abasement, and order. The fourth group had the highest peak on the order scale. The impressiveness of these differences led to a conceptualization of the significance of the patterns of research style in terms of problems in early development that were differently mediated by family values and the integration of the family in the community. Protestant socialization was hypothesized to create vulnerabilities in the area of autonomy versus shame and self-doubt. Families not fully integrated into the community—for reasons of ethnic background, lack of father, or something else—were hypothesized to present problems in the area of initiative versus guilt, the rationale being that the barrier between the family and the community would intensify the problems of relationship within the family that are characteristic of the "Oedipal" period. These and other hypotheses received some support, and the four patterns were illustrated with case histories.

Among women, confident inventiveness seems to have been encouraged by family values and by social support in achieving independence from ties to parents. This fact is important because it suggests that the sex difference in confident inventiveness may also have a significant social component (Block 1973; Mitchell 1974).

Each of the three creative subgroups of women had its strengths and its weaknesses; each met with discrimination or handicap because of sex. The fact that there were three creative subgroups shows that women with a variety of personality syndromes can do creative work in mathematics. Reducing the rigidity of sex roles should be helpful for all of them.

Nevertheless, Group I, the women high in confident inventiveness, has been the most productive. A style low in ego-assertiveness may be very creative, and it may be the only one available to individuals who, for one reason or another, are excluded from full participation in their society. Women as a group have been in this position. The low-assertive style needs protection and respect; with it individuals may reach insights that others would not. However, it does not fit well into the high-pressure academic setting. Many of the creative women mathematicians would have been more productive if their personal motivations had been supported by institutional nutriment; and they could have obtained this support more readily if they had been less ambivalent or less aloof. Understanding and experiment are needed on both the institutional side and the individual side.

The women of Group II, low on both order and confident inventiveness, are of special interest, not only because their research style is the least common among male mathematicians but also because they were found to be younger and to have had more responsibility for young children than the other women in the sample. Most members of Group II finished graduate school during the 1950s, so they present an interesting case of the interaction between a personality syndrome and a social context at a particular stage in the life cycle. The Group II women vary considerably in the degree to which they have become assimilated into academic life. Unfortunately, the present study does not help us to understand individual differences within subgroups.

Members of Group C, the core comparison group, were older on the average than other subjects and were the most likely to be childless. These demographic characteristics point to another distinctive cohort of women. One may imagine a succession of cohorts, each coming into mathematics with motivations that articulate with the subject-matter, conditions of employment, and social climate at a given time. Mathematics may have a "demand character" such that the personality types attracted to it are limited. If so, one would expect to find over time a varying distribution across a few personality syndromes rather than a succession of new syndromes. Today there is a generation of young women mathematicians with new options, new pressures, perhaps a new ethnic composition. How different it is in personality and research style is an interesting question.

REFERENCES

Barron, F. X. 1969. *Creative person and creative process.* New York: Holt Rinehart & Winston.

Block, J. 1961. *The Q-Sort method in personality assessment and psychiatric research.* Springfield, Ill.: Charles C. Thomas.

————. 1973. Conceptions of sex role: some cross-cultural and longitudinal perspectives. *American Psychologist* 28: 512-26.

Campbell, D. P. 1974. *Manual for the Strong-Campbell interest inventory: T325 (merged form).* Stanford: Stanford University Press.

Datta, L. 1973. Family religious background and early scientific creativity. In *Science as a career choice: Theoretical and empirical studies,* ed. B. T. Eiduson and L. Beckman, pp. 94-102. New York: Russell Sage Foundation.

Erikson, E. 1963. *Childhood and society.* New York: Norton.

Gough, H. G. 1957. *Manual for the California Psychological Inventory.* Palo Alto: Consulting Psychologists Press.

Gough, H. G., and Heilbrun, A. B., Jr. 1980. *The Adjective Check List manual.* Rev. ed. Palo Alto: Consulting Psychologists Press.

Helson, R. 1967. Sex differences in creative style. *Journal of Personality* 35: 214-33.

_____. 1968. Generality of sex differences in creative style. *Journal of Personality* 36: 33-48.

_____. 1971. Women mathematicians and the creative personality. *Journal of Consulting and Clinical Psychology* 36: 210-20.

_____. 1975. Personality characteristics and sex, in science. In *Research issues in the employment of women: Proceedings of a workshop,* pp. 61-82. Washington, D.C.: National Research Council.

_____. 1977. The creative spectrum of authors of fantasy. *Journal of Personality* 45: 310-26.

_____. 1978. Creativity in women. In *The psychology of women: Future directions of research,* ed. J. Sherman and F. Denmark, pp. 553-604. New York: Psychological Dimensions.

Helson, R., and Crutchfield, R. S. 1970. Mathematicians: The creative researcher and the average Ph.D. *Journal of Consulting and Clinical Psychology* 24: 250-57.

Holland, J. L. 1973. *Making vocational choices: a theory of careers.* Englewood Cliffs: Prentice-Hall.

Kuhn, T. S. 1963. The essential tension: Tradition and innovation in scientific research. In *Scientific creativity: Its recognition and development,* ed. C. W. Taylor and F. X. Barron, pp. 341-54. New York: Wiley.

Lesser, G. S. 1976. Cultural differences in learning and thinking styles. In *Cognitive styles and creativity in higher education,* ed. S. Messick, pp. 137-60. San Francisco: Jossey-Bass.

MacKinnon, D. W. 1962. The nature and nurture of creative talent. *American Psychologist* 17 (7): 484-95.

MacKinnon, D. W., and Hall, W. B. 1973. Intelligence and creativity. In *Science as a career choice: Theoretical and empirical studies,* ed. B. T. Eiduson and L. Beckman, pp. 148-52. New York: Russell Sage Foundation.

Mitchell, J. 1974. *Psychoanalysis and feminism: Freud, Reich, Laing, and women.* New York: Pantheon.

Osgood, C. E.; Suci, G. S.; and Tannenbaum, P. 1957. *The measurement of meaning.* Urbana: University of Illinois Press.

Rosenberg, M. 1965. *Society and the adolescent self-image.* Princeton: Princeton University Press.

Sarason, S. B. 1973. Jewishness, Blackishness, and the nature-nurture controversy. *American Psychologist* 28: 962-72.

Tryon, R. C., and Bailey, D. E. 1970. *Cluster analysis.* New York: McGraw-Hill.

Welsh, G. S. 1975. *Creativity and intelligence: A personality approach.* Chapel Hill: Institute for Research in Social Science, University of North Carolina.

Williams, K. B., and Williams, J. E. in press. The assessment of transactional analysis ego states via the Adjective Check List. *Journal of Personality Assessment.*

II

*Sex Differences in Mathematics
Achievement and Course-taking*

4

IS MATHEMATICS
A SEXIST DISCIPLINE?

John Ernest

ABSTRACT

A study of enrollment in mathematics courses at the University of California at Santa Barbara documented sex differences in mathematics course-taking at the college level. Evidence of differential participation and achievement in mathematics at the graduate and professional levels was also provided. In this chapter, stereotypes and attitudes of high-school students and teachers that may contribute to these sex differences will be explored, and the need for eliminating sexism in the classroom and in the job market will be emphasized.

The thesis of this paper comprises four assertions: First, sex differences in mathematical ability, or at least in achievement, exist. This phenomenon pervades employment patterns and mathematics education and training at every level. Second, the measured differences imply substantial restrictions on the participation of women in mathematical and technological development. As such they not only represent a "women's problem" but constitute a serious and urgent issue for the entire scientific community. Third, the deeply ingrained attitudes and stereotypes concerning women and mathematics are a major causative factor of the observed sex differences. Fourth, the scientific community has not recognized the gravity of the situation. Mathematics professionals, both educators and researchers, must accept the responsibility for developing an effective nationwide effort to eradicate the prevalent prejudices and stereotypes.

SOME FACTS

In a study of 1,324 school children in grades two through twelve, no statistically significant sex differences were found in reported enjoyment of mathematics (Ernest 1976). Nevertheless, when mathematics becomes optional (in high school and college), very few women choose it.

At the University of California at Santa Barbara (U.C.S.B.), for example, sex differences in the enrollment rates in mathematics courses are enormous. Although 55 percent of the 1976 entering freshmen class were female, almost twice as many men as women enrolled in the beginning calculus course. At U.C.S.B. there is a three-quarter calculus sequence and a five-quarter calculus sequence. The shorter sequence begins with math 34A; the longer sequence begins with math 3A. If one examines the change in enrollment, over the years, in the first quarter of the shorter sequence (34A) (see table 4.1), one might think that more women are beginning to take calculus. Unfortunately, this is not the case. If one combines the figures for the two calculus courses, one finds that the men have consistently made up about 64 percent of the calculus enrollment, in spite of the fact that men represent only 45 percent of the total freshmen class. Thus, a male freshman is more than twice as likely to take calculus as a female freshman. If there is any tendency at all, it is that more women are opting for a shorter calculus sequence, which is designed for the behavioral sciences and biology. The longer sequence is designed for the hard sciences, such as physics, chemistry, and engineering. These extreme sex differences in enrollment figures are (at least partially) attributable to the inadequate mathematics training of women at the high-school level—a sad state of affairs, which is described further by Lucy Sells in chapter 5 of this book. One might also conjecture that men take more mathematics not because they like mathematics more than women do but because, whether they like it or not, they are aware that such courses are necessary prerequisites to the kinds of future occupations they envision for themselves—in medicine, technology, or science.

In spite of the initial restricted female enrollment, it was still found, in both sequences, that at the end of each quarter the attrition rate was always higher for women. If we compare attrition rates for students in 1974 with those three years earlier, we see a considerable overall improvement. Unfortunately, the basic sex differences in these attrition rates have not changed (see table 4.2). The honors section of calculus has even lower female enrollment; often it has no women at all.

Attrition among U.C.S.B. mathematics majors is also higher for women. This pattern of higher attrition for women continues at each step of the academic ladder in mathematics—among math majors who go to graduate school, among master's students who continue toward the Ph.D. (Ernest 1976). In the last four decades about 7 percent of the Ph.D.'s in mathematics were earned by women. In the last two years we have begun to see a slight upward turn, the current figure being about 10 percent (American Mathematical Society 1975).

A similar phenomenon occurs in fields that require a considerable mathematics background. In the period 1972-75 the percentage of Ph.D.'s

TABLE 4.1. Fall enrollment in calculus sequences, by sex

Sex	Freshman class		Math 34A		Math 3A	
	Number	Percentage of total	Number	Percentage of total	Number	Percentage of total
1971						
Male	1,001	45	133	63	328	64
Female	1,228	55	78	37	184	38
1978						
Male	1,172	44	166	60	373	66
Female	1,475	56	112	40	190	34
1975						
Male	1,256	45	159	52	428	68
Female	1,549	55	146	48	199	32

TABLE 4.2. Attrition rates in calculus sequences, by sex

Quarter	Point of drop	Rates for	
		Males	Females
Fall 1971	3A → 3B	33%	37%
Winter 1972	3B → 3C	26	35
Spring 1972	3C → 4A	30	51
Fall 1972	4A → 4B	22	41
Fall 1974	3A → 3B	23	33
Winter 1975	3B → 3C	14	19
Spring 1975	3C → 4A	21	43

earned by women was below 10 percent in the following fields: agriculture, applied mathematics, astronomy, atmospheric science, business administration, computer science, economics, engineering, geography, geology, mathematics, operations research, physics, and religion. In contrast, in the same period, women received more than 25 percent of the doctorates in each of the following fields (most of which require little mathematical training): anthropology, art history, classics, comparative literature, education, English, Germanic languages, health sciences, home economics, library science, linguistics, microbiology, psychology, Romance languages, social work, sociology, and speech (McCarthy and Wolfle 1975).

The higher attrition rates for women, evident at every rung of the mathematics education ladder, continue with the professional success ladder. As previously indicated, about 7 percent of the mathematics Ph.D.'s are held by women (although at the 1976 graduation the figure was 10 percent). For all doctorate-granting mathematics departments in the United States, women comprise 4.8 percent of the regular ladder faculty. The percentage is slightly smaller (4.5 percent) when we restrict ourselves to the tenured faculty. If we examine the next rung of the success ladder and look at the figures for only the twenty-seven most prestigious research-mathematics departments, the percentages are almost halved. Women make up 3 percent of the ladder faculty but only 2 percent of the tenured faculty. The attrition rate for women, which we have observed to be higher than for men at every rung of the success ladder, takes its final toll at the very top. At the most prestigious schools women represent only 1.6 percent of the full professors of mathematics. (All of these figures are for the 1975-76 academic year.) In table 4.3 one can see the percentages of women among the tenured faculty in 1974-75 and 1975-76.

In 1975-76 the mathematics department at U.C.S.B. had two female mathematicians on the faculty, both employed as temporary lecturers. Thus, there were no women on the regular ladder faculty, that is, there were no women among the tenured associate professors and full professors and assistant professors who will be considered for tenure. Regular ladder

TABLE 4.3. Female percentage of faculty in U.S. math departments

Math departments	1974-75	1975-76
Granting doctorates		
Ladder faculty	4.7%	4.8%
Tenured faculty	4.6	4.5
At twenty-seven most prestigious schools		
Ladder faculty	2.2	3.0
Tenured faculty	2.3	2.0
Full professors		1.6

SOURCE: American Mathematical Society 1975.

faculty does not include instructors, lecturers, those holding temporary or terminal positions, or visiting professors. This same situation prevailed at other schools in 1975-76—at the University of Chicago, Princeton, Yale, Harvard, and M.I.T., to mention a few of which the author is personally aware.

There are numerous stereotypes concerning women and mathematics. One is that female mathematicians are less feminine than nonmathematicians. This preposterous claim has unfortunately influenced many young women when considering their career options. Many studies have proven the falsity of that silly assertion (Helson 1971; Lambert 1960). Some mathematicians, nevertheless, argue the point, typically basing their findings on a sample size of one. By remarkable coincidence, their random samples always consist of Emmy Noether (1882-1935), probably the greatest female mathematician in history. In making her way to the top of a male-dominated profession, she may not have met everyone's expectations of the way a woman should look and behave. To my knowledge, no researchers have concerned themselves with the similar momentous question, Are male mathematicians more or less masculine because they are mathematicians?

Hermann Weyl, eulogizing Emmy Noether, wrote: "No one could contend that the Graces had stood by her cradle, but if we in Gottingen often chaffingly referred to her as '*der* Noether' (with the masculine article), it was also done with a respectful recognition of her power as a creative thinker who seemed to have broken through the barrier of sex" (Kimberling 1972).

The appellation *der* Noether and the notion of the necessity of "breaking through the barrier of sex" to be a creative mathematician indicate as much about the frame of mind of the (male) mathematical community at Göttingen as they do about Emmy Noether herself. Although it was P. S. Alexandroff who dubbed her *der* Noether, he nevertheless spoke highly of her feminine characteristics: "her femininity appeared in that gentle and subtle lyricism which lay at the heart of the farflung but never superficial concerns which she maintained for people, for her profession, and for the interests of all mankind. She loved people, science, life, with all the warmth, all the cheerfulness, all the unselfishness, and all the tenderness of which a deeply sensitive—and feminine—soul is capable" (Kimberling 1972).

✳A second stereotype is that women are so "poor at figures" that they can't even balance a checkbook. As an example of how pervasive this nonsense has become, a major car-rental firm ran an ad showing a long line of men (apparently women don't rent cars) waiting impatiently while a young woman struggles through the arithmetic of the rental agreement. (The point of the ad was that this company now uses computers rather than relying on women.) The caption under the illustration read: "Now let's see . . . if *Billy* had 3 oranges and *Tommy* took 2 of them away. . . ."

Unfortunately, this copyrighted advertisement cannot be reproduced here. Permission to use it in this paper was denied with the following explanation: "Since our telephone conversation we have had much reaction to that ad from the ladies of America and all of it has been bad." It is certainly a hopeful sign that women are no longer passively accepting this stereotype and are beginning to react strongly against it.

The discipline of mathematics generates a curious conglomeration of attitudes in parents, teachers, and students. For example, in most homes it is the father who helps with the mathematics homework (starting about the time the child is in seventh grade), while the mother will help with most other subjects, such as English (Ernest 1976). In a small sample of elementary and high-school teachers, almost half believed that boys were better in mathematics than girls; not even one believed that girls were better than boys (Ernest 1976). These attitudes persist among the students themselves. In a sample of 506 high-school students (grades 9-12), some 32 percent felt that boys were better at mathematics, while only 16 percent felt that girls were better at mathematics (Ernest 1976). These parental, teacher, and peer-group attitudes have a major impact on a young woman's self-attitude. Stanford sociologist Sanford Dornbusch recently surveyed 1,886 high-school students and found that "female students in every ethnic group in San Francisco were more than three times as likely to give, 'I'm not good in math' as the basis for a poor grade as 'I'm good in math' as the basis for a good grade. This pattern was found in no other subject for females and in no subject for males" (Dornbusch 1974).

With attitudes, expectations, and stereotypes so widespread, it would not be surprising to find substantial sex differences in achievement levels. Nevertheless at U.C.S.B. we did not find any sex differences in the distribution of grades in mathematics courses (Ernest 1976). An excellent survey of the research on sex differences in mathematical ability indicates that the findings of educational and psychological researchers are very mixed (Fennema 1974). In some cases boys seem to do better, in others girls do better, and in still others no differences are found. The conclusion stems partially from the fact that the measuring instruments vary enormously and thus assess quite different faculties, such as computational skill, imaginative problem solving, geometric intuition, or logical reasoning. The consistently reproducible results involve highly specialized types of intellectual functions that *may* be related to mathematical ability and are quite probably the result of cultural conditioning. Nevertheless even here there is far more variation within each sex group than there is between the sexes.

SOME QUESTIONS

The above facts suggest many queries. Some follow.

1. So many substantial sex differences have now been recorded that one cannot avoid formulating the question, Is there an underlying sexist prejudice pervading the entire discipline of mathematics? The question is not raised in a judgmental or a rhetorical spirit. The question is a crucial one, for if the answer is yes, then this sexism must be fully reckoned with, especially in programs that are aimed at correcting the sexual imbalance in the field.

2. Much research continues to revolve around the question, Are there significant sex differences in mathematical ability? But what exactly is meant by *mathematical ability?* There is a wide range of measuring instruments, each assessing only one specialized facet. Creative mathematical ability is a rich and complex mixture of interrelated components, involving motivation, perseverance, the ability to withstand frustration, an esthetic sense, courage, intelligence, imagination, and many kinds of competencies, including computational, spatial, algebraic, and verbal. Let us first try to define what we mean by *mathematical ability,* in all its subtle intricacy, before we claim to have measured significant sex differences in that faculty.

3. The vitality of mathematics research depends on changes and new directions, without which it becomes routine and inbred. To what extent will the nature and quality of mathematics research change when sex equality becomes a reality in the profession? While this question is fascinating, it is basically academic, since we will only begin to observe any such developments as the increased participation of women in mathematics becomes a reality.

4. The final question is not at all academic; it is pragmatic. Given the facts surveyed above it is perhaps the most pressing and urgent issue before us: What projects and procedures will be most effective in changing the pervasive stereotypes, attitudes, and prejudices of parents, teachers, counselors, and students?

SOME SUGGESTIONS

The scientific community in general, and mathematical and educational professionals in particular, must accept the responsibility for uncovering and eliminating sexism wherever it might appear—at every stage of mathematics training, as well as in employment. Affirmative-action procedures are one such effort at the employment level; they deserve our earnest support.

Accountability is the paramount word in education today. It is usually interpreted to mean that the teacher is responsible for making sure Johnny can add quickly and accurately. Rarely is this interpreted as meaning the teacher is also responsible for seeing that *both* Johnny *and Mary* have a positive self-image concerning mathematics ability and approach mathematics challenges with curiousity and eagerness.

There is a mathematics course at U.C.S.B. designed specifically for future elementary-school teachers. On the basis of questionnaires distributed to one such class of seventy-five students, it was found that 26 percent of the potential teachers were indifferent toward mathematics, while another 14 percent actually disliked or hated it. Thus, 40 percent of these prospective teachers are likely to transmit to their students something less than a positive attitude towards mathematics (Ernest 1976). Many female students have related personal experiences of intimidation or even humiliation in a mathematics class. Many learned never to raise questions, lest they be subject to ridicule. Others tell of sitting in a class in constant fear that they would be called upon. It would be difficult to deny that such things occur, at all levels of mathematics education. Something *must* be happening in those classes to cause the consistently higher attrition rates for women in mathematics courses. Teachers should be held accountable for this. Sexism and intellectual sadism must be rooted out of our classrooms. A few sarcastic teachers must not be permitted to inflate their egos at the expense of children's natural curiosity. When teachers admit to disliking mathematics, they should not be permitted to teach it. Some alternative must be provided, such as the employment of eager and competent specialists carefully trained and highly sensitive to the prevailing sexist attitudes concerning mathematics. In particular, they would encourage girls to enjoy and excel in mathematics. If most of these mathematics specialists were women, then we would have the added advantage of presenting female students with a positive role model.

Effective procedures are needed for uncovering sexism in the classroom, at all levels. Anonymous teacher-evaluation forms should include such items as, Do you feel you were ever treated differently in class because you are a girl (or boy)? Explain. Were you afraid to ask questions? Why? Did you ever feel ridiculed or humiliated in class? Explain. Do you feel the instructor helped you to form a positive attitude toward the subject? Explain. Answers to questions such as these, analyzed for sex differences, might tell us how effectively we are meeting the requirements of the new (Title IX) federal law. More crucially, they might help to identify those few teachers who are doing the greatest damage to our young people. For the vast majority of competent, hard-working, and conscientious teachers, such information will represent helpful feedback on this difficult aspect of pedagogy.

As researchers aware of the facts, we have a particular moral responsibility to join together in demanding that extensive and effective steps be taken to eliminate sexism in our school and university system in general and in all forms of mathematical training in particular. Only then can we expect equal opportunity in science and technology to become a reality. Our culture and our children deserve no less.

REFERENCES

American Mathematical Society. 1975. Nineteenth annual AMS survey. *Notices of the American Mathematical Society* 22: 303-8.

Dornbusch, S. M. 1974. To try or not to try. *Stanford Magazine* 2 (2): 50-54.

Ernest, J. 1976. Mathematics and sex. *American Mathematical Monthly* 83 (8): 595-614.

Fennema, E. 1974. Mathematics learning and the sexes: A review. *Journal for Research in Mathematics Education* 5: 126-39.

Helson, R. 1971. Women mathematicians and the creative personality. *Journal of Consulting and Clinical Psychology* 36: 210-20.

Kimberling, C. H. 1972. Emmy Noether. *American Mathematical Monthly* 79: 136-49.

Lambert, P. 1960. Mathematical ability and masculinity. *Arithmetic Teacher* 7: 19-21.

McCarthy, J. L., and Wolfle, D. 1975. Doctorates granted to women and minority group members. *Science* 189: 856-59.

5

THE MATHEMATICS FILTER
AND THE EDUCATION OF
WOMEN AND MINORITIES

Lucy W. Sells

ABSTRACT

A student's level of high-school mathematics achievement acts as a critical filter for undergraduate college admission for blacks and limits choices of an undergraduate major for women in general once they are admitted to college. This effectively limits the opportunities of both these groups in the world of work. The data suggest solutions to the problems, particularly the dissemination of these facts to students, parents, teachers, counselors, and administrators in the educational system and to political decision-makers on the local, state, and federal levels.

Colleges and universities vary considerably in the amount of high-school mathematics preparation they require or recommend for entering freshmen.[1] This institutional variation in requirements and recommendations of high-school mathematics has important implications for freedom of access to undergraduate college admission and for freedom of choice of undergraduate major for those admitted. Students whose arithmetic skills are too far below grade level in high school are effectively barred from first-year

---

[1] A check of recent university catalogs shows the following variation: Iowa State University requires one year of high-school algebra for admission. Students are required to have two years of high-school mathematics—generally one year of algebra and one year of plane geometry—at the University of California (all nine campuses), Columbia, Georgetown, George Washington, Illinois, Indiana, Johns Hopkins, the State University of New York, Pennsylvania State, the University of Pittsburgh, Purdue, Temple, the University of Washington, Washington State, and the University of Wisconsin. Two years of algebra and one year of plane geometry are required by Cornell, Michigan, the City University of New York, Northwestern, Rochester, Vanderbilt, and Yale. While it only requires the first three years, Yale strongly recommends the fourth, as do Harvard and the University of Pennsylvania. Princeton and M.I.T. require four years of college-preparatory mathematics in high school.

high-school algebra, which is the minimal mathematics preparation required by most colleges and universities. Students who have had three and a half to four full years of high-school mathematics are immediately eligible for the standard freshman calculus sequence at any college or university in the country. Until very recently those students who had not pursued the second year of algebra and trigonometry in high school had no way of catching up before entering as freshmen and thus could not qualify for the standard calculus sequence.

The calculus sequence is generally required for undergraduate majors in every field except education, the social sciences, and the humanities. Even some of the social sciences are beginning to require more mathematics. For example, the calculus sequence is increasingly required for sophisticated, job-relevant work at the doctoral level in economics, political science, sociology, and psychology. Employers of social scientists from the bachelor to the doctoral level are looking for people with accounting and managerial skills, which would normally be developed in upper-division courses in schools of business administration. Access to upper-division courses in administration is limited to those who qualify for the standard freshman calculus sequence, thus restricting the potential options for blacks and women.

There is a rapidly growing literature on the importance of mathematics as a critical filter in shutting off opportunities for women and non-Asian minority students (see Dornbusch 1974; Ernest, chapter 4 in this volume; Fox and Cohn, chapter 7 in this volume; Helson, chapter 2 in this volume; Hilton and Berglund 1974; Jacklin 1977; Levine 1976; Maccoby and Jacklin 1974; Osen 1974; Sells 1973; and Tobias 1976). Because the filtering effect works to bar minorities from access to college and university admission earlier than it tends to close off choice of undergraduate major for women in general, minorities will be examined first.

LACK OF MATHEMATICS ACHIEVEMENT
IN HIGH SCHOOL AS A BARRIER TO MINORITIES

A 1973 study of San Francisco students shows a pattern of greater ethnic differences than sex differences in attitudes, behavior, and performance in mathematics (Fernandez, Espinosa, and Dornbusch 1975). Only among eighth-grade blacks was there a large and statistically significant sex difference in performance, in the opposite direction from what one would predict: While 69 percent of the males scored below the 5.2-grade level, only 38 percent of the females scored below that level.

At the tenth-grade level this sex difference had all but disappeared; and more than half the blacks performed at less than the 6.6-grade level, compared with 17 percent of the Chicanos, 8 percent of the whites, and 1 percent of the Asians. The percentage of blacks with ten or more unexcused absences during the previous semester was 39, compared with 28 percent of the Chicanos, 17 percent of the whites, and 8 percent of the Asians. The percentage of blacks reporting spending two or more hours a week on mathematics homework was 28, compared with 31 percent of the Chicanos, 44 percent of the whites, and 60 percent of the Asians. The percentage of blacks who received *A*'s and *B*'s in mathematics was 18, compared with 33 percent of the Chicanos, 38 percent of the whites, and 53 percent of the Asians.

The study has important implications for ethnic differences in undergraduate admission. More than half of the Asian students earned mathematics grades high enough for admission to most colleges and universities. Less than one fifth of the black students earned high enough mathematics grades. Further research needs to be conducted on differences in the experiences of Asians and blacks—in the home, on the schoolyard, on the streets, and in the classroom—to discover why the differences in attitude, behavior, and performance in mathematics are so great.

The evidence from this 1973 sample of San Francisco high-school students is supported by data on nationwide twelfth-grade median test scores in mathematics in 1965 (Coleman et al. 1966). The median achievement score of black twelfth-grade students was 41.8, compared with 51.8 for white students, a difference of one standard deviation.

Data from a 1978 study of enrollments in a California high school show that 79 percent of Asian students were enrolled in mathematics courses leading to calculus, compared with 72 percent of white students, 25 percent of Hispanic students, and 20 percent of black students. Blacks comprised 40 percent of the total mathematics enrollment. They comprised 79 percent of the enrollment in remedial courses with no access to algebra and geometry; 58 percent of the enrollment in terminal algebra and geometry (for students not expected nor not expecting to go beyond these courses); 21 percent of the enrollment in regular algebra and geometry; 11 percent of the enrollment in second-year algebra; and only 5 percent of the enrollment in trigonometry, elementary functions, and calculus (Sells 1979).

These three studies demonstrate the difficulties of opening opportunities for minorities at the post-secondary-school level through affirmative action without first addressing the problem of equalizing skills at the primary- and secondary-school levels.

LACK OF MATHEMATICS ACHIEVEMENT
IN HIGH SCHOOL AS A FILTER FOR WOMEN

It has been shown that girls start out equally with boys in the development of arithmetic skills (Maccoby and Jacklin 1973). Most studies show no sex differences in mathematics ability up to adolescence, but differences that are found tend to favor boys. The literature shows that after about age thirteen, boys start to move ahead in mathematics ability, and the gap widens with each additional year of schooling (Maccoby and Jacklin 1973, 1974; Poffenberger and Norton 1963; Very 1967). There is a need for further research on the distinctions between arithmetic, which involves memorizing skills of addition, subtraction, multiplication, and division, and mathematics, which involves abstract thinking and analytical skills.

The whole question of the impact with respect to mathematics achievement of puberty on girls, particularly since this occurs at the time of their first exposure to male teachers, in junior-high-school mathematics courses, needs to be further researched. Although the San Francisco study gives cross-sectional data rather than longitudinal data, one could infer possible effects of puberty on black females from the shift from 38 percent in the bottom fifth of all students at the eighth-grade level to 59 percent in the bottom fifth of all students at the tenth-grade level, an increase of 21 percent.

In addition to possible biological and psychological effects of puberty on mathematics achievement, there was, until the final Title IX Regulation Implementing Education Amendments of 1972, which prohibited sex discrimination in education, a universal tracking of seventh-grade girls into cooking and sewing and of seventh-grade boys into mechanical drawing, wood shop and metal shop. There is work being done at the University of California, Los Angeles, that shows the importance of mechanical drawing in the development of spatial-relationship abilities (Alspektor 1975). Spatial-relationship abilities are crucial for survival and progress in high-school mathematics. Perhaps sex differences in mathematics achievement are partially a result of sex differences in the development of spatial-relationship abilities.

In 1973 the author conducted a pilot study to test the hypothesis that inadequate high-school mathematics preparation places a serious constraint on a woman's choice of undergraduate major in college. The University of California system admits the top 12.5 percent of high-school graduates in the state. Presumably, they are better prepared in mathematics than high-school graduates who ranked below the top 12.5 percent. On the basis of the minimal mathematics requirement for admission, it was hypothesized that women accepted for admission would be less likely to have taken advanced mathematics in high school than men and therefore would be barred from various undergraduate majors, particularly in the sciences.

A systematic, random sample of names was drawn from the computer print-out of people accepted for admission as freshmen at the University of California at Berkeley for fall 1972. Their folders were pulled from the files and coded by sex and number of years of high-school mathematics preparation. Some students had taken only the minimum two-year entrance requirement, some had taken three years of mathematics, and some had taken the three and a half years required for admission to the standard freshman calculus sequence. The distribution of males and females by

TABLE 5.1. Years of high school math studied by 1972 Berkeley freshmen in percents, by sex

Years of mathematics studied	Men (N = 42)	Women (N = 39)	Total (N = 81)
2.0	7%	36%	21%
3.0	36	56	46
3.5	57	8	33
Total	100	100	100

SOURCE: Office of Admissions, University of California.
NOTE: $p < .001$; $\chi^2 = 25.066$, with two degrees of freedom.

number of years of high-school mathematics studied is shown in table 5.1. If we break this down according to sex, 57 percent of the men had sufficient high-school mathematics preparation to qualify for freshman calculus, compared with 8 percent of the women, a difference of 49 percent.

This fact of the high-school mathematics filter has frequently been interpreted as proof of discrimination against high-school girls, even while teachers and counselors have interpreted it as proof of self-selection on the part of students. When this information is presented in workshops to groups of parents, teachers, or school administrators or in testimony to congressional, state, or local hearings, someone invariably asks why the fact of sex and ethnic differences is a problem. They suggest that maybe girls and blacks don't take advanced algebra and trigonometry because they don't want to, and they ask, Isn't freedom of choice a good thing?

The crucial point is that freedom of choice rests on access to information about the options available and about the consequences of closing those options by choosing not to take as much mathematics in high school as one can handle. The leverage for changing the mathematics filter comes from two levels: (a) dissemination of information about the mathematics filter and its consequences to students, parents, teachers, administrators, and political decision-makers at local, state, and federal levels; and (b) identification of differences in the experiences of girls and boys, of blacks, Chicanos, whites, and Asians, at home, among peers, and in the primary- and secondary-school classrooms, that lead to their choosing to take or not to take advanced mathematics in high school and that shape and determine their ability to perform and achieve in those courses.

The evidence is strong that the ostensible freedom of choice not to take as much mathematics as one can handle operates to close off opportunities for minorities and women. To test the hypothesis that climates of expectation and social support might influence decisions to take or not to take advanced mathematics in high school, a questionnaire was distributed to members of an upper-division social-science class at Berkeley in 1973. It contained questions about performance in elementary-school arithmetic and high-school mathematics and about expectations and encouragement by peers, parents, and teachers; and it asked whether the respondent had

TABLE 5.2. Females who pursued advanced high-school mathematics, by reported social support

Pursuit	Some social support reported	No social support reported
Took advanced math	13	7
Did not take advanced math	1	17

SOURCE: Questionnaire survey of upper-division social-science class, University of California, Berkeley, spring 1973.
NOTE: $Q = .94$; $\chi^2 = 15.17$; $p < .001$, with one degree of freedom.

TABLE 5.3. Performance in advanced high-school mathematics, by reported social support

Performance	Some social support reported	No social support reported
A's and B's	13	3
C's and D's	—	4

SOURCE: Questionnaire survey of upper-division social-science class, University of California, Berkeley, spring 1973.
NOTE: $Q = 1.00$; $p < .001$, with one degree of freedom.

taken mathematics beyond the mininal, two-year entrance requirement. The distribution of responses is presented in table 5.2.

There is a strong relationship between having reported social support from peers, parents, or teachers, and taking advanced mathematics in high school ($Q = .94$). There is a similarly strong relationship between having reported social support for taking advanced mathematics courses and the level of performance in those courses. Table 5.3 shows that all of those who reported some social support for taking advanced high-school mathematics courses received A's and B's, and more than half of those reporting no such social support received C's and D's. While it is not possible to generalize beyond this small sample of social-science undergraduates, the magnitude of the relationship between reporting social support, taking advanced high-school mathematics courses, and performing well in them suggests the need for further research and action to increase levels of social support for blacks and for young women in high school.

Table 5.4 shows the differential enrollments, by sex and ethnic group, in majors in the physical sciences, life sciences, and mathematics. Note that the percentage of Asian women in these fields exceeds the percentage of white or black men, which is consistent with the findings of the San Francisco high-school study.

Coleman's national study in 1966 and the 1973 study of San Francisco students showed that more than half of the high-school blacks were barred from access to major colleges and universities by poor performance in arithmetic skills. The 1978 study of one high school showed one third of blacks and Hispanics barred from access to major colleges and universities

TABLE 5.4. Students majoring in physical sciences, life sciences, and mathematics, by sex and ethnic group

	Men		Women			Total	
Ethnic group	N	Percentage majoring	N	Percentage majoring	Sex difference	N	Percentage majoring
Asian	615	68	538	45	23*	1,153	58
White	4,094	41	3,040	17	24*	7,134	31
Black	697	37	412	17	20*	1,109	30
Total	5,406	44	3,990	21	23*	9,396	34
Ethnic Difference		31*		28*			28*

SOURCE: Student-response survey, University of California, Berkeley, spring 1972.
*p < .05.

and almost half of each group restricted by enrollment in terminal algebra and geometry. The 1973 study found that 92 percent of women at one major university were barred from access to undergraduate majors that required the freshman calculus sequence in the first year.

CONSTRUCTIVE INTERVENTION PROJECTS
TO OPEN THE MATHEMATICS FILTER

In recent years a number of constructive intervention projects have sprung up around the country to change the impact of the mathematics filter on blacks and women. These include:

1. Project S.E.E.D. (Special Elementary Education for the Disadvantaged). This project, initiated by the faculty at the University of California at Berkeley in 1965, eight years before the study described in this chapter suggested the importance of the mathematics filter, exposes disadvantaged youngsters to mathematical concepts during their elementary-school years. It hires mathematics specialists from the university and private industry to teach mathematics through discovery to full-size elementary classes.

2. Mathematics for Girls Project, University of California at Berkeley. This project offers small, after-school and weekend classes to help elementary-and junior-high-school girls discover that mathematics can be fun (Kreinberg 1976).

3. Pre-calculus Laboratory, conducted by the computer science-mathematics department at Mills College. This laboratory familiarizes students with the language of calculus before they get involved in its operation (Blum 1975).

4. Overcoming Math Anxiety, a consulting and training program, in Washington, D.C.

5. EQUALS, University of California at Berkeley, a teacher-education program to promote sex-fair mathematics instruction and counseling, funded by the U.S. Office of Education, Title IV. Now in its third year, this project works with 250 northern California elementary and secondary educators to provide materials fostering positive attitudes toward mathematics and to promote awareness of nontraditional careers for women. Teachers attend five days of in-service workshops and conduct presentations in their district.[2]

CONCLUSION

In using the data in this paper to elicit theories about what is happening in the home, the schoolyard, and the classroom to produce the sex and

[2] A handbook detailing the format, content, and methods used in the training is available from Nancy Kreinberg, Director, EQUALS Project, Lawrence Hall of Science, University of California, Berkeley, California 94720.

ethnic differences in mathematics achievement, the following results have occurred: Some people have been quick to infer lower ability levels on the part of blacks and females; some have been quick to infer freedom of choice and lack of interest in the subject matter by blacks and females; some have been quick to infer discrimination against blacks and females; and some have been quick to inquire how to intervene constructively to free students, parents, and teachers from the constraints of their respective sex- and ethnic-role expectations. This last group will contribute most effectively to changing attitudes, behavior, and performance, independently of their sex, ethnicity, or status in the educational, economic, and political system.

REFERENCES

Alspektor, R. A. 1975. A comparison of traditional and non-traditional practical arts programs in two schools and the effects upon mathematical attitudes, performance and spatial perception. Senior honors thesis, University of California.

Blum, L. 1975. An action program in progress. *Association for Women in Mathematics Newsletter.* May-June.

Coleman, J. S., et al. 1966. *Equality of educational opportunity.* Washington, D.C.: National Center for Educational Statistics.

Dornbusch, S. M. 1974. To try or not to try. *Stanford Magazine* 2 (2): 50-54.

Fernandez, C.; Espinosa, R. W.; and Dornbusch, S. M. 1975. *Factors perpetuating the low academic status of Chicano high school students.* Research and Development Memorandum no. 138. Stanford Center for Research and Development in Teaching.

Hilton, T. L., and Berglund, G. W. 1974. Sex differences in mathematics achievement: A longitudinal study. *Journal of Educational Research* 67: 231-37.

Jacklin, C. N. 1977. Sex differences and their relation to sex equity in learning and teaching. Washington, D.C.: National Institute of Education.

Kreinberg, N. 1976. *Furthering mathematical competence of women.* Bulletin of the Institute of Governmental Studies, vol. 17, no. 6. Berkeley: University of California.

Levine, M. 1976. *Identification of reasons why qualified women do not pursue mathematical careers.* Report to the National Science Foundation, Grant no. GY-11411. August.

Maccoby, E. E., and Jacklin, C. N. 1973. Sex differences in intellectual functioning. In *Assessment in a pluralistic society, proceedings of the 1972 invitational conference on testing problems,* pp. 37-55. Princeton: Educational Testing Service.

————. 1974. *The psychology of sex differences.* Stanford: Stanford University Press.

Osen, L. M. 1974. *Women in mathematics.* Cambridge, Mass.: M.I.T. Press.

Poffenberger, T., and Norton, D. 1963. Sex differences in achievement motivation in mathematics and related to cultural change. *Journal of Genetic Psychology* 103: 341-50.

Sells, L. W. 1973. High school mathematics as the critical filter in the job market. In *Developing opportunities for minorities in graduate education.* ed. R. T. Thomas, pp. 37-39. Proceedings of the conference on minority graduate education University of California, Berkeley, May 11-12. Berkeley: Graduate Minority Program, University of California.

Tobias, S. 1976. Math anxiety. *MS Magazine* 5 (3): 56-59.

Very, P. S. 1967. Differential factor structures in mathematical ability. *Genetic Psychology Monographs* 75: 169-207.

6

SEX-RELATED DIFFERENCES IN MATHEMATICS ACHIEVEMENT: WHERE AND WHY

Elizabeth Fennema

ABSTRACT

Many studies that have reported male superiority in mathematics learning have compared achievement scores of males and females without controlling for differential mathematics course-taking. Since males have usually elected to study more mathematics than have females, a better mathematically educated group (males) has been compared with a less mathematically educated group (females). When amount of course-taking is controlled, few sex-related differences in achievement are found. Cognitive, affective, and educational variables that may contribute to differential mathematics course-taking are explored in this chapter. The need for intervention programs that are designed to increase women's participation in mathematics and that include both male and female students, their teachers, and their counselors is stressed.

Mathematics educators have used sex as a variable in research concerned with mathematics achievement for a number of years, and many summaries of mathematics achievement have been published that include information about comparative learning of mathematics by women and men. Basically, all reviews published before 1974 concluded that while there might not be a sex-related difference in mathematics achievement in young children, male superiority was always evident by the time learners reached upper elementary school or junior high school. In addition, males were definitely superior on higher-level cognitive tasks: "The evidence would suggest to the teacher that boys will achieve higher than girls on tests dealing with mathematical reasoning" (Glennon and Callahan 1968, p. 50); "from junior high school and beyond . . . boys now surpass girls in studies involving science and mathematics" (Suydam and Riedesel 1969, p. 129); "sex dif-

Portions of this chapter were prepared under a grant from the National Institute of Education.

ferences in mathematical abilities are, of course, present at the kindergarten level and undoubtedly earlier" (Aiken 1971, p. 203).

Reviews published since 1974 do not show the same consensus about male superiority. In a 1974 review synthesizing information from thirty-six studies, the conclusion was that there were no sex-related differences in elementary-school children's mathematics achievement and little evidence that such differences exist in high-school learners. However, there was some indication that boys excelled in higher-level cognitive tasks and girls excelled in lower-level cognitive tasks (Fennema 1974). Callahan and Glennon (1975) agreed with this conclusion, while Maccoby and Jacklin, in a highly quoted review (1974), disagreed. They stated that one "sex difference that [is] fairly well established . . . is that boys excel in mathematical ability" (pp. 351-52). From these reviews it is evident that currently there is not a consensus on whether sex-related differences in mathematics achievement exist.

The question of whether there are sex-related differences in mathematics achievement is more complicated than it at first appears. While there is no doubt that many more men than women are involved in post-high-school mathematics study and in adult occupations that involve mathematics, whether this unequal representation is due to less adequate knowledge of mathematics on the part of women or to their deliberate choice not to study mathematics has been unclear. Both of these issues will be addressed here.

SEX-RELATED DIFFERENCES
IN MATHEMATICS ACHIEVEMENT

In order to clarify the reality of sex-related differences in mathematics achievement, four major studies of sex-related differences in mathematics achievement will be specifically noted: Project Talent, the National Longitudinal Study of Mathematical Abilities (NLSMA), the First National Assessment of Educational Progress (NAEP-I), and the Fennema-Sherman studies. In addition, some studies from other cultures will be briefly reviewed, as well as the Stanley study of mathematically precocious youth and scores on college boards.

Data for Project Talent were gathered about 1960 (Flanagan et al. 1964). This study assessed (among many other things) the mathematics achievement of a random sampling of high-school students in the United States ($N \simeq 440,000$). The data indicated that in ninth grade, sex-related differences in mathematics achievement were negligible but that by twelfth grade boys tended to do better. The mean difference at the twelfth-grade level, although statistically significant, may have little educationsal significance, since one item may account for the difference. Also, no attempt was made to control the number of mathematics courses the subjects had taken previously. Higher percentages of boys than of girls were enrolled in college-preparatory courses, so males undoubtedly had taken more mathematics courses and were more apt to say they were preparing for a career in which mathematics was needed. Undoubtedly a population of boys with more mathematical background was being compared with a population of girls with less mathematical background.

In 1975, a follow-up to the 1960 Project Talent study was done. Data were collected from approximately 1,800 students in grades nine through eleven in seventeen of the original schools (Flanagan 1976). Careful statistical checks on reliability of the comparisons, as well as adjustments for any change in the schools' socio-economic status, were made, and the following conclusions were reached (see table 6.1): (1) While the mathematics test scores were fairly stable from 1960 to 1975, the differences between females and males had been reduced; (2) male scores on computation tasks had declined 17 percent, while female scores had declined 11 percent, and the female mean score was 8.2 points higher than the male mean score; (3) and quantitative-reasoning scores declined 8 percent for each sex, and females scores were 0.6 points lower in 1975. A close inspection of these data makes it difficult to conclude that the mathematics achievement of males was much higher than that of females in 1960 or 1975.

Support for the belief that females do not achieve as well as males in mathematics could come from the NLSMA data that were gathered from 1962 through 1967. In these multitudinous studies, sex was used as a control variable. Analyses were done independently by sex whenever significant interactions between sex and any other variable were found. Unfortunately, the results from these studies have been inadequately reported and interpreted, making the knowledge they could contribute to the study of sex-related differences largely unavailable. However, a summary statement says: "Differences favoring girls were for variables at the comprehension level (the lowest cognitive level tested) and the differences favoring the boys were for variables at the application and analysis level" (Wilson 1972, p. 94). The number of mathematics courses that had been taken previously by the subjects in the NLSMA studies was controlled, so the conclusion reached undoubtedly was statistically valid in 1967. The size of the differences between the mean female performance scores and the mean male performance scores and the educational significance of that difference are unknown.

The 1972-73 mathematics data collected by the NAEP-I have received much publicity, and one statement has been widely quoted: "In the mathematics assessment, the advantage displayed by males, particularly at older ages can only be described as overwhelming" (Mullis 1975, p. 7); inspection of these data, shown in figure 6.1, confirms that males did outperform females at ages seventeen and between the ages of twenty-six and thirty-five. However, at ages nine and thirteen, differences were minimal and sometimes in favor of females. The problem of comparable populations is a concern here, as it was with the Project Talent data. The population was

TABLE 6.1. Project Talent 1960 and 1975 mathematics results

	Males				Females			
	Raw score		Tenth-grade Percentile difference		Raw score		Tenth-grade Percentile difference	
Skill	1960	1975			1960	1975		
Computation	25.7	18.7	−17%		30.8	26.9	−11%	
Mathematics	10.5	10.7	+2		9.9	10.3	+3	
Quantitative reasoning	8.5	7.8	−8		8.0	7.2	−8	

SOURCE: Abstracted from Flanagan 1976.

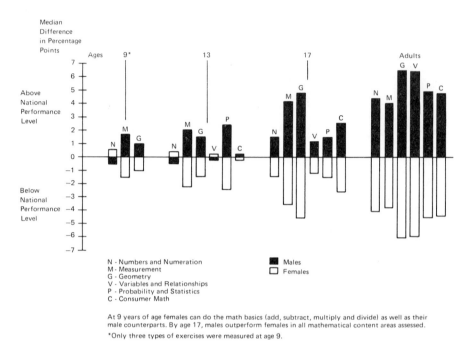

N - Numbers and Numeration
M - Measurement
G - Geometry
V - Variables and Relationships
P - Probability and Statistics
C - Consumer Math

■ Males
□ Females

At 9 years of age females can do the math basics (add, subtract, multiply and divide) as well as their male counterparts. By age 17, males outperform females in all mathematical content areas assessed.

*Only three types of exercises were measured at age 9.

FIGURE 6.1. Median-difference in performance between males and nation and females and nation on mathematics content areas.

selected by sophisticated random-sampling techniques but without control for educational or mathematical background. Since males have traditionally studied mathematics more years than have females, once again a population of males with more background in mathematics was being compared with a population of females with less background. At ages nine and thirteen, when the educational and mathematical backgrounds of boys and girls were similar, their levels of achievement were also similar.

The Fennema-Sherman study, data for which were collected in 1975 and 1976, investigated mathematics achievement in grades six through twelve (Fennema and Sherman 1977, 1978; Sherman and Fennema 1977). This National Science Foundation-sponsored study investigated a variety of levels of mathematics learning, as well as cognitive and affective variables hypothesized to be related to differential mathematics achievement by females and males. The results of this study can be widely generalized because of the diverse, carefully selected sample. In grades nine through twelve (N = 1,233)—carefully controlling subjects' mathematics back-grounds—significant differences in achievement in favor of males (approximately two items) were found in two of four schools. In grades six through eight (N = 1,330), significant differences in achievement were found in favor of females in a low-cognitive-level mathematical task in one of four school areas tested. In another of the four school areas significant differences were found in favor of males in a high-cognitive-level mathematical task.

Sex differences in mathematics have also been found on the Scholastic Aptitude Test (SAT), a college-entrance examination with a verbal component and a mathematics component, usually administered to high-school seniors. According to the publishers of the test, the mathematics required is that which is taught in grades one through nine. Over a period of years women have scored lower than men on this test. However, the following trend is interesting: "In 1960, the mathematical component means were 465 for women, 520 for men. Twelve years later, the average for women was virtually unchanged, but the average for men had dropped by 14 points (to 506)" (Wirtz 1977, p. 16). Although the advisory panel appointed to review the decline in SAT scores concluded that one reason the scores declined between 1962 and 1970 was that more women were taking the test (Wirtz 1977), the data do not confirm that women's scores dropped.

Once again, however, conclusions about male superiority are being drawn from populations in which males and females have studied different amounts of mathematics. Even though the mathematics required for the SAT may be taught before disparity in enrollment between the sexes is evident, continued use of such mathematics in advanced high-school classes undoubtedly aids one in solving items of the type included on the SAT.

In summary, the following can be concluded about sex-related differences in mathematics learning in the United States in 1978: (1) No sex-related differences are evident—at any cognitive level, from computation to problem solving—at the elementary-school level (this conclusion has been accepted for a number of years); (2) after elementary school, differences do not always appear; (3) starting at about the seventh grade, if differences appear, they tend to be in the males' favor, particularly on tasks involving mathematical reasoning; (4) there is some evidence that sex-related differences in mathematics learning in high school may not be as great in 1978 as they were in previous years; and (5) conclusions reached about male superiority have often been gathered from old studies or from studies in which the number of mathematics courses taken was not controlled. Therefore, males with more mathematics background were being compared with females with less mathematics background. In reality, then, the comparison was not between females and males, but between students who had studied mathematics from one to three years in high school and students who had studied mathematics for two to four years in high school.

An examination of cross-cultural differences in mathematics performance is interesting. In Australia, Clements and Watanawaha report female superiority on problem-solving and computation tasks in grades five through eight, while males performed at high levels in space tasks (in

Clements and Foster 1977). However, Keeves (1973) reports male superiority in mathematics achievement within all the ten countries that participated in the First International Study of Educational Achievement.

A different perspective on sex-related differences in mathematics achievement is noted if one examines performances of highly precocious males and females. In the Stanley Study of Mathematically Precocious Youth, many males outperformed any female; for example, in the 1973 talent search, junior-high-school youths who had scored above the ninety-eighth percentile on subtests of standardized achievement tests were asked to volunteer to be tested on a college-entrance examination. Seven percent of the boys scored higher than any girl, and the boys' mean score was significantly higher than the girls' mean score (Fox 1976; See also the chapter by Fox and Cohn in this volume, chapter 7).

SEX-RELATED DIFFERENCES
IN THE STUDYING OF MATHEMATICS

There *are* sex-related differences in the studying of mathematics. This is indicated by females choosing not to enroll in mathematics courses in high school and by the paucity of females in university mathematics courses (see the chapters by Ernest and Sells in this volume, chapters 4 and 5, respectively). Undoubtedly, the most serious problem facing those concerned with equity for the sexes in mathematics education is how to ensure that females will continue their study of mathematics. In support of this statement, consider some data from Wisconsin. During the 1975-76 academic year, while approximately the same number of females and males were enrolled in algebra, many more males were enrolled in the advanced courses (see table 6.2).

Although only symptomatic of the effect of many variables, electing not to study mathematics in high school beyond minimal or college requirements is the cause of many females' nonparticipation in mathematics-related occupations. The one variable that can be positively identified as causing sex-related differences in mathematics learning is the differential number of years females and males spend formally studying and using mathematics. Such a simplistic explanation of such an important problem seems too good to be true. However, this author believes strongly that if the amount of time spent learning mathematics were somehow equated for females and males, educationally significant sex-related differences in mathematics performance would disappear.

CONTRIBUTING FACTORS

In order to gain an understanding of why so many males leave educational institutions knowing a great deal more mathematics than do females, selected cognitive, affective, and educational variables will be discussed.

TABLE 6.2. Males and females enrolled in mathematics courses in Wisconsin

Course	Males	Females
Algebra[a]	41,404	41,579
Geometry	20,937	20,280
Algebra II	11,581	9,947
Pre-calculus	3,234	1,917
Trigonometry	4,004	2,737
Analytic geometry	1,752	970
Probability/statistics	1,113	581
Computer mathematics	3,396	1,481
Calculus	611	262

SOURCE: Konsin 1977.
NOTE: Data obtained from Wisconsin Department of Public Information Enrollment Statistics, 1975-76.
[a] Students enrolled in one-year and two-year courses.

Cognitive Variables

"Mathematics is essentially cognitive in nature; and the principle, distinguishing goals or objectives of mathematics instruction are (and should be) cognitive ones" (Weaver 1971, p. 263). Since mathematics is a cognitive endeavor, the logical place to begin to look for explanatory variables of sex-related differences in mathematics performance is in the cognitive area. It is within this area that the most important variable can be found, that is, the amount of time spent studying mathematics. This variable, as well as its impact, has already been discussed.

Another cognitive variable that may help explain sex-related differences in mathematics performance is spatial visualization, a particular subset of spatial skills. Spatial visualization involves visual imagery of objects, movement by the objects themselves or change in their properties. In other words, objects or their properties must be manipulated in one's mind's eye--or mentally. Even though the existence of many sex-related differences is currently being challenged, the evidence is still persuasive that in the American culture male superiority on tasks that require spatial visualization is evident beginning during adolescence (Fennema 1975; Maccoby and Jacklin 1974). However, even this difference appears to be moderating.

The relationship between mathematics and spatial visualization can be logically demonstrated. In mathematical terms, spatial visualization requires that objects be (mentally) rotated, reflected, and/or translated. These are important ideas in geometry. In fact, James and James (1968), in defining geometry and "the science that treats of the shape and size of things . . . the study of invariant properties of given elements under specified groups of transformation" (p. 162), are describing accurately most of the conditions that are met by items on spatial-visualization tests.

Many mathematicians believe that all of mathematical thought involves geometrical ideas. According to Bronowski (1947), the total discipline of mathematics can be defined as the language for describing those aspects of the world that can be stated in terms of "configurations." Meserve (1973) believes that each person who makes extensive use of all areas of mathematics uses the modes of thought of geometry at every turn and that "even the most abstract geometrical thinking must retain some link, however attentuated, with spatial intuition" (p. 249). In the Russian literature, mathematics and spatial abilities are regarded as inseparable (Kabanova-Meller 1970). Therefore, if spatial-visualization items are geometrical in character and mathematical thought involves geometrical ideas, spatial visualization and mathematics are inseparably intertwined.

Not only are spatial-visualization activities similar to ideas within the structure of mathematics, but spatial representations are increasingly being included in the teaching of mathematics; for example, the Piagetian conservation tasks, which are becoming a part of many preschool programs, involve focusing on correct spatial attributes before quantity, length, and volume are conserved. Most concrete and pictorial representations of arithmetical, geometrical, and algebraic ideas appear to rely heavily on spatial attributes. The number line, which is used extensively to represent whole numbers and operations on them, is a spatial representation. Commutativity of multiplication, illustrated by turning an array ninety degrees, involves a direct spatial-visualization skill. Many other examples could be cited.

Although the relation between the content of mathematics and spatial-visualization skills appears logical, results from empirical studies that have explored the relationship are not consistent. Many factor-analytic studies have explored this relationship, and several authors have reviewed the literature. Some investigators have concluded that spatial skills and learning of mathematics definitely are not related. In 1967, Very concluded: "Research on spatial ability has failed to produce any significant correlation of [the spatial factor] with any facet of mathematics performance" (p. 172). Fruchter (1954) stated that "spatial ability is unrelated to academic performance with the possible exception of a few very specialized courses such as engineering drawing" (p. 2). Smith (1964) concluded that although "there are several studies which indicate consistently that spatial ability is important in tests which are genuinely mathematical as distinct from those which involve purely mechanical or computational processes . . . the question whether the mathematical ability is dependent on the visual factor (or factors) has not been definitely answered" (pp. 127 and 68, respectively).

Even in geometry, where one would expect to find the strongest relationship, empirical findings do not indicate clearly that the two are related. Lim concluded in 1963, after a thorough review of relevant literature, that the evidence for a relationship between geometric ability and spatial visualization was inconsistent and unreliable. Werdelin (1971) was not willing to conclude definitely that spatial-visualization ability and geometric ability were related; however, he felt that "there is strong pedagogical reason to believe in a connection between the ability to visualize and geometric ability" (p. 39).

Other authors have felt that research indicated a positive relationship. In 1951, Guilford, Green, and Christensen concluded that spatial-visualization ability helped in solving mathematics problems. French (1951, 1955) showed that successful achievement in mathematics depended to some extent on spatial-visualization skills. In a more recent review, Aiken (1973) concluded that spatial-perceptual ability was one of the "most salient" mathematical factors extracted in various investigations. Obviously, the relationship between learning in mathematics and spatial ability is not clear, and the need for more data is great.

Even less is known about the effect that differential spatial visualization has on the mathematics learning of females and males. One indication that the relationship between the learning of mathematics and spatial visualization is an important consideration is the concurrent development of sex-related differences in favor of males in mathematics achievement and spatial-visualization skills. No significant sex-related differences in either mathematics achievement or spatial-visualization skills have been consistently reported in subjects four through eight years old. Sex-related differences in performance on spatial-visualization tasks become more pronounced between upper elementary years and the last year of high school (Maccoby and Jacklin, 1974). Sex-related differences in mathematical achievement also appear during this time (Fennema 1974). Perhaps less adequate spatial-visualization skills may partially explain sex-related differences in mathematics achievement.

The Fennema-Sherman study specifically investigated the relationship between mathematics achievement and spatial-visualization skills. The data from this study do not support the idea that differences in spatial-visualization ability are helpful in explaining sex-related differences in mathematics achievement. In this study of females and males (grades six through twelve) enrolled in mathematics courses, few sex-related differences in either mathematics achievement or spatial-visualization skills were found. The two were related ($r \simeq .5$) similarly for both sexes, and spatial-visualization ability appeared to influence both females and males equally to continue studying mathematics.

Affective Variables

The confidence-anxiety dimension in mathematics. One tends to do those things that one feels confident to do and to avoid activities that arouse anxiety. This confidence-anxiety dimension, as it relates to mathematics learning, is one of the more important affective variables that helps explain sex-related differences in mathematics learning. The relationship of anxiety and mathematics learning has been explored by a variety of methodologies and with instruments purported to measure debilitative or facilitative anxiety in general and/or specific to mathematics. Callahan and Glennon (1975) concluded that "anxiety and mathematics are related," that "in general high anxiety is associated with lower achievement in mathematics" (p. 82). Reports from NLSMA indicate that between grades four and ten, facilitating anxiety decreased; females' scores decreased more than males'. Debilitating anxiety increased for females between these grade levels (Crosswhite 1975).

Confidence per se as it relates to mathematics has not been given specific attention except in the Fennema-Sherman study. However, self-concept, which appears to be defined in many scales as self-confidence, has received much study. Leviton (1975) and Primavera et al. (1974) reviewed the literature dealing with self-concept, and both concluded that a positive relationship exists between academic achievement and self-esteem. Brookover and Thomas (1964) offer evidence that self-concept is not generalizable but is related to specific academic areas. Gallahan and Glennon (1975) concluded that there is a positive relationship between self-esteem and achievement in mathematics. Others have also recognized the importance of academic self-concept in learning mathematics (Bachman 1970; Fink 1969).

Although confidence and anxiety have been defined as separate traits, it appears that in relation to mathematics, they are very similar. In the Fennema-Sherman study an attempt was made to measure both confidence and anxiety. A high rating on the confidence scale correlated highly ($r = .89$) with a low rating on the anxiety scale. While it may be possible to talk about the two independently, it doesn't appear to be useful.

The literature strongly supports the belief that there are sex-related differences in the confidence-anxiety dimension. It appears reasonable to believe that lesser confidence, or greater anxiety, on the part of females is an important variable that helps explain sex-related differences in mathematics course-taking. Crandall et al. (1962) concluded that girls underestimate their own ability to solve mathematical problems. Others have concluded that females feel inadequate when faced with a variety of intellectual, problem-solving activities (Kagan 1964). Maccoby and Jacklin (1973) reported that "girls tend to underestimate their own intellectual abilities more than boys do" (p. 41).

In the Fennema-Sherman study, at each grade level from grade six through grade 12, boys were significantly more confident in their ability to deal with mathematics than were girls. In most instances this was true when there were no significant sex-related differences in mathematics achievement. In addition, confidence in learning mathematics was more highly correlated with mathematics achievement than was any other affective variable ($r \simeq .40$). Confidence was almost as highly related to achievement as were verbal ability and spatial visualization.

Stereotyping mathematics as a male domain. It is commonly accepted that mathematics is stereotyped as an activity more appropriate for males than for females. It has been believed that the sex typing of mathematics as male began in elementary school, became stronger during adolescent years, and was solidly entrenched by adult years. However, Stein (1971) and Stein and Smithells (1969) provide evidence that mathematics is not considered masculine by females and males until adolescent years, and even during these years it is not ranked as as highly masculine as are spatial, mechanical, and athletic tasks. Bobbe (1971) found that among fourth- and sixth-grade subjects, arithmetic was judged to be feminine by girls, while boys judged it to be appropriate for both sexes. Among adults, it is a fact that the use and creation of mathematics is predominantly a male domain. Stein and Smithells (1969) offered evidence that in the twelfth grade, females perceived this fact and were responding to the reality.

The Fennema-Sherman study indicated that females in grades six through twelve deny that mathematics is a male domain. While the males in the study did not strongly stereotype mathematics as a male domain, at each grade they stereotyped it at significantly higher levels than did females. This is an interesting and highly significant finding. The cross-sex influence on all aspects of behavior is strong during adolescent years. Since males stereotype mathematics as a male domain, they undoubtedly communicate this belief in many subtle and not so subtle ways to females, which influences females' willingness to study mathematics. This has strong implications for the development of intervention programs designed to increase female participation in mathematics.

Usefulness of mathematics. A different kind of affective variable is belief in the personal usefulness of mathematics. Hilton and Berglund (1974) and the Fennema-Sherman study provided data indicating that females believe that mathematics is personally useful to a lesser degree than do males. The difference was not as great, however, in the Fennema-Sherman study as it was in the Hilton-Berglund study. This may indicate that the beliefs of females are becoming more similar to those of males in this respect.

Effectance motivation in mathematics. One variable that has been hypothesized to show a sex-related difference is effectance motivation. This motive can be "inferred specifically from behavior that shows a lasting formalization and that has characteristics of exploration and experimentation" (White 1959, p. 323). It is closely related to problem-solving activity and is often called intrinsic motivation. This motivation would encourage learners to participate in mathematics activities at high cognitive levels. Some believe that females are not so involved in problem-solving activities as are males (Carey 1958; Kagan 1964); however, the Fennema-Sherman study found no sex-related difference in this variable at any grade level from grade six through twelve. It appears that the belief that females are not as intrinsically motivated in mathematics as males is merely a myth.

Educational Variables

There are sex-related differences in the final outcome of mathematical education due in large part to females' reluctance—if not refusal—to elect to study mathematics. Some intervention is essential at the present time to ensure equity in mathematics education for both sexes; however, before effective intervention can be planned, more information is needed about critical school variables that are amenable to change and important in the educational process.

Teachers. Teachers are the most important educational influence on students' learning of mathematics. From kindergarten to high school, learners spend thousands of hours in direct contact with teachers. While other educational agents may have influence on educational decisions, it is the daily contact with teachers that is the main influence of the formal educational institution. Part of the teachers' influence is in the learners' development of sex-role standards. These sex-role standards include definitions of acceptable achievement in the various subject areas. It is believed that this influence by teachers is exerted through their differential treatment of the sexes as well as through their expectation of sex-related differences in achievement.

Many studies have indicated that teachers treat female and male students differently (Schonborn 1975). In general, males appear to be more salient in the teachers' frame of reference. Teachers' interaction with males is greater than their interaction with females in both blame and praise contacts. Teachers also reinforce in both females and males sexually stereotypic behavior (Sears and Feldman 1966). Brophy, Good, and their colleagues—whose main interest has been teachers' treatment of males—have been the major investigators of teachers' treatment of females and males. In several studies they have concluded that girls and boys receive equal treatment. The data from one of their major studies, however, show that while the sex of the teacher was unimportant, high-achieving high-school boys received significantly more attention in mathematics class than any other group (Good, Sikes, and Brophy 1973). Another study involving first-grade reading replicated this trend at nonsignificant levels (Good and Brophy 1971). They concluded from these studies that teacher bias was not evident. One must question why no conclusion was reached about inequitable treatment of high-achieving females.

The investigation of the relationship between teacher behavior and sex-related differences in mathematics appears to be crucial to understanding why females do not participate in higher-level mathematics. In particular, information in the following areas would be helpful: (1) What are the effects of differential teacher treatment and expectations on achievement in and election of mathematics courses? (2) Do teachers differentially reinforce males and females for specific kinds of mathematical and/or sexually stereotypic activities? Are males being reinforced more for problem-solving activities, while females are reinforced for computational activities? (3) What is the effect of sex of teacher on mathematical achievement of boys and girls? While O'Brien (1975) reports no sex-of-teacher effect, Good, Sikes, and Brophy (1973) and Shinedling and Pederson (1970) report that male students do best in quantitiative scores when taught by male teachers.

School organization. There is some evidence, and much belief, that schools do influence sexual stereotypes. Minuchin (1971) concluded that children who attended schools categorized as traditional differed in their sex-typed reactions from those who attended schools categorized as modern. The interaction of the sexes was different in those schools, also. In the most traditional school, boys became leaders in problem solving, while girls became followers. This was not so in the less traditional schools. The sex-role behavior of children attending traditional schools was more rigid than that of children attending liberal schools.

Some schools are remarkably more effective in persuading females to attempt high achievement in mathematics. Casserly identified thirteen high schools that had an unusually high percentage of females in advanced-placement mathematics and science classes. The schools had identified these girls as early as fourth grade, and the girls' teachers and peers were supportive of high achievement by females. (Casserly's study is summarized in chapter 9 of this volume.) Rowell (1971) pursued the same type of investigation in attempting to identify schools and school characteristics that produced females with high achievement in science. Studies identifying and describing schools that are particularly successful in encouraging females to enroll in mathematics beyond minimal requirements are needed.

Many people are advocating that female-only classes will result in equity in mathematics education. The argument for this type of school organization goes something like this: Because peer pressure against female competitiveness is too strong a force, females will not compete against males in mixed-sex classrooms; female leadership (in problem solving, in this case) is only able to emerge when competition with males is eliminated; teachers will not have different sex-related expectations and behaviors if only one sex is present. Single-sex classrooms appear to provide a simple solution to a complex problem. However, the weight of evidence found does not support this type of grouping. Conway (1973) convincingly argues that throughout history separate education for the sexes has resulted in inferior education for females. Keeves (1973), after a careful and thorough review of mathematics and science education in ten countries, concluded that the "extent to which a community provides for education in single-sex schools would appear to indicate the extent to which it sees its boys and girls requiring different preparation for different societal roles" (p. 62). He argues that "in so far as a community has different expectations for different groups of its members and proceeds to mold its future members through different organizations, then it fails to provide equal opportunities for individual development" (p. 52).

Before single-sex classrooms are embraced as a panacea for educational equity for females, there must be careful examination concerning long-term effectiveness of such programs. In reality, this may be a partially nonresearchable problem. No one can foresee the implications for females fifty years from now of being isolated in their mathematical training. Because of what has happened to females as well as blacks over the last century, single-sex classrooms must be approached with caution.

CONCLUSIONS

What, then, is known about sex-related differences in mathematics and factors related to such differences? Certainly, when both females and males study the same amount of mathematics, differences in learning mathematics are minimal and perhaps decreasing. Far fewer females elect to study mathematics, and therein lies the problem. Factors that appear to contribute to this nonelection are females' lesser confidence in learning mathematics and a belief that mathematics is not useful to them and males' belief that mathematics is a male domain.

There is nothing inherent in females that keeps them from learning mathematics at the same level as do males (Sherman 1976). Intervention programs that will increase females' participation in mathematics can and must be designed and implemented within schools. Such programs must include male students, female students, and their teachers. Only when such intervention programs become effective can true equity in mathematics education be accomplished.

REFERENCES

Aiken, L. R. 1971. Intellective variables and mathematics achievement: Directions for research. *Journal of School Psychology* 9: 201-9.

————. 1973. Ability and creativity in math. *Review of Educational Research* 43: 405-32.

Bachman, A. M. 1970. The relationship between seventh-grade pupils' academic self-concept and achievement in mathematics. *Journal for Research in Mathematics Education* 1: 173-79.

Bobbe, C. N. 1971. Sex-role preference and academic achievement. Ph.D. diss., Yeshiva University.

Brookover, W. B., and Thomas, S. 1964. Self-concept of ability and school achievement. *Sociology of Education* 37 (3): 271-79.

Bronowski, J. 1947. Mathematics. In *The quality of education,* ed. D. Thompson and J. Reeves, pp. 179-95. London: Muller.

Callahan, L. G., and Glennon, V. J. 1975. *Elementary school mathematics: A guide to current research.* Washington, D.C.: Association for Supervision and Curriculum Development.

Carey, G. L. 1958. Sex differences in problem-solving performance as a function of attitude differences. *Journal of Abnormal and Social Psychology* 56: 256-60.

Clements, M. A., and Foster, J., eds. 1977. *Research in mathematics education in Australia.* Vol. 2.

Conway, J. K. 1973. Perspectives on the history of women's education in the United States. Paper presented at the annual meeting of the American Educational Research Association, New Orleans, 1973.

Crandall, V. J.; Katkovsky, W.; and Preston, A. 1962. Motivational and ability determinants of young children's intellectual achievement behaviors. *Child Development* 33: 643-61.

Crosswhite, F. J. 1975. Correlates of attitudes toward mathematics. National Longitudinal Study of Mathematics Achievement, report no. 20. Abstracted by L. R. Aiken. *Investigations in Mathematics Education* 8 (3): 38-40.

Fennema, E. 1974. Mathematics learning and the sexes: A review. *Journal for Research in Mathematics Education* 5: 126-39.

_____. 1975. Spatial ability, mathematics, and the sexes. In *Mathematics learning: What research says about sex differences,* ed. E. Fennema, pp. 33-44. Columbus, Ohio: Educational Research Information Center, Center for Science, Mathematics, and Environmental education, College of Education, Ohio State University.

Fennema, E., and Sherman, J. A. 1977. Sex-related differences in mathematics achievement, spatial visualization and affective factors. *American Educational Research Journal* 14 (1): 51-71.

_____. 1978. Sex-related differences in mathematics achievement and related factors: A further study. *Journal for Research in Mathematics Education* 9 (3): 189-203.

Fink, M. B. 1969. Self-concept as it relates to academic underachievement. *California Journal of Educational Research* 13: 57-61.

Flanagan, J. C. 1976. Changes in school levels of achievement: Project TALENT ten- and fifteen-year retests. *Educational Researcher* 5 (8): 9-12.

_____, et al. 1964. *The American high-school student.* Pittsburgh: University of Pittsburgh Press.

Fox, L. H. 1976. Sex differences in mathematical precocity: Bridging the gap. In *Intellectual talent: Research and development,* ed. D. P. Keating, pp. 183-214. Baltimore: The Johns Hopkins University Press.

French, J. W. 1951. The West Point tryout of the guidance battery. Research bulletin 51-12. Princeton: Educational Testing Service.

_____. 1955. The West Point tryout of the guidance battery, part 2. Research bulletin 55-6. Princeton: Educational Testing Service.

Fruchter, B. 1954. Measurement of spatial abilities: History and background. *Educational and Psychological Measurement* 14: 387-95.

Glennon, V. J., and Callahan, L. G. 1968. *A guide to current research: Elementary school mathematics.* Washington, D. C.: Association for Supervision and Curriculum Development.

Good, T. L., and Brophy, J. E. 1971. Questioned equality for grade one boys and girls. *Reading Teacher* 25: 247-52.

Good, T. L.; Sikes, J. N.; and Brophy, J. E. 1973. Effects of teacher sex and student sex on classroom interaction. *Journal of Educational Psychology* 65: 74-87.

Guilford, J. P.; Green, R. F.; and Christensen, P. R. 1951. A factor analytic study of reasoning abilities. II. Administration of tests and analysis of results. Report no. 3. University of Southern California Psychology Laboratory.

Hilton, T. L., and Berglund, G. W. 1974. Sex differences in mathematics achievement: A longitudinal study. *Journal of Education Research* 67: 231-37.

James, G., and James, R. C. 1968. *Mathematics Dictionary.* 3d ed. Princeton: Van Nostrand.

Kabanova-Meller, E. N. 1970. The role of the diagram in the application of geometric theorems. In *Soviet studies in the psychology of learning and teaching mathematics,* ed. J. Kilpatrick and I. Wirszup, trans. M. Ackerman, pp. 7-50, vol. 4. Stanford: School Mathematics Study Group, Stanford University.

Kagan, J. 1964. Acquisition and significance of sex typing and sex role identity. In *Review of child development research,* ed. M. L. Hoffman and L. Hoffman. pp. 137-67. New York: Russell Sage Foundation.

Keeves, J. P. 1973. Differences between the sexes in mathematics and science courses. *International Review of Education* 19: 47-63.

Konsin, M. A. 1977. Enrollment in Wisconsin high school mathematics classes, by sex, during 1975-76. Mimeographed. Madison: University of Wisconsin-Madison.

Leviton, H. 1975. The implications of the relationship between self-concept and academic achievement. *Child Study Journal* 5: 25-36.

Lim, H. 1963. Geometry and the space factors. Stanford: School Mathematics Study Group, Stanford University.

Maccoby, E. E., and Jacklin, C. N. 1973. Sex differences in intellectual functioning. In *Assessment in a pluralistic society: Proceedings of the 1972 Invitational Conference on Testing Problems,* pp. 37-51. Princeton: Educational Testing Service.

_____. 1974. *The psychology of sex differences.* Stanford: Stanford University Press.

Meserve, B. E. 1973. Geometry as a gateway to mathematics. In *Developments in mathematical education,* ed. A. G. Howson, pp. 241-53. Cambridge: Cambridge University Press.

Minuchin, P. P. 1971. Sex-role concepts and sex typing in childhood as a function of school and home environments. In *Social development and personality,* ed. G. C. Thompson, pp. 371-87. New York: John Wiley & Sons.

Mullis, I.V.S. 1975. *Educational achievement and sex discrimination.* Denver: National Assessment of Educational Progress.

O'Brien, C. W. 1975. Pupil achievement, attendance, and attitudes, and the relationship between teacher perception, teacher sex, and pupil sex. Ph.D. diss., University of Michigan.

Primavera, L. H.; Simon, W. E.; and Primavera, A. M. 1974. The relationship between self-esteem and academic achievement: an investigation of sex differences. *Psychology in the Schools* 11: 213-16.

Rowell, J. A. 1971. Sex differences in achievement in science and the expectations of teachers. *Australian Journal of Education* 15: 16-29.

Schonborn, B. G. 1975. *An investigation of the attitudes of elementary school teachers toward sex-role behaviors of elementary school children.* Ph.D. diss., University of Illinois.

Sears, P. S., and Feldman, D. H. 1966. Teacher interactions with boys and girls. *National Elementary Principal* 46 (2): 45-48.

Sherman, J. A. 1967. Problem of sex differences in space perception and aspect of intellectual functioning. *Psychological Review* 74: 290-99.

Sherman, J. A., and Fennema, E. 1977. The study of mathematics among high school girls and boys: Related factors. *American Educational Research Journal* 14 (2): 159-68.

Shinedling, M., and Pederson, D. M. 1970. Effects of sex of teacher and student on children's gain in quantitative and verbal performance. *Journal of Psychology* 76: 79-84.

Smith, I. M. 1964. *Spatial ability.* San Diego: Knapp.

Stein, A. H. 1971. The effects of sex role standards for achievement and sex role preference on three determinants of achievement motivation. *Developmental Psychology* 4: 219-31.

Stein, A. H. and Smithells, J. 1969. Age and sex differences in children's sex role standards about achievement. *Developmental Psychology* 1: 252-59.

Suydam, M. N., and Riedesel, C. A. 1969. *Interpretive study of research and development in elementary school mathematics, vol. I. Introduction and summary: What research says.* U.S. Department of Health, Education and Welfare final report, project no. 8-0586.

Very, P. S. 1967. Differential factor structures in mathematical ability. *Genetic Psychology Monographs* 75: 169-207.

Weaver, J. F. 1971. Seductive shibboleths. *Arithmetic Teacher* 18: 263-64.

Werdelin, I. 1971. *The geometrical ability and space factor in boys and girls.* Lund, Sweden: University of Lund.

White, R. W. 1959. Motivation reconsidered: The concept of motivation. *Psychological Review* 66: 297-333.

Wilson, J. W. 1972. *Patterns of mathematics achievement in grade 11: Z population.* National Longitudinal Study of Mathematical Abilities, no. 17. Stanford: Stanford University Press.

Wirtz, W. 1977. *On further examination: Report of the advisory panel on the Scholastic Aptitude Test score decline.* New York: College Entrance Examination Board.

7

SEX DIFFERENCES
IN THE DEVELOPMENT OF
PRECOCIOUS MATHEMATICAL TALENT

Lynn H. Fox and Sanford J. Cohn

ABSTRACT

In 1972 the Study of Mathematically Precocious Youth (SMPY) began its search to identify highly able mathematical reasoners. With some variations in the target population and the selection procedures, the talent searches have continued to the present. This chapter reviews the results of the 1972, 1973, 1974, 1976, 1978, and 1979 talent searches, with particular emphasis on sex differences. Follow-up data available on the 1972, 1973, and 1974 participants are analyzed, particularly as they relate to sex-role identity and willingness to accelerate. Attempts to foster precocious achievement in mathematics by means of special, accelerated classes for mixed-sex and same-sex groups are described.

Our knowledge of precocious mathematical ability and achievement in childhood and adolescence typically has been gleaned from retrospective study of the lives of eminent persons. Several famous scientists, mathematicians, and philosophers such as Pascal, Leibnitz, and Gauss, who dealt with quantitative topics, were reported to have been mathematically precocious children (Cox 1926). Since far fewer women than men have achieved eminence in mathematics, it is not surprising that there are few reports of genius and childhood precocity among women (Bell 1937; Cox 1926; McCurdy 1957; Stanley 1974; Stern 1971). There has been no evidence, however, to suggest whether precocious development is indeed more rare among females than it is among males or simply less visible.

Perhaps because of their assumed rarity, cases of precocious intellectual development and educational achievement have not been well-researched. Not even the monumental longitudinal study of intellectual giftedness by Terman (1925; see also Terman and Oden 1947, 1959) provides information concerning precocious mathematical talent and achievement among children designated as gifted by measures of global intelligence.

An ongoing study of mathematical precocity at The Johns Hopkins University offers some interesting insight into the question of sex differences in mathematical precocity. First, it provides information concerning the existence of precocious mathematical reasoning ability among adolescents, and second, it explores the question of how precocious achievement in mathematics can be fostered.

PRECOCIOUS MATHEMATICAL
REASONING ABILITY IN ADOLESCENTS

The Study of Mathematically Precocious Youth (SMPY) began in the fall of 1971 to search for junior-high-school-age students who were precocious in mathematical reasoning ability, as evidenced by very high scores on the Scholastic Aptitude Test Mathematics (SAT-M). In order to discover these talented students, SMPY conducted a talent search in each of the following years: 1972, 1973, 1974, 1976, 1978, and 1979. The rationale for the use of difficult pre-college-level tests to discover precocity is discussed in Keating 1974, 1976; Solano 1979; Stanley 1977; and Stanley, Keating, and Fox 1974. The results of each year of testing are summarized in the following sections.

The 1972 Contest

In March 1972, seventh-, eighth-, and young-in-grade ninth-grade students in the Greater Baltimore area who had scored at or above the 95th percentile on the numerical-concepts subtest of an in-grade standardized achievement test such as the Iowa Tests of Basic Skills were invited to participate in a contest. Three hundred ninety-six students (223 boys and 173 girls) accepted the challenge and took the SAT-M.

The results of the testing were startling. Twenty-two boys (about 10 percent) scored 660-790. This was better than the average Hopkins student scored as an eleventh or twelfth grader. Clearly, there are many mathematically precocious boys. The highest score for a girl, however, was 600. Although 44 percent of the contestants were girls, 19 percent of the boys scored higher than the highest-scoring girl. When the data were analyzed by grade, only 7.8 percent of the seventh-grade boys outperformed the highest-scoring seventh-grade girl, but 27.1 percent of the eighth-grade males scored higher than the highest-scoring eighth-grade girl.

The mean scores for boys and girls, by grade, are shown in table 7.1. Since the number of young-in-grade ninth graders was small, their scores

TABLE 7.1. Summary of gender-based differences in mathematical reasoning ability (SAT-M)

Talent Search	Grade	Sex	N	Mean SAT	S.D. SAT	t-test (df)	p <	Effect[c]	Percentage of males who outscored highest-scoring female
March 1972	7	Male	90	460	104	2.68 (165)	.005	0.42	7.8d
		Female	77	423	75				
	8a	Male	133	528	105	5.32 (227)	.001	0.71	27.1d
		Female	96	458	88				
January-February 1973	7	Male	135	495	85	5.14 (221)	.001	0.70	3.0d
		Female	88	440	66				
	8a	Male	286	551	85	5.18 (442)	.001	0.52	9.8d
		Female	158	511	63				
January 1974	7	Male	372	473	85	4.92 (592)	.001	0.42	3.0d
		Female	222	440	68				
	8a	Male	556	540	82	7.05 (923)	.001	0.47	2.2d
		Female	369	503	72				
December 1976	7b	Male	507	458	88	6.77 (871)	.001	0.46	2.0
		Female	366	422	65				
January 1978	7b	Male	1,549	448	87	11.55 (2,796)	.001	0.44	0.1e
		Female	1,249	413	71				
January 1979	7b	Male	2,046	436	87	15.61 (3,672)	.001	0.52	0.0f
		Female	1,628	404	77				

SOURCE: Study of Mathematically Precocious Youth (SMPY).

NOTE: The authors wish to thank Julian C. Stanley, director of SMPY, for his suggestions concerning the format of this table.

a Accelerated ninth graders and a few accelerated tenth graders were included in this category.
b Persons of seventh-grade age who were in higher grades were included in this category.

cEffect = $\frac{(\sqrt{\frac{1}{n} + \frac{1}{n}})t}{}$.

d These percentages are based on grouped frequency data. The actual percentages are probably higher than those indicated.

e One girl scored 760 on SAT-M. The second-highest-scoring girl earned a 640. If a score of 640 is taken as the basis of differentiation, 2.5 percent of the boys earned a higher score than the second-highest-scoring girl did.

f The highest-scoring boy earned a 790 on the SAT-M, the highest-scoring girl a 730. A second girl earned a 730. The third-highest-scoring girl earned a 670. If 670 is taken as the basis of differentiation, 0.8 percent of the boys earned a higher score than the third-highest-scoring girl did.

are reported with those of the eighth graders. The highest mean score for any group was five hundred twenty-eight for eighth- and ninth-grade boys. Seventh-grade boys had a mean score of 460, followed by eighth- and ninth-grade girls and seventh-grade girls whose mean scores were 458 and 423, respectively. Sex differences in scores on SAT-M were statistically significant at very stringent levels ($p < .005$ and $p < .001$ for seventh graders and eighth graders, respectively).

The 1973 Contest

In the winter of 1973 a second talent search was conducted. This time students were considered eligible for the contest if they had scored at or above the ninety-eighth percentile on an in-grade numerical-concepts subtest of a standardized test such as the Iowa Tests of Basic Skills. Wider publicity helped to increase the number of students who participated. There were 667 students in the contest (421 boys and 246 girls). The percentage of girls, however, had dropped from 44 percent in 1972 to 37 percent in 1973. This decrease in participation by girls may have been due in part to the fact that there were actually two contests in 1973, one for mathematics in January and one in the verbal area in February.[1] Students in both contests took the SAT-M and the SAT-V. Students were told they could enroll for either contest and be eligible for prizes in both. The total number of students in both contests was 953. There were 537 boys (56 percent) and 416 girls (44 percent).

The highest SAT-M score for a girl in the 1973 contests was 650, while two boys (one a seventh grader) attained scores of 800 (Stanley 1973). Seven percent of the boys in the 1973 contests scored 660 or more. No girl did. The mean scores on the SAT-M, by sex, grade, and contest entered, are shown in table 7.1. Note that only 3 percent of the seventh-grade boys outscored seventh-grade girls, while 9.8 percent of the eighth-grade boys did better than eighth-grade girls. For both grades the sex differences once again reached very stringent levels of statistical significance ($p < .001$).

The 1974 Contest

In January 1974 a third talent search for mathematics was held. Students throughout the entire state of Maryland who had scored at or above the ninety-eighth percentile on the numerical-concepts subtest of a standardized

---

[1] In 1972 the Study of Verbally Gifted Youth (SVGY) was begun at The Johns Hopkins University. Thus in the winter of 1973 there were two contests: SMPY held its contest in January, and SVGY held its in February. The SAT-M and the SAT-V were given at both contests. Students were told to register for the January contest if they were primarily interested in mathematics and for the February contest if they were interested primarily in the verbal area. Students were eligible for prizes in both contests, however.

achievement test were eligible for the contest. Testing was conducted in four centers across the state (The Johns Hopkins University, the University of Maryland at College Park, Salisbury State College, and Frostburg State College).

A total of 1,519 students took the SAT-M. Thirty-nine percent of the participants were girls (591). Sixty-one students scored 660 or above. Seven of those students were girls. One girl scored 700. The highest score earned by a boy was 760. In 1974, 3 percent of the seventh-grade boys scored higher than the highest-scoring seventh-grade girl, while 2.2 percent of the eighth-grade boys outperformed eighth-grade girls. Mean SAT-M scores in 1974 are shown in table 7.1. The pattern of mean scores in 1974 was similar to that of 1973. Within each grade group, there were statistically significant sex differences (p < .001) in favor of the boys.

The 1976 Contest

After a hiatus of nearly two years, SMPY held its fourth talent search in December 1976. Students were eligible to participate in that search if they were in the seventh grade or of seventh-grade age but in a higher grade and if they lived in Maryland or in the bordering regions of a state that shared a common boundary with Maryland (Delaware, Pennsylvania, Virginia, West Virginia, and the District of Columbia). Forty-two percent of the 873 participants in the 1976 talent search were girls. Mean scores by gender are shown in table 7.1. Only 2 percent of the boys scored higher than the highest-scoring girl, but while the highest-scoring male earned a 730, the highest-scoring female scored 610 (a difference of 120 points). Once again the sex differences reached stringent levels of statistical significance (p < .001).

The 1978 Contest

January 1978 saw a major change in SMPY's talent-search strategy. Seventh graders or students of seventh-grade age but in a higher grade were eligible if they lived in Maryland or in any part of a state bordering Maryland (Delaware, Pennsylvania, Virginia, West Virginia, and the District of Columbia). In order to accommodate participants from such a broad geographical region, SMPY arranged for the Educational Testing Service (ETS) to provide the study with its own code numbers for use during the regular January 1978 administration of the SAT. Students took the test at local testing centers, and their scores were reported to SMPY.

Of the total 2,798 participants in the 1978 talent search, 44.6 percent were girls. Boys continued to outperform the girls, 0.1 percent of the boys scoring higher than the highest-scoring girl. One girl scored 760 on the SAT-M; the girl scoring next highest earned a 640. If a score of 640 is taken as the basis of differentiation, 2.5 percent of the boys earned a higher score than the girl scoring second highest. Differences by gender reached stringent levels of statistical significance (p $<$ .001).

The 1979 Contest

The national administration of the January 1979 SAT served also as SMPY's sixth talent search. Eligibility criteria were exactly the same as they had been the previous year. Forty-four percent of the participants (3,674) were girls. In this most recent search for precocious mathematical reasoners only one boy scored higher on the SAT-M than the highest-scoring girl. Similar to the pattern of the previous five contests, however, sex differences on mean scores were 32 points (p $<$ .001).

Sex Differences

Boys and girls who participated in a voluntary mathematics contest (and who qualified for that contest on the basis of high scores on standardized tests of grade-level mathematics achievement) differed considerably with respect to performance on a difficult pre-college-level test of mathematical reasoning ability. Mean scores for boys in each of the six contests were at least 31 points higher than those for girls.

Thus as early as grades seven and eight, boys outperformed girls on difficult pre-college-level tests of mathematical reasoning ability, and the differences were particularly striking at the upper end of the distributions. In eight years of study SMPY has identified considerably more male than female highly precocious mathematical reasoners. The self-selection aspect of a contest may have contributed to the greater male participation, but this does not explain why the ratio of boys to girls who scored 660 or better on the SAT-M (14.4 to 1) was so much greater than the overall ratio of boys to girls in the contests (1.3 to 1).

Whether these apparent sex differences in mathematical aptitude are a result of biological differences or differential cultural reinforcement over time, or of a combination of the two, is not clear. One would expect to find a large gap at the upper end of the distribution of mathematical ability (as was found by SMPY) if the biological explanation of sex differences in mathematical ability, as suggested by Ellis Page in a previous volume in this series (Page 1976), is correct. At the present time, however, many researchers feel that there is too little known about the inheritance of specific abilities such as mathematical aptitude to justify such a conclusion (Astin 1974; Maccoby and Jacklin 1972).

The argument put forth by Fennema (in chapter 6 of this volume) that sex differences are a result of differential course-taking does not hold for this population. Many researchers believe, however, that the differences between the sexes in average performance on tests of specific abilities such as mathematics reflect differential cultural reinforcements over time that have shaped students' career and educational goals, interests, and achievements (Aiken 1970; Astin 1968*a*, 1968*b*, 1974; Hilton and Berglund 1974).

SMPY's study of the characteristics of mathematically precocious adolescents lends some support for the social explanation of sex differences at the higher levels of ability and achievement. Boys who scored 660 or more on the SAT-M had a stronger orientation toward investigative careers in mathematics and science and a greater theoretical-value orientation than their less mathematically precocious male and female peers (Fox 1973; Fox and Denham 1974). Many of the highly mathematically precocious boys reported studying mathematics and, sometimes, science textbooks systematically with the help of a parent or interested teacher, while others have worked informally with mathematical puzzles, games, and books. This extracurricular pursuit of knowledge appears to have been motivated by strong theoretical and investigative values and interests.

Even the most mathematically talented girls seem less eager than boys—particularly the most mathematically talented boys—to seek out special experiences related to mathematics and science. Girls tend to have values and interests that are more social than theoretical (Fox 1973; Fox and Denham 1974). Thus differential performance by the sexes on difficult pre-college-level tests of mathematical reasoning ability at grades seven and eight could be partially a result of differential exposure to and practice with mathematical problem-solving situations, which result from different interests and value orientations.

Girls may also receive less encouragement at home to consider scientific pursuits. In a small sample of gifted students studied by Astin (1974), boys' parents often had noticed their sons' interest in science at an early age. Parents of boys typically reported that they had discussed college careers in science, mathematics, medicine, and engineering with their son. These parents reported providing more scientific materials (such as toys, books, and games) for their child than did parents of girls. Very few parents of girls had noticed their daughters' interest in mathematics or science at an early age. The occupations that these parents had discussed with their daughters were more apt to be traditionally feminine ones, such as nursing and teaching. The girls' parents had given less thought to future educational plans than had the parents of boys.

The Initial Cohort from SMPY's First Follow-up Survey

In December 1976, SMPY surveyed participants from its first three talent searches who would have entered college (if they chose) by September 1976 if they had undertaken no educational acceleration. In this group were eighth graders from the 1972 contest, ninth graders from the 1973 search, and tenth graders from the 1974 contest, all of whom had scored at least 420 on the SAT-M (except for several 1972 science-contest participants, who were included via a separate eligibility criterion). Two hundred fourteen students were polled. Ninety-four percent of them (202) were located, and all but two boys responded to an extensive questionnaire concerning their educational activities up to that time and their plans for the future.

In order to assess the degree of educational acceleration each follow-up participant put to use, two variables were developed.[2] The first was an index of general educational acceleration, based on the student's birthdate and date of high-school graduation (or entrance full-time to college if high-

[2] In terms of data analysis, SMPY is interested ultimately in two measures of accelerative facilitation among its cohorts of identified, talented mathematical reasoners: (1) age at the time of receiving the bachelor's degree and (2) age at the time of earning the doctorate. Records of these age markers will depend upon two follow-up studies of these students, projected to be held in 1981-82 and 1986-87.

In the meantime several interim variables describing accelerative facilitation had to be devised. Since most of the intervention offered by SMPY to its participants is accelerative in nature, a general index of pace through the educational lock step was needed. In addition, a measure of the extent to which a student used educationally accelerative options in mathematics training was required.

In order to compute the general index (an age-acceleration variable), a student was said to be "right on time" in the typical American classroom if he or she had an eighteenth birthday on 1 July 1976 (plus or minus fifteen days); that is, he or she would turn eighteen years old during the calendar year when high-school graduation occurred. This is a stringent criterion because many states do not have 31 December deadlines for enrollment—sometimes the deadline is as early as 31 August.

If a student's eighteenth birthday came after 1 July 1976, he or she was said to have been "accelerated" by as many months as there were between the two dates. (If the difference in the fraction of a month was more than fifteen days, it was counted as a full month's difference.) Similarly, if a participant's birthday came before 1 July 1976, he or she was said to have been decelerated by as many months as there were between the two dates. This variable was named ACCAGE.

A measure of educational acceleration or deceleration, ACCAGE is a fairly precise general index of how fast one is progressing through the typical educational structures in our society. Using the number of grades skipped as one's general index would become confusing if a student additionally entered kindergarten or first grade early, and such a variable would provide less information than ACCAGE does.

By far the most often recommended and pursued accelerative activities from SMPY's smorgasbord of options are called collectively "subject-matter acceleration in mathematics." A number of alternative modes exist for accomplishing subject-matter acceleration in one's educational scheme, including: (1) starting the pre-calculus sequence early by taking algebra I before the eighth grade; (2) taking several high-school mathematics courses during a single year; (3) taking college mathematics courses while still in high school; (4) enrolling in fast-math classes; and (5) having a mentor use diagnostic and prescriptive teaching methods in mathematics. In order to account for the many subvariables making up a "subject-matter-acceleration-in-mathematics" variable, a rather elaborate point system was created. Each participant's sum of points then became the variable SBJACC. A detailed formulation of the variable SBJACC is provided in the following five steps: (1) Two points were credited for each grade before the eighth grade in which algebra I was taken. For example, if algebra I was taken in the sixth grade, the student was given four points. This subvariable was called YALG ($2 \cdot [4 - \text{ALGIG}]$), where ALGIG was a code for the grade in which algebra I was taken [5 = grade 9; 4 = grade 8; 3 = grade 7; 2 = grade 6]. If algebra I was not taken, YALG was equal to zero). (2) Points were given for each high-school mathematics course taken in the pre-calculus sequence according to the following scheme: Two points were given for algebra I, algebra II, and plane geometry; one point was given for college algebra, trigonometry, analytic geometry, elementary functions, matrices, and analysis. (The number of such courses was tallied as the subvariable TOCALI.) Three points were given for each mathematics course beyond and

school graduation was skipped). The second variable was a measure of the number and kinds of accelerative options the student used in studying mathematics, a subject-matter-acceleration variable of sorts.

In the case of both variables strong sex differences appeared that added considerable evidence to the instances cited earlier. Of particular note appears to be the relationship between level of mathematical reasoning ability (as measured at the time of the talent search) and the degree to which educational acceleration was applied subsequently in one's educational career.

Figure 7.1 demonstrates dramatically how differently accelerative techniques were used by boys and by girls. For the boys a strong positive relationship is shown between mathematical ability and the degree of general educational acceleration employed ($p < .001$). That is, on the average, the more able the boy was, the younger he tended to be when he graduated from high school (or when he entered college full-time if he skipped high-school graduation). No such relationship is evident for the girls. The sex differences in the degree to which mathematical ability is related to the general-educational-acceleration variable are highly significant ($p < .001$). Younger, more mathematically apt boys appear then to more frequently skip grades, enter kindergarten or first grade early, or in other ways speed up transit through the educational lock step than do girls.

With regard to using specific techniques of subject-matter acceleration in the study of mathematics, trends of sex differences similar to those

---

including calculus I: calculus I calculus II, calculus III, advanced topics, and so on. (The number of these courses was tallied as POCALI.) Several mathematics courses that were considered irrelevant to the precalculus sequence, to the actual calculus courses, or to higher-level mathematics following advanced calculus courses each were assigned one point value. Courses tallied under the subvariable ENRICH (worth one point each) were logic, computer mathematics, business mathematics, and probability and statistics. Points earned for completion of high-school mathematics courses were tallied as MACOUR = TOCALI + 3·POCALI + ENRICH. (3) In some instances students took college equivalents of high-school mathematics courses. The same tally system was applied, but students who took college mathematics courses earned twice as many points. The college-mathematics-course variable was called CACOUR (2·TOCALI + 6·POCALI + 2·ENRICH). (4) If calculus I was completed in high school, two points were presented for each year less than the typical four-and-a-half-year span from algebra I through calculus I. This subvariable was called QUIK (4.5 − [CALIG − ALGIG] + 1, where [CALIG − ALGIG] is the span of years from algebra I through the precalculus sequence). This number was then subtracted from the number of grades it would take to traverse this five-year course sequence in age-grade lock step, that is, four and one half grades.

In cases in which calculus I was taken as a college course while the student was in high school or in which grade(s) had been skipped between algebra I and calculus I, another variable, SQUEEZ, was defined as the number of actual years from starting algebra I to completion of college calculus I. If a student did not take calculus I, both QUIK and SQUEEZ were equal to zero. A dummy variable, SPEED, was used to select the appropriate QUIK or SQUEEZ, depending on when calculus I was taken or whether relevant grades had been skipped (If SQUEEZ was less than QUIK, then the equation SPEED = SQUEEZ was used; otherwise SPEED was equal to QUIK). In either case, two points were presented for each year (as a dummy variable SQUIK) under the usual four-and-a-half-year span from algebra I through calculus I (SQUIK = 2·SPEED). (5) All of the points earned by a student for subject-matter acceleration in math were summed as SBJAAC = YALG + MACOUR + CACOUR + SQUIK.

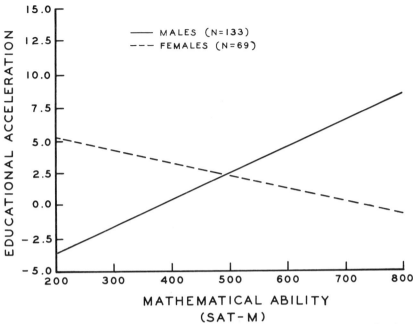

FIGURE 7.1. Comparison, by sex, of the regression lines for general educational acceleration (ACCAGE) on mathematical ability (SAT-M) among the initial cohort of SMPY's first follow-up survey. The *y*-axis represents months of acceleration.

shown for general educational acceleration are demonstrated in figure 7.2. Once again the more talented a boy was mathematically, the more he tended to take advantage of special, "fast-math" classes, college courses while still in high school, and the many other options for moving ahead in mathematics as rapidly as he could. Girls, on the other hand, manifested no such logical relationship between ability and the degree to which they chose to develop it. The difference between the two regression lines shown in figure 7.2 is statistically significant ($p < .01$).

The evidence presented in this section strongly suggests that in spite of whatever sex differences in mathematical reasoning ability appeared at the time of the talent search, girls tended to develop their abilities to a considerably lesser degree than boys. Thus not only are there sex differences in mathematical ability appearing at about age twelve, but there are sex differences as to how those abilities will be developed.

Sex-role Identity

An important factor in considering sex differences is sex-role identity, or the degree to which a person sees himself or herself as typical of a

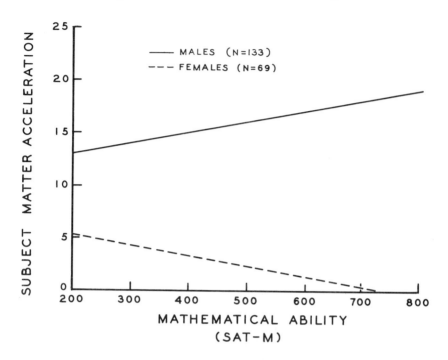

FIGURE 7.2. Comparison, by sex, of the regression lines for subject-matter acceleration in mathematics (SBJACC) on mathematical ability (SAT-M) among the initial cohort of SMPY's first follow-up survey. The *y*-axis represents points gathered on the subject-matter-acceleration variable (see n. 2, this chapter).

stereotypic male or female, regardless of the person's actual gender; it has received increasing attention among social psychologists (Bem 1974; Spence and Helmreich 1978). An important step in the development of this construct was a rejection of the view of sexual identity as a single dimension with masculinity at one end and feminity at the other. Instead, masculinity and feminity are conceived as independent dimensions. A boy, for example, could score high in masculinity and low in feminity, in which case he would be "same-sex typed." On the other hand, he could score high in feminity and low in masculinity, in which case he would be "cross-sex typed." He even could score relatively low in both dimensions ("undifferentiated") or high in both ("androgynous").

The Bem Sex-Role Inventory (BSRI) was administered to the top-scoring third of the 1976 talent-search participants (188 males and 90 females), who had been invited to take an extensive series of cognitive and affective tests so that SMPY could counsel them educationally. The BSRI yields a masculinity score and a feminity score. From those scores, Sanford Cohn has devised a technique by which the degree of sex-role differentia-

TABLE 7.2. Gender-based differences in sex-role differentiation and orientation for students in the top third of SMPY's 1976 talent search

	Males (N = 188)	Females (N = 90)	*t*-test (*df* = 276)	p <
Orientation (in radians)				
Mean	.702	.774	6.18	.000
S.D.	.093	.086		
Differentiation				
Mean	6.74	6.89	1.85	.065
S.D.	.65	.68		

tion and orientation can be determined.[3]

Table 7.2 summarizes the results of this study. Note that the higher one's sex-role-differentiation score, the more well defined one's sex-role identity is. The higher one's sex-role-orientation score, the more cross-sex-identified one is. In short, the girls were somewhat more differentiated in terms of sex-role identity than were the boys (p < .07). This is to be expected among students who are thirteen years old (on the average), since girls tend to mature earlier than boys. A more interesting observation, however, is that the girls in this group are more cross-sex-identified than the boys (p < .001); the girls in this group appeared to be significantly more masculinely sex-role identified than the boys were femininely sex-role identified. This finding is consistent with the fact that mathematics is

[3]Cohn suggests the following method as a measure of sex-role differentiation and orientation, using as its basis masculinity and femininity scores.

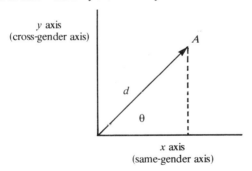

x axis
(same-gender axis)

Sex-role differentiation is rather simple, consisting of finding the geometric sum of the masculinity and femininity scores. That geometric sum is graphically illustrated here as a vector (*d*) from the origin to point *A*. The length of this vector is a measure of how well differentiated one's sex-role identity is; the higher the value of *d*, the better differentiated one is.

Note that the *X* axis is always the same-gender axis, and the *Y* axis is always the cross-gender axis. For boys, then, the masculinity score would be plotted on the *X* axis, and the feminity score, on the *Y* axis (and vice versa for girls). The greater the angle θ is, then, the more cross-sex identified a person is. In terms of degrees, one might consider a range of θ from 0° to 30° as describing same-sex identified; a range from 31° to 60°, androgenous; and a range from 61° to 90°, cross-sex identified. Hence θ becomes a measure of *sex-role orientation*. In table 8.2, however, sex-role orientation (θ) is expressed in radians rather than in degrees.

considered in our culture to be a masculine pursuit.

Perhaps girls are being discouraged away from developing their mathematical talent in an attempt by their parents and educators to make them fit more closely to feminine stereotypes. In light of this possibility, it might be wise to offer effective role models to girls several years before they turn twelve years old in order to offset their more rapid rate of sex-role differentiation and give them greater security in pursuing the development of their precocious mathematical ability traditionally identified as masculine.

FOSTERING PRECOCIOUS ACHIEVEMENT

Although it is difficult to draw conclusions about the relative influences of biological and social factors upon the performance on measures of aptitude (for example, some would even argue the possibility that some of the differences in test performance are artifacts of biased test materials), there is clear evidence that precocious achievement in mathematics can be directly influenced by environmental factors. SMPY's attempts to foster acceleration in mathematics provide some insight into the dynamics of precocious achievement among bright adolescent boys and girls.

Through 1974 SMPY sponsored three experimental accelerated-mathematics classes on the Johns Hopkins campus and two classes in a public junior high school (the details of these classes are reported in depth in Fox 1974*a*, 1974*b;* George and Denham 1976; and Stanley 1976). A summary of the results of these five classes and their implications for understanding the differences between the sexes with respect to precocious achievement is presented in the following sections.

Class 1—boys and girls. In the summer of 1972 thirty end-of-the-year sixth graders (eighteen boys and twelve girls) were invited to a special, summer mathematics class that met two hours a week.[4] Fourteen boys (78 percent) and seven girls (58 percent) enrolled for the program. The initial success of the class in mastering algebra I with only eighteen hours of instruction was so great that the class continued to meet for two hours a week through the middle of the following summer. Of the twenty-one students who initially began the course, six boys (43 percent) and one girl (fourteen percent) completed their study of all the pre-calculus mathematics (algebra I, algebra II, algebra III, plane geometry, trigonometry, and analytic geometry). Six of the boys took calculus the following year in a senior high school.

Class 2—boys and girls. In the summer of 1973 eighty-five students (fifty-one boys and thirty-four girls) who had participated in the 1973 talent search and who had scored at least 500 on the SAT-M and 400 on the SAT-V were invited to a summer accelerated-mathematics class. Most of

---

[4]Thirty students were invited. One was an end-of-the-year third grader. Another was an end-of-the-year eighth grader. The remaining students were end-of-the-year sixth graders.

these students were eighth graders who had completed algebra I. Twenty-two boys (43 percent) and nine girls (29 percent) enrolled. Fourteen boys (64 percent) and none of the girls completed all the pre-calculus mathematics by the middle of the following summer, meeting only two hours a week during the school year and four hours a week during the second summer (George and Denham 1976).

Although these classes were highly successful in promoting precocious achievement in mathematics among boys, both were far less successful with girls. First, more boys than girls were eager to enroll in such a program. Second, girls who did enroll tended to drop out of the classes before their completion. Interviews with the girls indicated that one major reason for dropping out was a reluctance to become accelerated in their placement in school. Many of the girls seemed to fear being labeled as different from their friends by virtue of becoming somewhat accelerated. Girls also reported that the class meetings were dull, and some made references to the boys in the classes as "little creeps." The overall reaction to the classes by the girls was that it was socially unappealing and might have negative social consequences in school.

It has been reported that even very bright girls often select themselves out of advanced mathematics classes in high school (Haven 1972) and that few women ever pursue doctoral degrees in mathematics (in 1969, for example, only 7 percent of the doctoral degrees awarded in mathematics were earned by women [Bisconti and Astin 1973]). Until this present study, however, it was not known that bright girls in junior high school would be far more reluctant than boys to participate in special accelerated-mathematics programs and, especially, to persist in them.

Class 3—all girls. The results of testing values and interests of boys and girls in the 1973 contest suggested that even the most mathematically able girls were likely to prefer social activities to theoretical ones. In combination with the results of the first two accelerated-mathematics classes, this suggested that to interest girls in learning mathematics faster it would be important to consider the social aspects of a program.

Thus in the spring of 1973 an accelerated algebra I class was organized for seventh-grade girls who had been in the 1973 contest and who had scored at least 370 on the SAT-M (the average for female juniors in high school).[5] (The details of the program for girls are reported in chapter 10 of this volume.) In brief, the class was designed to appeal to the social interests of girls in a number of ways. It emphasized social cooperation rather than competition and was taught by a woman rather than by a man. Male and female scientists and mathematicians spoke to the girls about exciting

[5] Two girls who had not participated in the 1973 contest were later tested on the SAT-M and allowed to take the course. One of these girls scored 350 on the SAT-M. Since she had been eligible for the first class but had not enrolled, the decision was made to let her be in the all-girls class. Her score of 350 was considered to be an underestimate of her ability. The following year she scored 570 on a different form of the SAT-M.

careers in mathematics and science (such as operations research, health statistics, and social-science research) that deal with social problems as well as theoretical ones. This approach to an accelerated program was considerably more effective in recruiting girls. Of the thirty-four girls invited, twenty-six (76 percent) enrolled; eighteen girls (69 percent) completed the course. Not all the girls, however, chose to accelerate their mathematics in school the following year, and a few actually met with school resistance to their acceleration. Eleven did take algebra II the following year; ten of these (38 percent of the total female enrollees) were considered to have been successfully accelerated.

The emphasis on the social interests of girls was moderately effective in promoting greater achievement in mathematics for girls than the two mixed-sex, more theoretically oriented classes had. This approach, however, did not promote the same extent of acceleration for the girls that the other two programs did for the boys. Five of the girls from the all-girl class indicated some interest in becoming further accelerated in mathematics (by as much as two or three years) by the time they complete high school and enter college.

Classes 4 and 5—city public school. In the winter of 1974 Roland Park School, in Baltimore City, asked SMPY to set up in that school a fast-paced mathematics class based on the principles learned from the first three classes. Twelve boys and twelve girls in grades four through seven were selected to participate. On the basis of past experience, SMPY suggested that there be two fast-paced classes, one for boys, taught by a male college professor, and one for girls, taught by a female college professor. One boy and one girl dropped out of the program. Both classes made rapid progress through algebra I, meeting two hours a week for a total of thirty-seven hours the first year, and all who remained in the school the following year elected to continue in the fast-paced class to study algebra II. Although on the average the girls were somewhat less able than the boys, the two groups performed about equally well on a standardized algebra I test at the end of the first year. Both classes were considerably more successful in mastering algebra I than the class of eighth graders in a regular, full-year algebra I program (Stanley 1974).

The success of these two classes in fostering high achievement at an accelerated pace suggests that special programs of this type may be more successful for girls when they are conducted within the context of the regular school. Further research is needed to determine just how successful these programs can become for both boys and girls if they are implemented on a large scale within public schools or school systems. Whether sex segregation and female teachers as role models are actually crucial for the success of girls needs to be studied systematically within school settings.

These five classes represent prototypes that have been used, modified, and revised for students from the last three talent searches. With the establishment of the Intellectually Gifted Child Study Group (IGCSG) at Johns Hopkins, mathematically precocious girls have a specialized group with whom to consult. Although SMPY continues to sponsor fast-math classes for its highest-scoring students regardless of gender, it works predominantly with mathematically talented males.

CONCLUSIONS AND IMPLICATIONS

On the basis of SMPY's research on the mathematically precocious, it appears that males are more likely than females to perform at a very high level on pre-college-level tests of mathematical reasoning ability (at least in a voluntary contest situation). The sizable gap between the sexes on mean SAT-M scores and at the upper end of the distribution as early as grade seven suggests that there may be biological differences between the sexes with respect to mathematical aptitude. There are, however, strong indications that some of the apparent differences are related to environmental factors. Whether greater efforts to encourage and develop mathematical interests among women in childhood and adolescence could eliminate or reduce this sex difference at the higher levels of ability is not known.

Clearly it is much more difficult to foster precocious achievement and acceleration in mathematics among girls than among boys. In structuring learning environments to foster accelerated achievement among young women some attention to their social interests appears to increase their rate of participation and success. To date, however, SMPY has not effectively helped to accelerate any girl as far or as fast as most of the boys in its programs. This should not be interpreted as meaning that it is unprofitable to work with bright girls. Although mathematical precocity (both in measured ability and in achievement) is far more evident among young males, SMPY's efforts to foster greater achievement among very bright students suggests that girls can be helped to develop their quantitative potentials more fully.

Even if there are biological differences between the sexes that account for much of the differing degree of precocity between the sexes, it is still desirable to develop ways of fostering greater achievement among both men and women. It would appear, however, that our instructional strategies and classroom environments should be more systematically studied and regulated to avoid unnecessarily discouraging young women from developing their mathematical potentials to the fullest.

The fact that at the present time mathematical precocity appears to be not only less visible but rarer among female adolescents than among males can lead us to one of two approaches for future educational planning and development: First, we could concentrate all efforts to find and foster high-level achievement and talent in mathematics on boys, since they will be easier to find and to work with (which would be very much like what is occurring, perhaps unintentionally, in most schools today). The second approach would be to try to identify talented young women, as well as young men, but to modify or restructure instructional strategies for girls in order to optimize their chances for high-level achievement. The long-term benefits of this second approach could be quite gratifying.

REFERENCES

Aiken, L. R. 1970. Attitudes towards mathematics. *Review of Educational Research* 40(4): 551-96.

Astin, H. S. 1968a. Career development of girls during the high school years. *Journal of Counseling Psychology* 15(6): 536-40.

_____. 1968b. Stability and change in the career plans of ninth grade girls. *Personality and Guidance Journal* 46(10): 961-66.

_____. 1974. Sex differences in mathematical and scientific precocity. In *Mathematical talent: Discovery, description, and development,* ed. J. C. Stanley; D. P. Keating; and L. H. Fox, pp. 70-86. Baltimore: Johns Hopkins University Press.

Bell, E. T. 1937. *Men of mathematics.* New York: Simon and Schuster.

Bem, S. L. 1974. The measurement of psychological androgeny. *Journal of Consulting and Clinical Psychology* 42: 155-62.

Bisconti, A. S., and Astin, H. S. 1973. Undergraduate and graduate study in scientific fields. *ACE Research Report* 8(3).

Cox, C. M. 1926. The early mental traits of three hundred geniuses. *Genetic studies of genius,* vol. 2. Stanford: Stanford University Press.

Fox, L. H. 1973. Values and career interests of mathematically precocious youth. Paper presented at meeting of the American Psychological Association, Montreal, September 1972.

_____. 1974a. A mathematics program for fostering precocious achievement. In *Mathematical talent: Discovery, description, and development,* ed. J. C. Stanley; D. P. Keating; and L. H. Fox, pp. 101-25. Baltimore: Johns Hopkins University Press.

_____. 1974b. Facilitating the development of mathematical talent in young women. Ph.D. diss., The Johns Hopkins University.

Fox, L. H., and Denham, S. A. 1974. Values and career interests of mathematically and scientifically precocious youth. In *Mathematical talent: Discovery, description, and development,* ed. J. C. Stanley; D. P. Keating; and L. H. Fox, pp. 140-75. Baltimore: Johns Hopkins University Press.

George, W. C., and Denham, S. A. 1976. Curriculum experimentation for the mathematically talented. In *Intellectual talent: research and development,* ed. D. P. Keating, pp. 103-31. Baltimore: Johns Hopkins University Press.

Haven, E. W. 1972. Factors associated with the selection of advanced academic mathematics courses by girls in high school. Research bulletin 72-12. Princeton: Educational Testing Service.

Hilton, T. L., and Berglund, G. W. 1974. Sex differences in mathematics achievement: A longitudinal study. *Journal of Educational Research* 67: 231-37.

Keating, D. P. 1974. The study of mathematically precocious youth. In *Mathematical talent: Discovery, description, and development,* ed. J. C. Stanley; D. P.

Keating; and L. H. Fox, pp. 23-46. Baltimore: Johns Hopkins University Press.

————, ed. 1976. *Intellectual talent: Research and development.* Baltimore: Johns Hopkins University Press.

Maccoby, E. E., and Jacklin, C. N. 1972. Sex differences in intellectual functioning. In *Assessment in a pluralistic society: Proceedings of the 1972 Invitational Conference on Testing Problems,* pp. 37-55. Princeton: Educational Testing Service.

McCurdy, H. S. 1957. Childhood patterns of genius. *Journal of Elisha Mitchell Scientific Society* 73: 448-62.

Page, E. B. 1976. A historical step beyond Terman. In *Intellectual talent: Research and development,* ed. D. P. Keating, pp. 295-307. Baltimore: Johns Hopkins University Press.

Solano, C. H. 1979. The first D: Discovery of talent (discovery of intellectually talented youths, especially those who reason extremely well mathematically). In *New voices in counseling the gifted,* ed. N. Colangelo and R. T. Zaffran, pp. 89-106. Dubuque, Iowa: Kendall/Hunt.

Spence, J. T., and Helmreich, R. L. 1978. *Masculinity and femininity: their psychological dimensions, correlates, and antecedents.* Austin, Tex.: University of Texas Press.

Stanley, J. C. 1973. Accelerating the educational progress of intellectually gifted youth. *Educational Psychologist* 10(3): 133-46.

————. 1974. Intellectual precocity. In *Mathematical talent: Discovery, description, and development,* ed. J. C. Stanley; D. P. Keating; and L. H. Fox, pp. 1-22. Baltimore: Johns Hopkins University Press.

————. 1976. Special fast-mathematics classes taught by college mathematics professors to fourth through twelfth graders. In *Intellectual talent: Research and development,* ed. D. P. Keating, pp. 132-59. Baltimore: Johns Hopkins University Press.

————. 1977. Rationale of the Study of Mathematically Precocious Youth (SMPY) during its first five years of promoting educational acceleration. In *The gifted and the creative: A fifty-year perspective,* ed. J. C. Stanley; W. C. George; and C. H. Solano, pp. 75-112. Baltimore: Johns Hopkins University Press.

Stanley, J. C.; Keating, D. P., and Fox, L. H., eds. 1974. *Mathematical talent: Discovery, description, and development.* Baltimore: Johns Hopkins University Press.

Stern, Aaron. 1971. *The making of a genius.* Miami, Fla.: Hurricane House.

Terman, L. M. 1925. Mental and physical traits of a thousand gifted children. *Genetic studies of genius,* vol. 1. Stanford: Stanford University Press.

Terman, L. M., and Oden, M. H. 1947. The gifted child grows up: Twenty-five years follow-up of a superior group. *Genetic studies of genius,* vol. 4. Stanford: Stanford University Press.

————. 1959. The gifted group at mid-life. *Genetic studies of genius,* vol. 5. Stanford: Stanford University Press.

III

Facilitating Women's Achievement in Mathematics

8

An Experiment in Mathematics Education at the College Level

Carolyn T. MacDonald

ABSTRACT

Women's career choices traditionally have been limited, in part because of women's inadequate mathematics background. In an attempt to reverse this trend, an intervention project was conducted at the University of Missouri-Kansas City during the 1974-75 academic year. The project, which was centered around a special introductory mathematics course for female students only, was designed to open career options for women by helping them acquire basic mathematics skills and by assisting them in overcoming various social and cultural barriers to their success. There were several areas in which the project was successful. Participants in the special program earned higher grades, had more positive attitudes about mathematics, and were less likely to withdraw from the introductory mathematics class and more likely to continue to the next-level mathematics class than were non-participants.

Many complex psychological and sociological factors have limited women's career choices, and changing some of these factors can be a very slow and difficult process. One factor, however, that lends itself to correction quite readily is women's frequent lack of the mathematics preparation necessary for admission to many college programs. In chapter 5 of this volume, sociologist Lucy Sells discusses how high-school mathematics has acted as a critical filter in the job market, since many career options are effectively closed to someone who does not have a solid background in basic mathematics. Proficiency in mathematics is a requirement for a career in the natural sciences, and an understanding of at least lower-level mathematics is necessary for a great many other careers. Increasingly mathematics is

This project was supported by a grant from the National Science Foundation, GY-11326.

necessary for work in the social sciences or business administration.[1] Traditionally, women more than men have been handicapped by deficiencies in their mathematics backgrounds. Because of these deficiences, women have been precluded from considering many career options, not only in the sciences but in many other areas as well.

In an attempt to reverse this trend, an intervention project was conducted at the University of Missouri-Kansas City during the 1974-75 academic year. The central part of the experimental project was a special, two-semester introductory mathematics course for female students, team-taught by two female instructors, supplemented by personal assistance and group-tutoring sessions.

The project was designed to encourage women to consider academic programs in science areas by helping them acquire basic mathematics skills and by assisting them in overcoming various social and cultural barriers to their success, thus providing them with the skills and self-confidence necessary to enter fields typically dominated by men. Interpreted more broadly, the project was designed to open career options for women. An additional goal of the project was to measure the effectiveness of the program and to try to develop methods that might be used with female students elsewhere.

INTRODUCTORY MATHEMATICS AT
THE UNIVERSITY OF MISSOURI-KANSAS CITY

The University of Missouri-Kansas City is one of four campuses of the University of Missouri system. It is an urban, commuter campus of almost twelve thousand students, located in a metropolitan area with a population of 1.5 million. The percentage of minority students in 1974 was 8.5 percent. The age distribution of students is characteristic of that of most urban schools, including a significant number of older students, many of them women returning to school. Because there is an extensive metropolitan junior-college system, almost 60 percent of new students enter as transfer students.

There is no high-school mathematics requirement for admission to the university, although three years of mathematics is "strongly recommended." One third of the students come from the immediate inner-city school district of eleven high schools, whose eleventh graders in 1972-73 ranked at the twenty-fourth percentile on national norms on the mathematics portion of the Iowa Tests of Basic Skills. In 1973-74 the state of Missouri dropped completely any mathematics requirement for high-school graduation. Thus, many students, especially the female students, enter the university with a limited mathematics background.

---

[1] For example, an undergraduate major in the School of Administration at the University of Missouri-Kansas City must take three full years of mathematics and computer programming, beginning with college algebra.

The university offers a single, first-semester introductory mathematics course, Fundamentals of Mathematics I, which is approximately the equivalent of college algebra, including probability and emphasizing theory and structure.[2] This course is effectively a basic-skills graduation requirement for students who have not completed four years of high-school mathematics. There are three options for students who continue with further mathematics. Most students select Fundamentals of Mathematics II, which is the equivalent of trigonometry and analytic geometry. The alternative courses are a geometry course designed for elementary-education majors and a finite-mathematics course designed for social-science majors.

The Fundamentals of Mathematics I enrollment includes students with backgrounds ranging from zero to four years of high-school mathematics. Of the students who completed the course in the fall of 1974, about 90 percent had completed first-year high-school algebra, three fourths had taken geometry, and about half had completed a third year of high-school mathematics.

The fundamentals-of-mathematics courses are taught in large, coordinated lecture sections of up to eighty students, but averaging fifty-five to sixty students, about half of whom are women. Each section is taught by a single instructor, who may be a regular faculty member, a nonregular instructor, or a graduate assistant. The mathematics department keeps a tutoring room open several hours a day, where any student enrolled in one of the introductory courses may obtain free tutoring from the graduate assistants who staff the sessions. There is a uniform examination and grading system for all the sections. One-hour examinations are given every three to four weeks, preceded by a review examination that is discussed in the tutoring sessions or in class. The examinations consist of a computer-scored, multiple-choice section and a problems section. Some instructors also give short quizzes regularly. Grading is on a standardized percentage basis, with 90 to 100 percent equal to an *A;* 80 to 89 percent, a *B;* 70 to 79, a *C;* 60 to 69, a *D;* and 0 to 59, an *F.*

EXPERIMENTAL PROJECT

The core of the experimental project was a special section of the introductory-mathematics sequence, Fundamentals of Mathematics I and II, for a group of specially selected female students. Thirty-two regular students plus an auditor enrolled in the first-semester course, and twenty-two students enrolled in the second-semester course.

Sixty percent of the first-semester participants were identified from the files of entering freshmen. The project director and a student assistant

[2] During the 1975-76 school year, the mathematics department began a revision of the format of the fundamentals-of-mathematics sequence.

reviewed the applications of all women admitted to the university as freshmen for fall of 1974. Possible participants were selected from those students who seemed able but who did not have a strong background in mathematics. A special attempt was made to include minority students from the inner-city high schools. The student assistant spoke individually to each potential participant who attended the small, group freshmen-orientation sessions held throughout the summer and presented the project as being designed to help each student to acquire basic skills in mathematics and to open her career options. Each potential participant was given a brief written description of the project. All but one of the students whose schedule permitted enrollment elected to participate.

Twenty percent of the participants were identified by academic advisers as advanced-standing students who would benefit from special attention and assistance in mathematics. The remaining 20 percent were students who enrolled in the special section due to an error at registration. Because their needs and problems were in many ways similar to the specially identified students, they were allowed to remain in the course. In addition to the thirty-two regular participants, a woman who had taken Fundamentals of Mathematics I from the project director the previous year audited the first semester of the experimental course in order to be adequately prepared for regular enrollment in the second semester of the project.

The class composition for the first semester was rather heterogeneous. Slightly over half of the students were freshmen entering the university directly from inner-city, suburban, or small-town high schools. The remainder, divided among the sophomore, junior, and senior classes, included transfer students as well as women who had returned to school after an absence of from one to twenty years. Ages ranged from seventeen to thirty-nine years, about half of the students being nineteen or under and one fifth being over thirty. Approximately half of the students expressed an interest in a science major, broadly interpreted.

Twenty-two students enrolled in Fundamentals of Mathematics II, the second semester of the course. There were sixteen participants and one auditor who continued from the first semester and five new participants, who had requested admission to the class. In addition, one first-semester participant enrolled in a different section.

The mathematics course was team-taught by the project director, who is a regular faculty member with a broad science and mathematics background, and by an advanced doctoral student in mathematics.[3] Primary instruction was alternated in three-week units, the primary instructor for a unit being responsible for class sessions, quizzes, and examinations for that unit (after consulting with the other instructor). Both instructors attended

[3]The project director, Carolyn MacDonald, was at the time chairman of an interdisciplinary science program offering courses primarily for non-science majors; she has graduate degrees in mathematics, chemistry, and physics. The second team teacher, Barbara Currier, has since completed a Ph.D. in mathematics and taught at the college level.

the daily, one-o'clock class session, the secondary instructor for a unit interjecting helpful comments when appropriate.

Each regular class meeting was preceded by an optional one-hour tutoring session by an undergraduate mathematics major. The noon-hour session was held in a laboratory room adjacent to the classroom that was furnished with tables seating four to six persons.[4] The students worked in small groups and helped each other, obtaining assistance from the tutor when necessary. The instructors shared an office across the hall from the tutoring room and were always available to give individual assistance to students. The sessions took on both social and academic aspects; some of the students brought their lunch and ate and visited together while they worked on mathematics. Several participants who were unable to continue with the second semester of the course still stopped by occasionally during the tutoring sessions.

Essential Mathematics, by Keedy and Bittinger (1972), was used as the text the first semester, together with various supplementary materials. There were weekly fifteen-minute, ten-point open-book quizzes, and approximately every three weeks there was a one-hour, hundred-point closed-book examination. Both quizzes and examinations had a problem format. Each one-hour examination was preceded by a comprehensive, take-home review examination that was graded and returned prior to the in-class examination. No other homework was collected, although students were expected to work problems on a daily basis. The highest ten out of fifteen quiz scores were totaled and counted as an additional examination score. Each student was permitted to take each examination a second time if she showed a later mastery of the material after an initial poor performance. Only the second score was counted if the student's performance improved; otherwise, the two scores were averaged. A comprehensive, three-hour examination was given at the end of the semester. Course grades were determined on the same percentage basis as in the regular sections.

Because many of the students had weak mathematics backgrounds, it was necessary to spend the first four weeks of the semester on basic arithmetic. In order not to bore the better prepared students, the review was integrated with instruction on the use of the slide rule.[5] Several class sessions were devoted to practical exercises, such as determining the proper size air conditioner for a particular room and calculating the travel time to various locations.[6] The students worked on these activities in small groups,

[4] The laboratory was chosen as the tutoring room because the project director had the authority to determine the schedule of the room and because the room was conveniently located. Although not a factor in the original choice, the furnishing of the room with tables rather than with individual desks was a definite asset, since it encouraged small-group interaction.

[5] Electronic calculators were too expensive for general student use at the time.

[6] Many of the activities were suggested by Elizabeth Berman, a Kansas City-area mathematician who has since published a basic mathematics textbook: *Mathematics Revealed,* published by Academic Press in 1979.

while the tutor and both instructors circulated freely in the classroom, offering assistance when necessary. There were also several handouts of puzzle-type problems, designed to illustrate key mathematical concepts and challenge the better students. The arithmetic review was followed by material on linear equations and inequalities; polynomials and fractional expressions; exponents, powers, and roots; quadratic equations; and combinatorial algebra and probability.

For the second semester, *Algebra and Trigonometry: A Functions Approach,* also by Keedy and Bittinger (1974), was used as the text. Topics covered by the entire class included functions; polynomials; analytic geometry; exponential functions and logarithms; sequences, series, and mathematical induction; a brief introduction to computer programming; and elementary trigonometry. For the last three-week period the instructors divided the class into two groups, approximately half of the students choosing to study more advanced topics in trigonometry and the other half choosing to study systems of linear equations.

Four class periods during the fall semester and one class period during the spring semester were devoted entirely to supplementary activities. During the third week of the fall semester, an assistant professor from the political science department spoke on the socialization of women. The next week, four women who hold administrative and counseling positions at the university informed the class about services available to students. The students then divided into four discussion groups led by the women and shared experiences and concerns. In order to encourage free discussion about the mathematics course, the instructors left during the discussion period. Later the instructors met with the four discussion leaders and received feedback about student concerns. Near the end of the first semester a research assistant from Midwest Research Institute discussed her undergraduate mathematics background and her job and then arranged a tour of the institute for interested members of the class. After a short classroom introduction to computer programming in the spring semester, part of the class visited the university's computer center.

Occasionally the instructors commented in class about social and cultural issues and personal experiences. During one class period, there was a brief discussion of the booklet *Mathematics and Sex,* written by John Ernest and a student research team (1975).

RESULTS

The success of the program in several areas can be demonstrated by comparing participants and nonparticipants with respect to grades earned and rate of withdrawal, continued enrollment in mathematics, and attitudes about mathematics and the program.

Grades Earned and Rate of Withdrawal

Participant performance for the first semester as measured by grades earned was very high; half of the students received *A*'s, and one fourth received *B*'s. Several comparisons of student performance as measured by final grades are shown in table 8.1. The first four columns give the grade distribution for fall 1974, comparing the 32 women participating in the experimental section with 684 nonparticipants in the twelve standard sections.

In the fall of 1972 the project director had taught a standard section of Fundamentals of Mathematics I. The grades given in this section are listed in the next three columns. In the fall of 1973 she had taught a "negatively selected" section, one of two sections to which academic advisers referred many of the students needing special attention because of weak mathematics backgrounds. The grades for this section are listed in the last three columns. The thirty-nine female students in this section had backgrounds most similar to those of women in the experimental group.

Perhaps as important as the much higher grades received in the experimental section was the much lower rate of withdrawal. Only 3 percent of the participants withdrew, compared with 22 percent of the women in the 1974 standard sections and 15 percent of the women in both the 1972 and the 1973 sections.

In addition to the performance of the students as represented by the letter grades earned, there are several other indications that the students in the experimental section learned considerably more than their letter-grade counterparts in the standard sections offered during the fall of 1974 and in the 1972 and 1973 classes.

The problem format of the examinations given to the experimental section made it possible to test more rigorously the mathematical understanding of the students than the standard examination format, containing primarily multiple-choice questions, would have. In addition, considerably more material was covered by the experimental section (40 percent of the comprehensive final exam covered topics not included in the regular course). Participants also observed the difference, commenting that they appreciated covering the additional material because of its usefulness in their other courses. The auditor frequently commented that her level of understanding and knowledge was much higher than what she had acquired in the regular Fundamentals of Mathematics I course, which she had completed with an *A*, from the same instructor the previous year.

The grades earned by the participants for the second semester are shown in table 8.2. The first four columns give the grade distribution for spring 1975, comparing the 22 women participating in the experimental section with the 285 nonparticipants in the 6 regular sections. The nonparticipants comprised two subgroups, 116 students who had been enrolled

TABLE 8.1. Percentage distribution of course grades for Fundamentals of Mathematics I

| Course grade | Fall 1974 | | | | Fall 1972[a] | | | Fall 1973[b] | | |
| | Participants | Nonparticipants | | | | | | | | |
	Women (N = 32)	Women (N = 340)	Men (N = 344)	Total (N = 684)	Women (N = 33)	Men (N = 45)	Total (N = 78)	Women (N = 39)	Men (N = 25)	Total (N = 64)
A	53%	29%	21%	25%	30%	24%	27%	23%	12%	19%
B	25	19	16	17	27	33	31	18	28	22
C	6	11	18	14	15	16	15	21	36	27
D	9	9	6	7	6	4	5	10	4	8
F	3	7	9	8	6	13	10	13	0	8
W	3	22	27	25	15	9	12	15	20	17
I	0	1	3	2	0	0	0	0	0	0
Audit	0	1	0	1	0	0	0	0	0	0

[a]Standard section with a standard format, taught by the project director.
[b]"Negatively selected" section with a standard format, taught by the project director.

TABLE 8.2. Percentage distribution of course grades for Fundamentals of Mathematics II

| Course grade | Spring 1975 | | | | Summer 1973[a] | | |
| | Participants | Nonparticipants | | | | | |
	Women (N = 22)	Women (N = 108)	Men (N = 177)	Total (N = 285)	Women (N = 3)	Men (N = 13)	Total (N = 16)
A	41%	39%	23%	29%	0%	54%	44%
B	32	20	23	22	0	15	13
C	5	15	18	16	0	23	19
D	0	10	10	10	0	0	0
F	0	6	11	9	33	0	6
W	9	10	14	13	33	8	13
I	14	0	0	0	0	0	0
Audit	0	0	2	1	33	0	6

[a]Standard section with a modified format, taught by the project director.

in Fundamentals of Mathematics I the previous semester and 169 students who had not. The latter group included students who had entered the university with high-school mathematics backgrounds that permitted them to enroll in Fundamentals of Mathematics II or who had completed college algebra at other schools, as well as students who had completed Fundamentals of Mathematics I during a previous year. Because there was almost no difference in the performance of the two subgroups, their grades are combined in table 8.2.

In the summer of 1973, the project director taught a standard section of Fundamentals of Mathematics II with a modified format, intermediate between the standard format and the format used in the experimental section. The grades given in this section are listed in the last three columns of table 8.2. Generally there was little difference between the second-semester grades earned by the participants and those earned by the non-participants.

All of the withdrawals and incompletes in the experimental section were the result of health and personal problems, not academic problems. Two students withdrew from school during the semester. The top student from the first-semester course withdrew because of medical problems but planned to return to school as soon as possible. Another student who withdrew because of injuries suffered in an accident has since returned to school and completed Fundamentals of Mathematics II in a regular section. An additional three students were unable to complete the work by the end of the semester because of medical and personal problems, and they received incompletes.

None of the three women who took Fundamentals of Mathematics II from the project director in the summer of 1973 completed the course; two withdrew, and one switched to auditor status because of academic deficiencies that perhaps were exaggerated by the faster pace of summer-school classes. The performance of men in that class was very high, in part because several of the men had backgrounds that were better than usual for students enrolled in that level course—they were taking the summer class as a review before enrolling in calculus in the fall.

Rate of Continuation to a Second Semester of Mathematics

Another measure of the effectiveness of the program is the percentage of students originally enrolled in Fundamentals of Mathematics I who continued with a second semester of mathematics the following semester. Several comparisons of the rate of continuation are shown in table 8.3. The first four columns compare participants and nonparticipants with respect to the percentage of students enrolled in Fundamentals of Mathematics I in the fall of 1974 who continued with one of the three second-semester mathematics courses the next semester. Results are shown for the per-

TABLE 8.3. Percentage of students enrolled in Fundamentals of Mathematics I who continued mathematics the following semester

| Course | Fall 1974 | | | | Fall 1972a | | | Fall 1973b | | |
| | Participants | Nonparticipants | | | | | | | | |
	Women (N = 32)	Women (N = 340)	Men (N = 344)	Total (N = 684)	Women (N = 33)	Men (N = 45)	Total (N = 78)	Women (N = 39)	Men (N = 25)	Total (N = 64)
Enrolled in second-semester mathematics										
Fundamentals of Math II	53%	14%	19%	17%	30%	22%	26%	5%	32%	16%
Finite math	0	0	3	1	0	9	5	3	12	6
Geometry	3	3	0	2	0	0	0	0	0	0
Total[c]	56	17	23	20	30	31	31	8	44	22
Received C or better in second-semester mathematics										
Fundamentals of Math II	38	11	13	12	24	13	18	3	20	9
Finite Math	0	0	3	1	0	9	5	0	12	5
Geometry	3	2	less than 1	1	0	0	0	0	0	0
Total[c]	41	13	16	14	24	22	23	3	32	14

[a] Standard selection with a standard format, taught by the project director.
[b] "Negatively selected" section with a standard format, taught by the project director.
[c] The totals include several students who are counted twice because of dual second-semester enrollment.

centage enrolling in the second-semester course and also for the percentage who completed the second-semester course with a grade of *C* or better. The remaining seven columns give the rate of continuation of students who took Fundamentals of Mathematics I from the project director in fall 1972 and fall 1973. Several students, including one participant, are counted twice in the totals because they simultaneously enrolled in two different second-semester courses.

Participants had a much higher rate of enrollment in and completion of the second-semester course than nonparticipants. Forty-one percent of the participants completed a second-semester course with a grade of *C* or better, compared with 13 percent of the nonparticipant women and 16 percent of the nonparticipant men the same semester. The contrast with the women in the fall 1973 section was more marked. Only 3 percent of the female students in this group, who had backgrounds similar to the participants', successfully completed another mathematics course the following semester.

The higher rate of continuation of participants can be attributed in part to their lower rate of withdrawal and their higher grades in Fundamentals of Mathematics I. Students receiving a grade lower than a *C* generally are not interested in nor capable of continuing with a second mathematics course. To correct for this effect, an additional set of comparisons was made, in which the population was restricted to students who received a *C* or better in Fundamentals of Mathematics I (see table 8.4). Although this correction partially reduced the relative difference between participants and nonparticipants, there was still a definite contrast. Almost half of the participants completed a second course, compared with less than a fourth of the nonparticipant women.

Attitudes about Mathematics and the Program

Several questionnaires were administered to the participants during the first semester. In a questionnaire given to the participants during the last week of the fall semester, they were asked to comment about various aspects of the course. Thirty of the thirty-one students still enrolled in the course, plus the auditor, completed the questionnaire.

Comments about other students in the class emphasized the cooperation and the friendships that developed. One participant wrote, "I feel like it was a big family." Another wrote, "We were a team!" However, two of the participants felt this was not the case and referred to vicious competition among women. *Great* was the word most frequently used to describe the tutorial sessions and individual assistance from the instructors. Many also stressed the patience exhibited.

When asked whether the project was worthwhile and whether it should be continued, one student replied that a special program should not be

TABLE 8.4. Percentage of students receiving a grade of *C* or better in Fundamentals of Mathematics I who continued mathematics the following semester

| | Fall 1974 | | | | Fall 1972a | | | Fall 1973b | | |
| | Participants | Nonparticipants | | | | | | | | |
Course	Women (N = 27)	Women (N = 200)	Men (N = 188)	Total (N = 388)	Women (N = 24)	Men (N = 33)	Total (N = 57)	Women (N = 24)	Men (N = 19)	Total (N = 43)
Enrolled in second-semester mathematics										
Fundamentals of Math II	59%	20%	31%	25%	38%	27%	32%	4	37%	19%
Finite math	0	0	5	2	0	12	7	4	16	9
Geometry	4	5	less than 1	3	0	0	0	0	0	0
Total[c]	63	25	36	30	38	39	39	8	53	28
Received C or better in second-semester mathematics										
Fundamentals of Math II	44	18	20	19	33	18	25	4	26	14
Finite math	0	0	5	2	0	12	7	0	16	7
Geometry	4	4	0	2	0	0	0	0	0	0
Total[c]	48	22	25	23	33	30	32	4	42	21

[a] Standard section with a standard format, taught by the project director.
[b] "Negatively selected" section with a standard format, taught by the project director.
[c] The totals include several students who are counted twice because of dual second-semester enrollment.

necessary. Another participant felt that the project was excellent for students without a good background and that she should have been in a higher-level course. The other twenty-nine indicated that they felt that the project was worthwhile and recommended that it be continued. Twenty-three participants commented that the project had positively affected their attitudes about mathematics, while two more said that they had always liked mathematics and this attitude had not changed. Four students said that their attitude had not been affected, although one woman commented that she understood mathematics better now. Nine participants responded that their career options had been broadened.

The students were asked to rate various aspects of the project on a five-point scale, ranging from "one of the best features" to "one of the worst." (The responses are summarized in table 8.5.) The instructors and the group-tutoring sessions were the most highly rated program aspects.

During the final-examination period a computer-scored questionnaire was administered to all students in all the sections of Fundamentals of Mathematics I (math 110). The questionnaire was completed by 24 of the 31 participants who took the final exam and by 461 of the 519 nonpartici-pants who took the final. Students who withdrew prior to the final exam were not included. The lower response rate of 78 percent in the experimental section, as compared with 89 percent in the regular sections, probably can be attributed to fatigue after a three-hour final examination, as compared with a two-hour one, and a growing saturation with question-naires. The questionnaire consisted of forty-six questions about the course, the instructor, and individual student backgrounds. The results for some of the key questions are summarized in table 8.6.

The participants reported a much greater increase in their performance and understanding of mathematics (question 7) than did nonparticipants (76 percent of the participants, as compared with 40 percent of the non-participant women and 47 percent of the nonparticipant men). Sixty percent of the participants expected their grade to be either much better or somewhat better than previous mathematics grades (question 6), as com-pared with 32 percent of nonparticipant women and 38 percent of the non-participant men. A partial explanation for this is that the participants generally spent more time studying mathematics. Twenty percent of the participants reported that they studied mathematics more than twelve hours per week outside of class, as compared with 5 percent of the non-participant women and 4 percent of the nonparticipant men, while only 8 percent of the participants reported that they studied less than three hours per week, as compared with 34 percent of the nonparticipant women and 43 percent of the nonparticipant men (question 3). The large number of students in the regular sections reporting less than three hours of weekly study reflects in part a significant number of students who should have enrolled in a more advanced course.

TABLE 8.5. Percentage distribution of ratings of aspects of experimental section of Fundamentals of Mathematics I[a]

Aspect	Rating					
	One of the best	Good	Fair	Poor	One of the worst	No response
Instructors	81%	16%	0%	0%	0%	3%
All-woman classes	35	35	19	3	0	6
Group-tutoring sessions	61	26	6	3	0	3
Textbooks	35	35	19	0	0	10
Supplementary handouts	16	55	13	6	0	10
Tests and quizzes	61	23	3	3	3	6
Guest lecturers and availability of counselors	32	29	19	6	13	0

[a] The questionnaire was completed by thirty of the original thirty-two participants, as well as by the auditor.

Sixty percent of the participants stated that they would recommend taking math 110 to friends (question 10), as compared with 23 percent of the nonparticipant women and 17 percent of the nonparticipant men. Although students in all sections were satisfied with their instructors, the ratings were higher in the experimental group—84 percent of the participants gave their instructor an overall rating of excellent, as compared with 53 percent of the nonparticipant women and 43 percent of the nonparticipant men (question 21). The "instructor" ratings the experimental section gave in table 8.6 were those for the project director. However, the questionnaire for this section included two separate evaluations, one for each of the team teachers. Most participants gave almost identical evaluations to both instructors, although there were two students who rated the instructors differently, one student preferring one of the instructors and the second student preferring the other instructor.

INDIVIDUAL CASES

In addition to the measures of group performance given in tables 8.1-8.6, examples of the effectiveness of the program can be provided by individual accounts. Although it is too early to predict the effect of the project on the eventual careers of the participants, several students have either altered their career plans or have received the assistance and reinforcement

TABLE 8.6. Selected responses to questionnaire administered to students in Fundamentals of Mathematics I at time of final exam, fall 1974

| | Participants | Nonparticipants | | |
	Women (N = 25)a	Women (N = 235)b	Men (N = 223)c	Total (N = 461)d
3. The approximate number of hours per week that I studied Math 110 outside of class was:				
1. 0-3 hours	8%	34%	43%	38%
2. 3-6 hours	48	36	35	35
3. 6-9 hours	12	18	14	16
4. 9-12 hours	12	7	3	5
5. 12 hours or more	20	5	4	5
4. When I first enrolled in Math 110, the grade I expected to receive was:				
1. A	24	25	20	23
2. B	28	38	46	42
3. C	40	31	29	30
4. D	4	4	3	4
5. F, W, or I	4	2	1	1
6. My grade in Math 110 is likely to be:				
1. Much better than most of my previous math grades	32	15	19	17
2. Somewhat better than most of my previous math grades	28	17	19	18
3. About the same as most of my previous math grades	28	45	41	43
4. Somewhat worse than most of my previous math grades	12	14	14	14
5. Much worse than most of my previous math grades	0	9	6	7

7. My current understanding of mathematics is:

1. Much better than before I enrolled in Math 110	76	40	47	43
2. Somewhat better than before I enrolled in Math 110	12	41	37	39
3. About the same as before I enrolled in Math 110	12	16	13	15
4. Somewhat worse than before I enrolled in Math 110	0	2	2	2
5. Much worse than before I enrolled in Math 110	0	1	1	1

8. My current interest in mathematics is:

1. Much higher than before I enrolled in Math 110	36	17	15	16
2. Somewhat higher than before I enrolled in Math 110	32	24	28	26
3. About the same as before I enrolled in Math 110	28	27	45	46
4. Somewhat lower than before I enrolled in Math 110	0	8	5	7
5. Much lower than before I enrolled in Math 110	4	3	6	5

10. I would recommend to my friends that:

1. They really ought to take Math 110	60	23	17	20
2. They might take Math 110	28	44	51	47
3. It does not matter whether or not they take Math 110	8	14	15	14
4. They might avoid taking Math 110	0	12	12	12
5. They really ought to avoid taking Math 110	4	6	6	6

21. I would give the instructor an overall rating of:

1. Excellent	84	53	43	48
2. Good	12	37	43	40
3. Fair	4	7	12	9
4. Poor	0	3	2	2
5. Very poor	0	0	0	0

a Twenty-five of the original thirty-two responded.
b Two hundred thirty-five of the original three hundred forty responded.
c Two hundred twenty-three of the original three hundred forty-four responded.
d This total comprised the 235 women, the 223 men, and 3 not identified with respect to sex; 461 of the original 684 responded.

necessary to stay with an original choice of a major in a traditionally male area requiring considerable mathematics.

A transfer-student participant planning to major in art history, who at the beginning of the project felt very unsure about her ability in mathematics, discovered that she was very capable and interested in mathematics. She excelled in the experimental courses and became a mathematics major. During the second semester of the project she also enrolled in geometry, and she completed first-semester calculus during the summer. She later studied second-semester calculus by correspondence when a move prevented her regular enrollment in school.

A prospective business major who had returned to school after twenty years and who had never taken high-school algebra acquired the background and confidence necessary to apply for and gain admission to the school of administration.

One young woman had been selected for participation primarily because the project director was intrigued by the student's application for admission to the university, in which she wrote: "I am very interested in the field of dentistry. I don't want to become a dentist, but rather something like a dental hygienist or dental lab-technologist." This student turned out to be extremely able. At the end of the fall semester she indicated that she was considering dentistry rather than dental hygiene because she had gained confidence in her own ability and qualifications. However, she had been discouraged somewhat by a visit to the dental school and was uncertain about her plans. If she did not continue with the second semester of the mathematics course, that would mean that she was proceeding with her original plans to be a dental hygienist; on the other hand, if she enrolled for the second semester, that would mean that she was aiming for later admission to dental school. On the first day of the second semester she was seated in the first row of the mathematics class. At the end of the project she commented that the encouraging and supportive environment of the special class had been an important factor in her realizing that she possessed the ability to modify her career plans.

Two of the women who had junior-high-school- and high-school-age children were delighted to have acquired skills enabling them to assist their children with mathematics. One of the women indicated that the project had affected two generations of her family: Not only was she able to consider more career options because of her increased knowledge in mathematics, but the mathematics grades of her children had improved during the year because of her positive attitude about mathematics and her ability to help them when they had difficulties.

An elementary-education major who had always done poorly in mathematics enrolled in Fundamentals of Mathematics I only under great protest. She had accidentally enrolled in the experimental section, but she requested permission to remain because she felt that she would benefit from the different format. During the semester she discovered that she could enjoy and excel in mathematics. She has since completed a mathematics-methods course and is eagerly looking forward to teaching mathematics as part of the elementary-school curriculum.

ANALYSIS OF EFFECTIVENESS OF DIFFERENT COMPONENTS OF THE PROJECT

There were a number of differences between the format for the experimental project and the format of the regular mathematics sections, and it is difficult to isolate the influence of individual components. There is some quantitative information available. In addition, there is considerable qualitative information available from the continual dialogue that took place between the instructors, the tutor, and the participants during the project, as well as occasional discussions after the project. Feedback about participants' perceptions after the conclusion of the project is also provided by information obtained when an outside evaluator for the National Science Foundation spent a day during the fall of 1975, the year after the project, interviewing a number of the participants and discussing the project with the instructors.

An all-female class was decided upon in order to reduce feelings of intimidation and to encourage free participation by all students. In mixed classes some students, especially older students, hesitate to ask questions, fearing that they will appear stupid. On the other hand, sometimes bright young women hesitate to speak up in a mixed class because they do not want to appear to be too smart.

Having only women in the class seemed to be an important factor in the success of the project, primarily because it made it easier for a special rapport and class spirit to develop. Students helped and encouraged each other, and many friendships developed between students and between students and instructors as well.

The reactions of others to an all-female class was at first often mild amusement. Many persons assumed that the class must be a remedial class. Several of the participants and the instructors discussed this reaction and speculated that had the section been all-male, many of these same persons might have assumed that it was an advanced section. However, the remedial designation quickly disappeared in most cases as it became evident that the experimental section was covering more material in a more thorough manner than the regular sections.

When a male student asked for admission to the second semester of the course, the question was put to the students. Although many of the women indicated that they did not care, a sufficient number reacted so adversely to the idea that the request was denied.

The women who were older than the traditional undergraduates seemed especially to benefit from the atmosphere of the class, perhaps because they generally had been more affected than their younger class-mates by the social and cultural factors that often act as barriers to women in the study of mathematics. Some appreciated the reinforcement of their decision to return to school and were encouraged by the presence of other women in situations similar to theirs.

The positive atmosphere of the class further stimulated the high level of motivation on the part of most of the participants. Students rarely missed class. One woman who originally had been very apprehensive about the course commented that she found herself enjoying the math class even more than the courses in her major. The instructors also found themselves looking forward to class because of the active participation and interest of most of the students.

During the first week of the course the instructors had been plagued with doubts. There was considerably more diversity of math backgrounds than they had expected; some of the students had extremely poor grounding in the most elementary fundamentals. Privately, the instructors wondered if they had made a substantial error in judgment in filling a class with so many potentially "marginal" students. Their greatest fear was that there might not be the few good students vital to any class for stimulating class discussion and challenging the other students. In addition, it was obvious that much more time would have to be spent on basic arithmetic than originally planned, and the projected amount of material to be covered in the first semester seemed far too ambitious. Of course, as the previously reported results have shown, the instructors could not have been more wrong, and their fears were rapidly dispelled.

The month-long review of basic arithmetic was absolutely essential for the students with the weakest backgrounds. However, rather than impeding class progress, the time spent on review ultimately enabled the class to cover more material than the regular sections. In the beginning, many of the participants were very anxious about mathematics because of emotional factors and their lack of skills. The first-month's program dealt with both of these areas. Students acquired the solid, basic background necessary for the remainder of the course, and many of the women also gained confidence in their ability to learn mathematics.

Group-tutoring sessions can provide highly effective and economical assistance to students with backgrounds similar to those of the participants. Many undergraduates can be competent tutors with minimal guidance. A tutoring session restricted to a single class is preferable to sessions open to all classes, even when they are available several hours each day. In addition to being more effective with respect to providing math assistance, the common time helped foster an atmosphere of friendship and cooperation among the participants and facilitated a feeling of class unity.

The instructors played an important role. Having a female instructor may be quite helpful for a female target population, but it is not mandatory. What is essential is that an instructor be competent, enthusiastic, supportive, encouraging, patient, and accessible to the students. Although the participants rated the instructors very highly, they were only part of the key to success of the project. A comparison of the performance of participants with the performance of students who previously had taken courses from the project director indicates that other factors also contributed to the success of the project.

The team teaching of the course by two instructors was an asset primarily to the instructors, since such courses require a great deal of instructor time. Their teaching styles were very similar, and they both attended all classes in order to be completely coordinated. The students received some positive benefit in that they had two instructors from whom they could seek assistance. Having two slightly different explanations of a difficult concept was sometimes helpful. The smaller class size permitted more individual assistance, although additional tutoring could offset some of the disadvantages of larger classes.

There were fewer guest lectures, counseling sessions, and field trips than originally planned. A few students very much appreciated these sessions, but many students indicated a general indifference to them, with some feeling that such extra activities took away important class time that could be used more profitably in doing mathematics. Another reason that these contributed less than expected was that the instructors and the tutor were already serving informally as role models, advisers, and counselors. The three women represented a range of roles, since they included a single undergraduate student, a married graduate student without children, and a married faculty member with three preschool- and school-age children. In a class taught by a male faculty member such supplementary activities might be of more benefit in providing role-model support and encouragement.

Students found the practical, problem-oriented nature of the textbooks by Keedy and Bittinger to be very helpful. In addition, the instructors used a number of supplementary practical exercises, especially during the arithmetic review, and pointed out applications that arose in other fields that the students might encounter.

Frequent quizzes and examinations that were graded and returned promptly provided the students with regular feedback. The weekly quizzes helped pinpoint weaknesses early and provided some students with additional incentive to keep up with the material.

The project director previously had experimented with a policy of permitting a retake of an examination. The policy was initiated for the project because one of the students had never had high-school algebra and in fact had not had any mathematics during the preceding twenty-five years. Typically she would do very poorly on an examination but would master the material from that examination about the time that the next examination was scheduled. She was provided with a special tutor to help her on a one-to-one basis. The extra tutoring and the incentive offered by the retake policy, as well as the policy itself, resulted in her mastering the material and receiving a *B* each semester. Had she been judged on what she knew at the regular test time rather than on what she knew at the conclusion of each course, she would have failed. For the other students, the retake policy was of benefit primarily because it provided psychological security; students knew that there was a second chance if necessary and that what was most important was, not the rate of mastery, but the final mastery.

The first semester of the experimental project seemed to have been sufficient to build up the necessary skills and confidence that would enable most of the students to succeed in later courses. Although there was little difference in the performance of participants and nonparticipants with respect to grades earned for the second semester, there was a marked difference in the student populations enrolled for the second course. The second-semester enrollment in the experimental section included many students who, on the basis of their previous background, would not have been expected to take an additional mathematics course.

The project was most successful with the older women. They seemed especially to benefit from the all-female class, the tutoring, and the supplementary activities. Their performance in terms of grades earned was on the average even higher than that of the younger participants, despite their generally weaker mathematics background.

Most of the minority students performed very well. However, the project did not succeed with two participants who were also in the university's transitional-year program, which is designed to assist disadvantaged inner-city students who seem to show promise but do not meet the university's normal admission requirements. After receiving a *D* in the first-semester course, one of the women continued with the second semester in a different section but failed the course. The other woman failed the first-semester course in the fall and repeated the course in a regular section the next semester but failed again. This appeared to be more a result of insufficient motivation and work than of ability. The women were not always conscientious about classroom attendance and studying but seemed capable when worked with individually. Some different or additional means of support for such women is needed.

CONCLUSION

The project has shown that it is possible for most college women, no matter what their background, to succeed in introductory mathematics. An encouraging and supportive environment such as can be provided by a sympathetic teacher, an all-female class, and supplementary tutoring sessions can assist the women in acquiring basic mathematics skills and in opening their career options. As more women of this generation experience success in mathematics, there will be less need for special projects for future generations.

REFERENCES

Ernest, J., et al. 1975. *Mathematics and sex.* Mathematics Department, University of California-Santa Barbara.

Keedy, M. L., and Bittinger, M. L. 1972. *Essential mathematics: A modern approach.* Reading, Mass.: Addison-Wesley.

_____. 1974. *Algebra and trigonometry: A functions approach.* Reading, Mass.: Addison-Wesley.

9

FACTORS AFFECTING FEMALE PARTICIPATION IN ADVANCED PLACEMENT PROGRAMS IN MATHEMATICS, CHEMISTRY, AND PHYSICS

Patricia Lund Casserly

ABSTRACT

In order to identify those factors that might encourage female participation in Advanced Placement (AP) high-school science and mathematics programs, as well as those that discoursage it, a study was conducted examining the curriculum, guidance policies, and student cultures of thirteen high schools. The high schools were selected both for their geographic and socioeconomic heterogeneity and also for the statistically strong proportion of girls among their AP candidates in college-level calculus, chemistry, or physics. The conclusions of the study were as follows: (1) The AP courses provide girls with a stimulus toward careers; (2) AP teachers are excellent agents for recruiting girls to AP courses and later careers; (3) much effective college and career counseling takes place in AP classes; and (4) many guidance counselors are poor sources of encouragement, while older girls are good sources for girls interested in mathematics and the physical sciences.

In the physical sciences, mathematics, and related fields, professional- and college-level output is limited by the pool of students in these areas at the secondary-school level. If we are concerned with national sources of preprofessional talent, we would hope to find girls represented in their natural proportion to boys in the initial pool. Unfortunately, relatively few girls are enrolled in high-school science and mathematics courses. Consequently, it is highly important to identify ways to encourage girls to develop their intellectual powers and particularly to enroll in high-school physical science and mathematics classes. What factors tend to encourage female participation? What factors tend to discourage it?

This study attempts to isolate some of these factors by studying a number of secondary schools that have had unusual success in attracting and holding young women in their mathematics and physical-science curricula, as evidenced by the proportion of girls to boys who take the College Board's Advanced Placement Examinations in these areas. It is our hope that the findings will be useful to those in schools elsewhere who wish to encourage and prepare greater numbers of young women to pursue scientific or technological studies at college and beyond.

Before going on to a discussion of the sample, a brief explanation of the Advanced Placement Program is in order. This program, sponsored by the College Board, is designed to stimulate advanced studies in secondary school for able, interested students and to ensure their appropriate reception, with credit and placement, at college. It operates through working committees of school and college teachers in thirteen fields commonly shared between the latter years of secondary school and the early years of college. The committees state each year their understanding of the curricular goals of a generality of introductory college courses in the field and set examinations of up to three hours in length to certify their attainment in self-nominating, participating schools. Participating colleges, in turn, normally grant qualified candidates placement, with appropriate credit, into advanced college courses. Repeated research studies, performed both at the Educational Testing Service and at participating colleges, have shown that qualified candidates outperform similar students in advanced college courses who did not take part in the Advanced Placement Program in high school and completed their first-year-college work at college. Students who have benefitted from Advanced Placement courses also have a higher tendency to persist in their fields of Advanced Placement study than do college freshmen in similar introductory courses (Casserly 1968; Fry 1973). For the student, the AP program can be said to "work," and for the researcher, its participating schools offer a visible, defined set of demonstrably strong programs in chosen fields.

THE SAMPLE

The sample was drawn in three stages during August 1974. Using data provided annually and routinely during the summer, after the annual May administration of the AP examinations, those schools that had twice the national proportion of girls to boys taking the AP examinations for calculus, chemistry, or physics were identified.[1] The sample was then narrowed to

[1]Nationally, in 1974 only 17.2 percent of the Advanced Placement candidates in chemistry were girls. Only 27.9 percent of those taking calculus AB examinations were girls, as were 21 percent of those taking the calculus BC examinations. Only 12.9 percent of those taking the physics B examinations were girls, as were 6.8 percent of those taking physics C.

those schools that had the desired proportion of girls in two of the three fields under study and/or at least five girls in one of the two other fields. Finally, socioeconomic variety and regional representation were considered. Initially, twelve high schools were asked to participate in the study. Additional funding by the College Board made it possible to add one more high school and AP teachers from seven others, as well as guidance counselors from several junior high schools.

About a third of the schools were in the midst of large urban centers and drew heavily from working-class neighborhoods. Another third were also urban, but they drew a greater number of middle-class students. The remaining third were suburban schools serving a high proportion of students from professional and upper-middle-class families.

PROCEDURES

In the fall of 1974 the schools were asked whether they would be willing to participate and, if so, to inform us of the number of girls enrolled in the appropriate AP classes. All were willing to take part in the study, but two schools had to be dropped, and substitutes found, because there was an insufficient number of girls in their physical-science and mathematics AP classes that year. In one case we were told that a number of parents had recently removed their daughters from the school because of federally mandated redistricting and bussing.

Visits to the schools were carried out from November 1974 through April 1975. With one exception, each visit lasted at least two days; at several schools visits lasted three days, and in one case, four days. School visits were often supplemented by interviews, at the appropriate board of education and at regional conferences for AP teachers.

The original plan had been to observe the appropriate classes in order to get a sense of teaching styles and of patterns of interaction and participation among students and to arrange individual interviews, lasting from a class period to over an hour, with the girls and with their teachers and guidance counselors. In the fourth school, however, the girls' schedules were so tight that the only time that could be arranged to talk with them was during the AP class (which fortunately lasted two periods); so we held a group discussion after the girls had each filled out a short biographical questionnaire hastily adapted from the outline designed for individual interviews. This shift from individual interviews to structured group discussion proved to enhance rather than diminish the quality and specificity of the girls' responses in many areas. The girls jogged each other's memories and sharpened one another's suggestions for the task at hand. The discussion format also gave a far richer picture of the girls' formal educational experiences and of the uniqueness of their particular school system than did individual interviews. Not least important was the fact that overblown generalizations and misinterpretations of classmates' perceptions and motivations and problems were corrected on the spot.

Because of the success of the initial group discussion, which had taken place out of necessity, group sessions were scheduled at the remaining schools to be visited for the study; thus, at nine schools both individual and group interviews were conducted. This flexibility provided an additional advantage in that it was possible to talk with all but three of the girls in the target population rather than with only five from each class. A total of 161 of the girls enrolled in AP classes participated in the study, and 70 of these were interviewed individually; the rest participated in group discussions only or were seen in both individual and group settings.

In all but one school, interviews with AP teachers were conducted individually, although on several occasions all the faculty members of a department were seen also in a group. When time and the occasion presented itself, teachers responsible for the pre-AP courses were interviewed. When time and the opportunity permitted, teachers outside the mathematics and science fields that were described by students, AP teachers, or members of the administration as having enhanced the aspirations of young women in the schools were also interviewed. All but two of these teachers were female. One of these women headed a drama department; several taught social studies and history; and one taught physical education. The two males were a guidance and career counselor and the chairman of an English department.

For additional information, forty-three former AP students who were recent graduates from nine of the high schools in the study were interviewed by telephone. In some cases the schools provided rosters with home or college addresses of all 1974 graduates, while at other schools only specific graduates were suggested because their college careers and aspirations were known by a particular teacher or someone in the administration. They were then, or were in the process of becoming, the school's "success stories." Because of the variety of methods used for choosing this graduate group of participants, no claim can be made that they are in any way a representative sample of their former AP classmates, although their perceptions did strengthen many of the suggestions made by their younger sisters still in secondary school.

THE CURRENT AP STUDENTS—A BIOGRAPHICAL DESCRIPTION

The 161 girls interviewed in the schools represented the usual age distribution, the average age being about seventeen.[2] Twelve were sophomores, fifty-eight were juniors, and ninety-one were seniors. Of the sophomores, three were in AP physics and six were in AP chemistry. Of the

[2] At the time they participated, fourteen were fifteen years old, thirty-nine were sixteen years old, seventy-one were seventeen years old, and thirty-seven were eighteen years old.

fifty-eight juniors, six were studying calculus, thirty-three were studying chemistry, and nineteen were studying physics; approximately half of the juniors were also taking an additional AP course, usually AP American history. Of the ninety-one seniors interviewed, sixty-one were studying or had studied calculus, forty-five were in an AP chemistry course, and twenty-six were studying physics. It should be pointed out that this means that roughly half these seniors were enrolled in two or more courses in the subjects of this study. In addition, twelve of these seniors were taking or had taken AP biology. And fifty-five of them were also taking or had taken other AP courses outside the math-science field. The greatest numbers were enrolled in AP English (twenty-five) or modern foreign languages (thirteen); five were studying either American or European history, and four were studying AP music or art, and two were in AP classics.

The girls appeared to be bright and highly motivated. Approximately four fifths of them expected to graduate with two or more AP courses behind them. A number of them expected to enter college with four or five AP courses to their credit.

What kinds of families do these girls come from? One hundred thirty-eight (86 percent) of the girls were native-born Americans, fourteen (10 percent) of whom had spent at least one but not more than three years in a foreign (English, French, or Swiss) school system. Twenty-three (14 percent) of the students were foreign-born. Of these, eighteen (78 percent) were Asian, thirteen coming from Hong Kong and five from Taiwan. The remaining five were English, Dutch, French, Hungarian, and Mexican. Each of the Asian girls had completed the equivalent of at least six years of schooling before immigrating to this country.

Two kinds of socioeconomic data (educational and occupational) were collected about mothers and fathers. The data, gross indicators as they are, are relatively complete in 125 cases. Occasionally the data collected from the girls were amended and augmented by information gleaned from school records or provided by guidance counselors. The girls had the most difficulty stating how many years of schooling their mothers had completed. For girls whose fathers were college graduates, another question almost as troublesome concerned the area of their father's degree and his precise occupation, especially if he worked for a large corporation. As one girl put it, "He works for Kodak, but I don't know whether he manages, sells, or develops."

The educational levels of both mothers and fathers of 125 girls, together with some data for comparison from U.S. census figures, are shown in table 9.1. An unusually high proportion of mothers had earned doctorates (8.8 percent) or had some graduate work beyond college (7.2 percent). Among this latter group were several mothers who had five-year nursing degrees. Several others had M.A. degrees in teaching. The remainder had taken "some courses" but had not, so far as their daughters knew, completed the requirements for an advanced degree. A slightly smaller percentage (14.4

TABLE 9.1. Education level of parents (N = 125)

Level of highest education	Mother		Father		Percentage of general population	
	Number	Percentage	Number	Percentage	Age 35-44[a]	Age 45-54[a]
Doctorate	11	8.8	18	14.4 }	15.1	11.4
Some graduate study	9	7.2	14	11.2		
Baccalaureate degree	18	14.4	30	24.0		
Some college	48	38.4	18	14.4	12.2	11.0
High-school degree	37	29.6	29	23.2	42.1	39.3
Some high school	2	1.6	9	7.2	17.0	17.8
Eighth grade or less	0	.0	7	5.6	13.6	20.5

[a]U.S. Bureau of the Census, Current Population Report, series P-20, 1973.

percent) of the mothers had stopped their formal education with a baccalaureate degree. All in all, almost a third of the mothers (30.4 percent) had completed college, while slightly more (38.4 percent) had some college experience. Most of the remaining third (29.6 percent) had graduated from high school; only two mothers (1.6 percent), who were foreign-born, had not.

Among the fathers, a greater proportion (14.4 percent) had achieved doctorates, and a slightly smaller group (11.2 percent) had completed master's degrees, usually in either engineering or business. Approximately another quarter (24.02 percent) of the fathers had earned baccalaureates, and a smaller group (14.4 percent) had had some college training. Almost a quarter of the fathers (23.2 percent) had completed high school, but one in eight (12.8 percent) had less than a high-school diploma.

The general educational level of the parents was quite high. Almost one third of the mothers (30.4 percent) and half of the fathers (49.6 percent) had at least completed college; and another large group of the mothers (38.4 percent) and a smaller group of the fathers (14.4 percent) had had some college. Roughly two thirds of each group had had "some college" or more—68.8 percent of the mothers and 64 percent of the fathers. According to the girls, a number of their mothers had stopped their formal education "to put Daddy through." This phenomenon is reflected in the figures of table 9.1. It is also of interest that although fewer of the mothers than fathers have college degrees, fewer mothers (1.6 percent) than fathers (12.8 percent) failed to graduate from high school.

An unusually high number of both fathers and mothers are employed in positions that require baccalaureate or advanced degrees, as shown in table 9.2. Just over one third (33.6 percent) of the fathers for whom data were available were so employed, as were slightly more than a fifth (21.6 percent) of the mothers. Many of the college-trained women, however, were among those who did not work outside the home, while only three fathers out of the total group were unemployed (only one, a Ph.D., was looking for work). At the other end of the scale (categories 8 and 9), approximately one fifth of the mothers (19 percent) and a roughly equal number of the fathers were working at blue-collar jobs. Both ends of the socioeconomic spectrum were represented in the sample on which there was complete information. Those students whose parents were not included in the tabular information seemed to come from families with low socioeconomic status. At one school the director of guidance volunteered that 75 percent of the students were eligible for the free-lunch program and suggested that the students not be asked about their parents directly. Thus, the girls who participated and did well in the Advanced Placement Program calculus and physical-science courses were not necessarily the offsprings of a socioeconomic elite, able to provide them with extracurricular opportunities and stimulation. The majority of parents were fairly well-educated, however, and 40 percent were employed in reasonably high positions.

TABLE 9.2. Occupational groups of parents (N = 125)

Occupation	Mother		Father	
	Number	Percentage	Number	Percentage
1. Professional requiring advanced degree (doctor, lawyer, college professor, researcher, etc.)	8	6.4	16	12.8
2. Professional requiring a bachelor's degree (engineer, teacher, social worker)	19	15.2	26	20.8
3. Owner or high-level executive of large business or governmental agency	1	0.8	12	9.6
4. Owner, manager, or partner in small business or lower-level governmental official	2	1.6	12	9.6
5. Sales or clerical worker	6	4.8	8	6.4
6. Skilled worker or craftsman (carpenter, printer, electrician, plumber, medical technician, potter, programmer)	1	0.8	14	11.2
7. Service worker (policeman, fireman, barber, noncommissioned military officer, paraprofessional in education or health field)	14	11.2	11	8.8
8. Semi-skilled worker (machine operator, longshoreman, assembler, etc.)	9	7.2	13	10.4
9. Unskilled worker (laborer, maid, janitor, warehouseman)	15	12.0	10	8.0
10. Unemployed or retired	50	40.0	3	2.4

THE FINDINGS

Countless factors lie behind the decisions, activities, and views of young women anticipating careers in mathematics and the physical sciences. Some of these influences were so general and banal as to be outside the purpose of this study. Others, on the other hand, were so unique and accidental as to defy generalization for other reasons. The attitudes and actions, however, of at least four groups of people—parents, teachers, guidance counselors, and other students—seemed to play a regular, visible, and important role in such young women's educations.

The following discussion will revolve around a number of recurrent themes that became evident from interviews at all the schools, focusing on those experiences—mostly within the schools—that students regard as either having enhanced their interest in science and mathematics or, although well-intended, as having had little or even negative effect. (Whatever their purpose, the "messages" of counselors and teachers are often "received" quite differently than they are "sent.") Throughout this discussion the aim is to provide practical suggestions for people committed to encouraging young women to develop their intellectual powers and interests.

Paths to Advanced-Placement Courses

The girls who had enrolled in the advanced courses had done so for many reasons. For some the courses were the capstones in secondary school of apparently natural sequences of courses serving their early, and later well-defined, interests.

"I guess we were always accelerated; at least we had been grouped together almost since the beginning of school. At first it wasn't that we necessarily did different things, but we did more."

"We were on the fast track from the fourth grade on. . . . These courses are just the culmination of a natural sequence that served our well-defined interests, you might say."

"Most of us have been together forever, it seems, We've grown up together, like a family."

A number of different curricular paths were traveled by the students on the way to their AP courses in high school. Most involved homogeneous grouping, at least in mathematics, as early as the fourth grade; but typically the curricular content of these courses was not differentiated until the seventh grade, when some of these students took pre-algebra in lieu of the usual sequence. Although formal acceleration for these girls usually didn't start until the seventh or eighth grade (some went right into algebra from the regular mathematics sequence, skipping pre-algebra), the girls generally agreed that homogeneous grouping in the lower grades had had distinct advantages. The most important of these were psychosocial, although a number of girls also spoke of the enrichment that had kept boredom at bay.

"Made us a group . . . who by junior high were pretty independent of the other high-school culture. We didn't mind being smart—in fact we really liked it."

"Yeah, we still do! We're really competitive with each other and the boys —but let one of *them* try to put anyone of us down and we close ranks."

". . . and help each other."

"Let's face it, we were different . . . where other girls were worrying about who was going to take them to the basketball game, we were worrying about how to get a ride to the county library (across town) or down to New Paltz for our projects."

"Junior high was the worst time for us—the absolute worst—with going to a new school and a whole different social scene. And lots of the other students thought us a bit weird—only boys had been in the pre-med club before."

Over and over again, girls remarked on the importance of girlfriends who shared "common school experiences and similar interests on similar levels" in dealing with the teasing and disapproval of boys, which "peaked at the ninth grade." Although boys who had come up with the girls in the accelerated group teased too, they did so "half-heartedly" or "good-naturedly." "They were used to us and we were used to them—they were really like brothers," and they remained so into the last years of high school. When asked whether or not their social groups outside of school mirrored their academic group in school, the vast majority of girls in all schools said that although many of their girlfriends were in the same classes, they preferred to date outside their AP classes in math and science, although a number dated boys in other AP classes. (This matter is discussed more in a later section.)

For the girls who were not tracked early, the potential placement into algebra in the eighth grade was often almost traumatic. Such girls reported that other girls in their class had rejected the option when it was presented, either on their own or because parental awareness and support were lacking. "It's an awkward age, and some girls feel like they're being singled out at a time they'd like to be anonymous." For girls already tracked, the option never arose, nor did the opportunity for a guidance counselor to ask, as some were reported to have done, "Why do you want to be ahead? You certainly don't need all that math for college." Such statements show ignorance of the prerequisites of upper-level high-school courses as well as of the demands of many college courses, and they close doors prematurely.

Three of the schools in the study gave strong students who had studied algebra in the ninth grade a chance to jump ahead (or to catch up with their more advanced classmates) by combining either tenth- and eleventh-grade or eleventh- and twelfth-grade mathematics. It was said, however, that many more boys than girls were encouraged to choose (and actually used) this option. Quotes from two students illustrate the feelings expressed by many that by ninth grade (often the last year of junior high school), "the school culture is such that mathematics suddenly seems 'harder' for girls than for boys," and "sex typing is at its peak, and it takes an unusually motivated and self-confident girl to buck it and say 'so what?'"

At two other schools several unaccelerated girls reported that they had caught up a year or two in mathematics by going to summer school. In one school this was no longer an option, since summer school was being dropped because funds were lacking. And in a school located down the hill from a highly selective university, several girls reported that they had studied mathematics "on the outside" since grade six "for fun" with a private tutor who brought his small groups of students up to college level in mathematics by the time they were age fifteen or so. This meant that they could take AP mathematics and AP physics with calculus as sophomores if they wished, and several were doing so.

The paths leading to the AP courses in the physical sciences reflected two divergent attitudes toward the secondary-school science curriculum. As it happened, they were almost equally represented in the schools under study. One group of schools thought it important to give a student interested in *any* science a good scientific background in *all* the scientific fields the school had to offer. The student had to study general science or physical science, followed by regular courses in biology, chemistry, and physics, before she could enter an AP course in any of those fields. This meant, effectively, that AP science courses were senior courses and that because of the laboratory time required, most students were limited to a single AP course in the sciences. Also the laboratory sections of the AP sciences were often scheduled for the same period, so that even if students were willing to put in the time for two AP science courses, scheduling was impossible.

In several of the schools employing this approach, some students — identified in junior high school by their mathematics and reading scores and by their interests — had been allowed to substitute biology for physical science in the eighth grade, just as most of them had substituted algebra for regular eighth-grade mathematics. This had gained them a year and meant they could take one AP science course in each of their last two years.

In two schools where general science was a part of the ninth-grade curriculum, followed successively by biology and the two physical sciences, AP students either had to take two regular sciences in one year or, in their senior year, one AP science and one regular science in order to satisfy the science department's requirements. In one school, every senior girl in AP chemistry was also enrolled in a regular physics class. None had wanted to study physics in earlier years, so concurrent enrollment in regular physics had been a condition for their enrollment in the AP chemistry class.

The concern for providing students with a broad science background that underlies such policies is understandable and well-intentioned. On the other hand, such policies had discouraged many other girls from continuing in the science of their interest on the AP level. There were indications that such requirements might work differently for girls and boys because of the prevailing culture. At least some girls thought so.

> "A lot of guys tend to be interested in science, *per se*—in any and all fields. But a number of my [girl] friends are interested in only one at the moment. Why can't we just do that?"

> "Besides, girls don't want to be known as science nuts by taking every science course around. I happen to like chemistry, but I hate dissecting, and figuring out trajectories bores me."

In an almost equal number of schools the science curriculum was less rigidly structured: There were no prerequisites for AP science courses beyond "one other science course." For a third of the girls this other course had been a regular course in the same field, although this pattern was sometimes discouraged. For another third the other science course had been the ninth-grade physical-science course. The final third presented credentials in more than one other course. How do students decide on AP science courses instead of regular precollege science courses if the latter are not prerequisites for the former? According to one science coordinator, "It's all there in the description of courses. We have a two-page course outline that spells out exactly what they'll be getting into and what level of mathematical competence is necessary. And we're careful to point out the extra time required outside of class and the trips to [other educational institutions] when they begin their research projects."

Students rely heavily on the extended course descriptions, offered by a number of schools, that point out the differences in the levels of difficulty among courses in the same field. The descriptions of AP courses include a statement of their possible benefits in college to those who do well on the AP examination. Such written statements are particularly important in attracting girls, since in only five schools did either students or teachers report that guidance counselors were of any help in identifying and encouraging well-qualified girls to enroll in the AP courses or to consider careers in mathematics or science. In the other schools girls and their AP teachers thought that the advice counselors gave eager and motivated girls about curricular choices seemed too conservative at best, and at worst, positively hostile.

Both of the curricular patterns outlined above have their specific advantages and disadvantages. The first provides a general science background but may turn some students off completely. Regular pre-college courses (often taught by the AP teacher) in the sciences taught within each curricular pattern give the teacher and the students time to evaluate one another, and they have some advantages for recruitment. On the other hand, students may not have the opportunity to take as many AP courses as they would if so many prerequisities were not imposed. The second pattern provides greater opportunity for students to pursue their interest in a science when they and the AP teacher feel they are ready to do the work. When students go on to other sciences after one AP course, it is by choice, not coercion.

Students from both curricular patterns do equally well in their AP courses and on the AP examinations. It is interesting that when teachers in each system were told about the other, they often expressed disbelief.

> "No one without a first course in physics could survive the AP physics course."

> "They'll get lopsided enough in college—there's still a place for general education, and it's here."

> "This girl (a junior AP physics student) has been fascinated with optics all her life and has done science-fair projects on some phase of it since seventh grade. And she's a whiz in math! Am I going to tell her she has to pith frogs?"

All in all, the more flexible curricular system, which does not require a full spectrum of science courses, seems more conducive to female participation in AP science courses than does the more rigid system. The latter system is sometimes seen as demanding a firmer commitment to science —all of it—than many girls are willing to make in high school, for both intellectual and social reasons.

So far we have been considering the sequences in schools that lead to the AP courses in the study. For many girls, school provides the only formal exposure to science or mathematics. For girls lucky enough to live near a university museum or a laboratory with a strong community outreach program, such as the now defunct Lux Lab or the Lawrence Laboratory in Berkeley, California, or in an area where the explorer scouts of the Boy Scouts of America are active, there are numerous opportunities for both formal instruction and work experience outside of school. About 30 percent of the girls in the study, but never more than half the girls in any AP class, had taken science (or math) classes outside of school. These activities usually started when the girls were between the ages of ten and eleven.

These courses covered a broad spectrum, as did the activities engaged in by any one girl. They ranged from mini-courses lasting several weekends or a week or two to six- or eight-week summer National Science Foundation projects to semester-long after-school endeavors. Many centered around environmental science projects, though the emphasis seemed to be on understanding ecosystems in general and did not focus on environmental problems per se. The most fequently mentioned courses of study were oceanography, marine biology, seashore management, and forestry. Geology was popular among girls living inland as well as among those living on the coasts, but only in California did girls report a special course in earthquakes. Ichthyology, herpetology, entomology, astronomy, space travel, and exploration were enjoyed by a number of others. These non-school courses seem particularly important, since when the girls were asked to compare their extracurricular science courses with those taken in school during the same period (late elementary- and junior-high-school years), the latter always suffered. Why?

"In school during those years [grades four through seven] we were learning something about science; after school we were doing science. . . . Oh, I don't mean we didn't have hands-on experiences in school. But they seemed somehow contrived and silly. At the museum, it was different; you sort of felt you were helping your leader with his science."

"We were junior partners in her quest. She was collecting data for her doctorate, which involved a census of the inhabitants of tide pools, and she impressed on us how important it was to observe and count accurately. . . . She hadn't been there before either and was relying on us."

The above comments, describing the attraction of voluntary activities under the direction of practicing scientists as compared with the compulsory science programs in the schools, could have been made as easily by boys as by girls. But those cited below help explain the girls' less positive reactions to school courses:

"Well, of course we had what you'd call laboratory sessions in school, which meant getting everything out of the storeroom and putting it back every day. And the teacher would always say, 'Now the boys will help me with the boxes while the girls tidy things up.' This was funny because the science equipment was on high shelves and the girls were as tall as or taller than the boys at that time [eighth grade]. Why couldn't she have said, 'Who wants to help?' or whatever? But here she was, a scientist supposedly! . . . And assigning tasks day after day that reflected sexual stereotypes rather than an objective evaluation of her students' abilities. Her denial of our obvious differences made us more self-conscious, not less."

"So this teacher came down from the high school to give a demonstration in physics and said, 'Now this is going to make a pretty big noise, so any of you girls who don't like loud noises better cover your ears.'"

"He said, 'Now this is going to be dirty, so we'd better have a boy do it.'"

"And he [a high-school science teacher performing a demonstration for a sixth-grade class] said, 'Now this will help you boys who fix your own bicycles, so pay attention!'"

"Yeah, don't girls have bicycles too? What are you expected to do? Wait till Daddy or your older brother gets home?"

"But supposing you don't have an older brother or a daddy? Which reminds me, do you have any idea how demeaning it is to ask your little brother's permission to play with his Lego set?"

This last comment started a heated discussion on toys that illustrated the kind of stereotyping many girls encounter in their earliest years and why they are especially sensitive to sex-stereotyping when they reach school. The discussion continued:

"Yeah, or his tinker toys and erector set."

"I got Lego the first Christmas I asked, but there are no boys in our family."

"Yeah—lucky you! I had to wait three years for a microscope and when I finally got it, I drove my parents wild because I went around scraping people's teeth for months."

Girls in other schools agreed with this group of girls that a chemistry set had been the hardest toy for most of them to get, either legally (by direct gift) or illegally (surreptitiously "borrowed") from a brother:

"How come your parents are so scared you'll drop everything and burn yourself?"

"Yeah, maybe what they're saying is that boys are more expendable" [group laughter].

"Yeah, if we were in such danger and so clumsy, how come they trust us in the kitchen with the cooking and the dishes?"

Girls who were only children, eldest siblings separated from younger brothers by four or more years, or first-born girls with sisters only faired much better in acquiring the desired toys than did girls in other family positions.

Advanced Placement Teachers

One girl, on her way to studying engineering at Rice University, summed up many girls' experiences with science in and out of school before senior high school in this way:

"In school, they [teachers] were trying so hard to relate to us and be chatty, they fell on their faces with 'Now, you girls and you boys.' They really talked down to us. But at the labs it was 'Who wants to?' or 'Who will?' And whoever was closest caught it. They were teaching the subject, not trying to ingratiate themselves. They assumed our interest because we were there, which is really funny, because a lot of us were sent because our parents thought we were unchallenged in school; they wanted to keep us out of our brothers' rooms or off the streets, I suppose. I mean, we didn't start off as scientific geniuses. But it wasn't long before we were hooked. Their enthusiasm was infectious."

Other girls from different schools augmented this theme of infectious enthusiasm when talking about their AP teachers and the reasons for taking the AP course:

"Well, he's known for being a stickler, but he just lives chemistry—I mean he loves it. And he gets such a kick out of teaching it, you don't mind working for him. I'd rather work than be bored with a teacher who's bored too."

"You just know he's doing exactly what he likes best. Oh, he tries to make jokes and mostly they're awful, but he tries so hard. He purposely botches things to keep us on our toes. He *cares* what we learn."

"The difference between Mr. V. and other teachers can be summed up easily. He always says to me, 'Now you'll really need this when you study _____.' He assumes everyone is as interested in chemistry as he is. Of course, he's dead wrong about some students, but that's a better way to err. My other science teachers sort of excuse the girls and say, 'Well, this would be important if you were going on.' The implication was that, of course, you're not going to, so why bother."

Girls turned to their female classmates for support and encouragement when adults in schools made similar remarks and were perceived by the girls to be either "putting them down" or applying sex-linked criteria for acceptable performance. "Peer-group solidarity is vitally important for girls interested in science in this school," noted one AP coordinator, "because this is a school of working-class kids. . . . they have no one at home to offer encouragement. All they have is their determination and their dreams."

He was wrong about the girls receiving no encouragement from their families. Most of the girls in this school (and an overwhelming number of girls in the study) felt that their parents were supportive, at least of their *general* goals. What was lacking on the working-class parents' part was an understanding of the specific steps that could be taken or needed to be taken in school in order for the girls to reach their objectives. Further, the girls rarely had any first-hand experience outside of school with an adult of either sex who was employed as a professional in a scientific field.

Disparaging remarks about one's abilities or goals, particularly those that reflect sexism, whether intentionally or not, are more easily dealt with if there is someone within or outside the school who knows both the girl and the requirements of the field and can help her put such potentially discouraging utterances in perspective. For the girls in whose lives there were such persons, it seemed unimportant whether they were male or female. What was important was that the older person could identify with the girl's frustrations about being a novice in a complex field and could support the girl's educational goals, however nonspecific they were in high school. The girls felt that AP teachers within the schools fulfilled this need well.

Recruitment

Girls for whom the AP class was not a natural option among a number of advanced senior courses after years of homogeneous grouping and acceleration attributed their enrollment largely to the recruitment efforts of AP teachers in lower-level science classes. Often AP teachers scanned rosters of ninth- and tenth-grade science and mathematics classes and asked the teachers of these courses to recommend potential candidates who might not show up on the basis of grades alone. "Any one with a good mind, but a bit dreamy and unconventional? Any one with a consuming interest in some aspect of science outside the curriculum? Any one who's bright but drives you up a wall?" asks one AP physics teacher of his colleagues. Then some of the AP teachers who actively recruit students make a presentation to whole lower-level science classes, explaining what the AP course is, what level of work is required, and what the advantages are to the student both in college (placement and credit) and in high school (a chance to get deeply involved in a subject, to do independent research and the like). Others arrange to see potential AP students individually, often more than a year before they will be ready for an AP course, to advise them on their curricular choices. A number of girls who were recruited in this way reported it was the first time they had shared their specific interests and goals with an adult at school. AP teachers tend to take over the role of college and career counseling of their students—or step into the vacuum left by the guidance department.

One AP physics teacher who is also the science coordinator at his school uses *all* the techniques I encountered elsewhere to recruit students to his and other science and mathematics classes. Two beliefs—that science study has value for all students and that scientific talent is distributed equally among the sexes—dominate his efforts and are reflected in enrollment figures. Each year approximately 40 percent of the student body is enrolled in some science course, and a third of these are in AP classes. There are three AP physics classes, as well as AP classes in chemistry and biology, and about half of the AP students in these classes are girls. "Enrollment in science classes should be representative of the total school population and, if it's not, I ask myself why . . . and double my efforsts." The attitudes and atmosphere he and his department have created are most effective in developing scientific talent regardless of sex and on whatever level it exists.

Indeed, it is hard to escape science at this school. Science trophies are purposely larger than athletic trophies and are displayed just as prominently in the main lobby. Large plaques honoring student teachers and laboratory assistants through the years hang on the walls outside the appropriate centers. Girls have shared these honors about equally with boys since this practice was initiated.

At this school, *every* year *every* student in *every* science class is counseled about science courses for the coming year and reminded of the advanced courses available. "We *assume* all students will continue in science. The only options we present are within the department . . . ," he chuckled. (The options include an array of courses in astronomy, geology and earth sciences, computer science, electronics, and the like, not covered by the AP program.) However, the more able students are strongly encouraged toward AP courses. "I'm against wasting time almost as much as wasting talent," he continues. "Students should get the basics (freshman college courses) out of the way in high school if they can, so they'll be able to move on when they get to college. Professional degrees take a long time in science and it's a young person's field."

Once a student is enrolled in AP physics, even less of the student's future is left to chance, that is, to lack of information about opportunities within the field. An extensive library within the classroom includes books on careers in specific fields, as well as science classics, biographies of scientists, and science fiction. A certain number of book reports are required during the school year. Catalogues of many colleges with strong science programs are prominently displayed nearby, and pamphlets outlining unusual programs and scholarship programs are distributed to *each* member of the class. On the day I visited, two such pamphlets had arrived, one about special programs in engineering for women in the midwest. These were passed out to all girls, and there was a special admonition to one of the girls: "Now see that your parents read this one. . . . Yes, I know you want to go to medical school, but this will help get your parents used to the fact that you may have to go outside this part of the country!" The girl later confirmed his perception of her situation: "My father says I can study anything I want to, to be anything I want to, as long as it's done within a radius of 150 miles, and that's going to be hard to do, but when the time comes Mr. _____ [her teacher] will come to the house and talk with him."

This teacher, like several others, called the parents of his students whenever he felt it was in the student's best interest; this meant whenever the student was more than a few days behind, or more frequently, when a parent needed to be persuaded to fill out the Parents' Confidential Statement (PCS), required by colleges for a student's consideration for financial aid or the like. Other teachers agreed that parental attitudes toward the PCS were a problem for many students, particularly girls from lower socioeconomic strata. A teacher from an urban school offered the following comments:

> "The father is often reluctant to share his financial affairs with the family. . . . I know most everyone in this school would qualify for financial aid, but there seems to be a cultural pattern of reluctance to apply, especially for

daughters. The father is the provider and he doles out the money. Even his wife may not know exactly how much he makes—and he thinks he's got to tell her and the student. Actually, he doesn't—he just has to put it on the form, which you know is strictly confidential. Also, sometimes pride is involved and he thinks the girl should go to _____ [a good, publicly supported college nearby], which he can afford. The father of one of the girls I had last year is a case in point. She is the most exceptional student I've had in seven years, and I knew M.I.T. would be glad to get her, but he wouldn't fill out the form. So, first I had to convince him that it *was* strictly confidential—no one would see it—not even his family, if he didn't want it, and then that the difference in the education she'd receive was worth it. I made him feel more guilty about the form than he was already feeling inadequate about not being able to pay for M.I.T. He's [an immigrant] terribly hard working and responsible. It was not like him to ask anyone for help. I convinced him he'd be doing the college and the country a favor. He just couldn't make that last big leap. It was o.k. for her to be a scientist if that's what she wanted. But he couldn't think of a girl being at the very top in her field and therefore, worth the investment to the college. I finally wore him down and there she is. Call her up."

This teacher and many others in the study were fulfilling three roles that were important in accounting for the numbers of girls in their classes—that of trusted older friend, that of respected mentor in their field of interest and, that of informed and aggressive counselor, interested in promising students whatever their sex.

Girls in a few other schools were lucky to have guidance counselors go to bat for them with their parents about the PCS and other matters relating to college choice, but in most schools counselors saw their students who were not in trouble for only a few minutes a year. They simply didn't know their students well enough to be helpful, had they wanted to be.

The Role of the Counselors

So far guidance counselors have been mentioned only in passing and then usually in a negative light. This is for the simple reason that in only five of the schools visited did either students or teachers think them a positive force in the students' lives. In two of those schools the guidance office was credited with sharing much of the responsibility for introducing the AP program into the school, as well as for many other programs for the "gifted" student, however it was locally defined. In those five schools the counselors also seemed committed to encouraging bright students of both sexes to follow the most rigorous curricular program they could manage. Interviews with guidance counselors in the remaining schools, however, confirmed the reports of the students and teachers that the guidance office was a poor place to regard as a resource for girls with interests in mathematics and science:

[A counselor in her early 30s:] "Well, if they bring me their registration card with [an AP science course] listed I'll check to see if that's really what they meant. . . but I would never encourage it. I mean, it's usually their last year and there are so many fun things going on. I think they'll be busy enough and they can get into the serious work in college."

[A counselor in her 20s:] "I just hate to see a girl get in over her head. I always try to place students at a level where I know they'll be successful. I mean, wouldn't it be frightful to spoil a beautiful record by doing poorly in a course your senior year?"

[A male director of guidance in his mid-40s:] "Sure, I'm for the AP program in general, but not for encouraging girls in science necessarily. Have you looked at the Bureau of Labor Statistics? It's a contracting market. There are men with Ph.D.'s in physics all over the place who can't get jobs. Why should we encourage girls? Why, if the're successful, they'd be taking jobs away from men who need them. No, it wouldn't be fair to the girls."

Unfortunately, these comments were not chosen because they were unique but because they represented all too well the attitudes of the counselors in many schools. It is no wonder that a science supervisor, when asked if counselors were helpful, responded in a meeting of AP science teachers, who agreed with him, "Helpful? All I can say is that it's too bad they outlawed hanging . . . yes, it's too bad. . . ." It is really too bad that counselors have little time to get to know the students who aren't in difficulty. Not being aware of the depth of a superior student's interests and aspirations is one problem. The fact that most guidance counselors have little or no background in the physical sciences is another, perhaps a more serious one. In some junior high schools this lack leads the counselors to try to dissuade girls from taking the industrial-arts and shop courses they desire (as well as higher-level math and science courses). Often a good physical-science course has given them their first taste of building apparatus and the use of tools, and they're anxious to expand their competencies. Yet the attitude lingers that while such courses are "practical and proper" for boys, "who will use those skills in their hobbies if not their jobs," they are superfluous for girls. There was the suspicion at some schools that since the boys' interest in such courses was more "legitimate," they were given preference when places were limited.

Strangely, science frightens many professional guidance counselors; and the long studies and training required to achieve professional status in such fields seem even longer to them. Rather than encourage girls to try AP courses and (it is hoped) save time and money in college, many counselors would rather redirect them into some other field, so that they would "not work too hard," "enjoy life while then can," and certainly not court "discouragement or possible failure." This latter concern is unrealistic, as counselors will admit when questioned. The many AP teachers with whom I discussed this matter were very carful to enroll only students who seemed qualified for their classes, and students who did get in over their heads or couldn't keep up were allowed to transfer to less demanding courses with no penalty. What many female counselors seem to be doing is projecting their own anxieties and the more limited options of their late adolescence on the young women of today. In cases where male counselors are fearful that women will take away men's jobs, it is doubly difficult for the science-oriented girl to get as far as she can in high school. In schools where such counselor attitudes prevail, the recruitment efforts of teachers become of paramount importance.

The Actual AP Course

When girls finally reached the AP courses with which this study is concerned, they frequently found the environment far different from the environment of previous classes. It was sometimes a shock and then a pleasant relief, particularly for those girls who were not products of long-time, homogeneous grouping. Sexual stereotyping had no place in the classroom, and the environment was one that allowed some girls a chance to become aware of the sex-related stereotypes they had unconsciously internalized.

> "Well John, would you lay out this problem the way Sue did or some other way?"
>
> "I don't know."
>
> "What do you mean you don't know? That you have no opinion?"
>
> "No, sir."
>
> "If you don't have a considered opinion, you don't belong in this class. Now, who agrees with Sue? Who has another way? Leslie?" [And so on through the rest of the class.]

The preceding exchange took place in an AP physics class. In talking about it afterwards, the girls said the class had been typical, and several remarked at how terror-struck they had been the first few weeks, when they were forced to contribute to the discussion, "to have an opinion." Other, more agressive girls had immediately welcomed the teaching style. "He's absolutely even-handed and you don't have to be right, you just have to have thought about it." For both shy and not-so-shy girls, it was the first time in any science class that they felt positive sanctions to speak up, much less to be wrong. They were wrong less often than they expected.

Girls in other schools often reported similar experiences that turned out to be freeing. Their teachers had told them, "Sometimes we learn more from mistakes than right solutions" and "Don't worry how it comes out the first time, but record your procedure exactly, then we'll see," or some variation. The girls with such teachers tended to have a more positive self-image than did girls with teachers for whom verbal participation was optional.

When girls were asked whether they were held back in speaking up because they were afraid of seeming too bright in front of boys, the vast majority of girls in classes in which participation was optional turned the question around: "Too bright? Oh no, I keep quiet because I'd seem too dumb." Over and over girls reported that they were "really at the bottom of the class" or "just holding on." Yet the teachers of these same girls said that *some* of these girls were at the top of their class, and many were reported to be "among the very best." Indeed, only 3 of the more than 160 girls in the study were reported as having academic difficulties.

Forced participation did cut down on much, but not all, of the girls' self-depreciation, and the girls' perceptions of the their abilities more nearly mirrored the teacher's. When the girls were asked how they felt about getting better grades than boys, no one denied that it happened, a response interesting in itself, since so many of them were, according to their own report, doing poorly in their AP courses.

For 60 percent of the girls in the study, getting better grades either didn't make any difference or was a "delight" or "the way it should be." Often such remarks were accompanied by smiles or laughter and "Right on, sister!" or "Yea, women!" But for the other 40 percent, high grades, although a source of personal pleasure, were best played down or denied in front of one's classmates, particularly one's non-AP classmates. "The boys in the AP class don't matter. But, if you want a date. . . ." Thus, most girls deliberately chose to date boys from outside their AP science or mathematics class. Some even preferred to date boys from other schools or older boys, "to whom we aren't any threat." It is impossible to tell how much girls' modest self-appraisal and sensitivity about high grades is a reflection of self-inflicted stereotyping and how much is the realistic appraisal of the stereotypes held by others.

The Girls' Plans for the Future

Remembering the hesitancy of many girls to speak up in class or to have their academic accomplishments known to male peers, one might expect that a good proportion of them would choose to continue their education at first-rate women's colleges. Such a choice would certainly allow them to separate, temporarily at least, academic accomplishment from male competition and scrutiny. It was surprising to find, however, that only slightly less than 10 percent had even considered going to a single-sex college. Only three of the graduating seniors were actually doing so. They were planning to enter Mt. Holyoke and Smith, but they had chosen them for reasons other than their histories of turning out eminent female scientists. Indeed, the girls were unaware of such colleges' reputations in this regard.

Although a great many of the girls' career plans were wisely tentative, most of them had already made up their minds that some branch of science or mathematics was (or was not) for them. Eighty percent were planning to continue in these fields, and 20 percent had fairly firmly decided on careers in other directions.

The most popular fields in science were architecture, biochemistry, engineering, forestry, marine biology, medicine, oceanography, and veterinary medicine (see table 9.3). Each of these fields was being seriously considered by five or more girls; eleven girls hoped to become veterinarians. Of the nonscience fields, only law attracted more than five girls.

The girls' choices being what they were, it was not surprising that almost all of the girls planning on careers in science or mathematics expected to find themselves still "in school" five years hence. Those considering some medical specialties and certain branches of physics could see themselves as probably still in school or just finishing up ten years later. But what would they *like* to be doing five or ten years into the future? For the most part, if expectations and hopes differed—and they did for about two thirds of the girls—the hope was to reach the desired goal sooner. They wished to be "already in practice" or "commanding an expedition" or "heading a task force to _____." For the others the desire was to be taking a year off for travel or, ten years later, to be thinking about "starting a family, if I decide to get married" or "if I'm married at that time."

A majority of girls did not spontaneously mention marriage in their future plans. When I brought the subject up as a follow-up to the question of what they expected, or hoped, to be doing, their responses were on the cool side. No one said that they took it for granted that they would get married. The kinds of comments they did make ranged instead from "perhaps" and "I suppose so, if the right guy has come along" to "Yes, if I can work it out with my professional life" and "Who needs to get married today?" One of the outstanding characteristics of these girls as a group was that they were not going to define their adult identity in terms of their husband. Marriage was acceptable, often hoped for, but not at the expense of abandoning the development of one's interests, competencies, and career.

As for children, a large number of the girls oriented toward science planned to postpone motherhood until they were "established" or until they had at least completed training in their chosen fields. Only a handful

TABLE 9.3. Career fields planned by girls of this study

Science and mathematics		Other fields
Architecture*	Marine biology	Art
Astronautics	Medical technology	English
Astrophysics	Medicine	French
Biochemistry*	Neurology	History
Biology	Nuclear	Journalism
Chemistry	Pediatrics	Law*
Computer science	Public Health	Music
Engineering*	Space	Teaching
Environmental science	Other*	Travel
Farm agriculture	Meteorology	
Forestry*	Nursing	
Genetics	Oceanography*	
Geology	Physics	
Mathematics	Psychology	
	Scientific writing	
	Veterinary medicine*	

*Mentioned by five or more girls.

were thinking of staying home full-time during their offsprings' early years. The majority, however, were planning to cut back their professional activities and work part-time for "two or three years." There was some (but not much) sentiment that mothers should stay home until their children reached school age. It should be pointed out that in their plans for combining motherhood with a career, many girls were voluntarily choosing the same patterns that their mothers had had to live because of economic necessity rather than because of interest and professional commitment, although there were many mothers in the latter category as well. In either case, the quality of "mothering" the girls had received seemed sufficiently satisfactory that no girl felt that she needed to change the pattern for her own children. On the other hand, one girl in a large discussion group received applause from her classmates when she remarked, "Besides, there's no one who can tune her children out as completely as a mother who's always home."

CONCLUSIONS AND RECOMMENDATIONS

AP courses in mathematics, chemistry, and physics provide girls with an excellent curricular stimulus and preparation toward professional careers in these and related fields. Eighty percent of the girls who participated in the study plan to continue in these fields. Yet many schools' AP science programs rest on a constricted set of assumptions and attitudes. It is strongly recommended, therefore, that schools be encouraged to offer AP courses in these fields; that girls' enrollment in them be actively sought out;

and that the strategy and tactics of this program be deliberately thought through—starting in the early years of junior high school—rather than simply be allowed to grow. AP teachers in mathematics, chemistry, and physics are excellent agents for recruiting girls to these fields for study and later careers, and the departmental role in soliciting and accepting enrollments should be visible, recognized, and strong. Much effective college and career counseling takes place in AP classes because often AP teachers are the only good source within the school of specific information about the financial, academic, and professional opportunities now open to young women in these fields. For this reason, schools should encourage and enable AP mathematics and science teachers to obtain appropriate materials to serve this purpose.

Many guidance counselors are poor sources of encouragement for girls interested in mathematics and the physical sciences. It is strongly recommended, therefore, that counselors become sensitized to their personal attitudes toward mathematics and the physical sciences and toward professional women in these fields and that they recognize their responsibility to keep options open for students and encourage all eligible girls (and boys) in early junior high school to accelerate in mathematics even if the students' interests in mathematics and science seem vague and undefined.

Current AP girls often credited older girls with encouraging their interest in science and mathematics and supporting their determination to continue in the field. This encouragement was particularly important during two critical periods in the girls' school years when sexual stereotyping on the part of some adults within the school led to lack of support for girls who wished to follow the most rigorous curricular path. The first period was in early junior high school, when the decision whether to take algebra in the eighth grade was made. The second was late in senior high school, when the choice was made between AP and regular college-preparatory courses. It would seem, therefore, that girls from AP classes should be invited to participate in science demonstrations for elementary-school students and in explaining the opportunities and advantages provided by various curricular choices to junior-high-school-girls. And former AP students continuing their mathematical and scientific studies in college should be invited to talk not only with girls currently in AP classes but with younger girls enrolled in science courses.

The girls who participated in the study represent diverse backgrounds and expectations and yet have shared common experiences in their AP science and mathematics classes. It is hoped that more schools will take advantage of the opportunity to encourage girls to go into mathematical and scientific fields of study by encouraging them to take Advanced Placement Courses.

REFERENCES

Casserly, P. L. 1968. To see ourselves as others see us: An evaluation of the Advanced Placement Program by students from 252 secondary schools at 20 colleges. CEEB Research and Development Reports, RDR 67-8, no. 5.

Fry, D. E. 1973. A comparison of the college performance in calculus-level mathematics courses between regular-progress students and advanced placement students. Ph.D. diss., Temple University.

10

An Accelerative Intervention Program for Mathematically Gifted Girls

Linda Brody and Lynn H. Fox

ABSTRACT

An intervention program designed to increase gifted girls' participation in mathematics was conducted at The Johns Hopkins University in the summer of 1973. The program consisted of a course in algebra I for twenty-six seventh-grade girls and included special attention to the social needs of the girls, female role models, some career awareness training, and an emphasis on the social applications of mathematics. Control groups of boys and girls who did not participate in the program were selected for purposes of comparison in assessing the program. In 1977, when the students had completed the eleventh grade, there were significant differences in mathematical acceleration between the control boys and the control girls and between the experimental girls and the control girls, but not between the experimental girls and the control boys. Differential values, career interests, and encouragement are explored as possible contributing factors to sex differences in course-taking behavior.

Sex differences in mathematics are most apparent in course-taking at the secondary and post-secondary levels and in the careers pursued. Fewer women than men pursue careers in mathematics and science, and girls are more reluctant than boys to take advanced mathematics courses. As Lucy Sells has shown, in chapter 5 of this volume, the level of high-school mathematics achievement acts as a "critical filter" for eligibility to a variety of college majors and careers. Since girls are less likely than boys to take advanced mathematics courses in high school, sex differences in mathematics at the college and career levels result.

There are two major hypotheses in the present study: First, gifted boys and girls from similar home backgrounds and of about equal ability in mathematics at grade seven will differ in the high-school years with respect to mathematics achievement as measured by the advanced mathematics courses taken. This difference will be a result of differential interests and encouragement. Second, girls who receive special encouragement and facilitation in mathematics in an accelerated algebra program will keep pace with or surpass their male and female cohorts with respect to achievement as measured by coursework. It is thus the premise of this paper that some type of intervention program in mathematics is necessary for gifted girls to ensure their persistence and success in advanced mathematics courses at the same rate as gifted boys. Because of internal and external barriers that discourage girls from achievement in mathematics, gifted girls need more encouragement than do gifted boys to pursue mathematics courses. In this study an attempt was made to influence later mathematics course-taking behavior of gifted girls by changing course-taking behavior in the eighth grade. A secondary consideration was to try to influence their attitudes and career interests in the hope that this too might affect later course-taking.

THE INTERVENTION PROGRAM

An experimental mathematics program was conducted for mathematically gifted end-of-the-year seventh-grade girls at The Johns Hopkins University in the summer of 1973. The class met two days a week for about two hours from May through July and covered a standard algebra I curriculum. It was hoped that a positive experience in mathematics at the junior-high-school level, when mathematics was becoming more abstract, along with the opportunity to accelerate one year in mathematics, would increase the likelihood that the girls would take advanced mathematics courses in high school.

An experience with an accelerated mathematics class for both boys and girls in the summer of 1972 suggested that attention to the social interests of girls was necessary to attract girls to the program and to help ensure their success (Fox 1976a). Thus the class was designed to provide social stimulation in several ways: The class was for girls only. In order that the girls might have role models, the teacher was a woman, and she was assisted by two female undergraduate mathematics majors. The structure of the class was informal, instruction being individualized and in small groups. Cooperative activities rather than competitive ones were stressed. Whenever possible, the teachers emphasized the ways in which mathematics could be used to solve problems. Some traditional word problems were rewritten in an attempt to make them more socially appealing. In addition to the classes, there was a series of speakers, both male and female, who met with the girls to talk about their careers in mathematics and science.

Students were selected for the program on the basis of performance on the mathematics subtest of the Scholastic Aptitude Test (SAT-M) in either the mathematics or the verbal contests (conducted by the Study of Mathematically Precocious Youth [SMPY] and the Study of Verbally Gifted Youth [SVGY], respectively, at The Johns Hopkins University in the winter of 1973) and geographic considerations. Thirty-two seventh-grade girls living in the Greater Baltimore area who had scored at least 370 on the SAT-M as seventh graders were invited to take part in the class. Two additional girls were invited on the basis of referral and subsequent testing. Twenty-six girls enrolled in the course.

Assessing the Intervention Program

The full impact of the intervention program cannot be assessed until 1983, the year that these students would be expected to complete a four-year bachelor's program. It is possible during the interim, however, to assess course-taking behavior in high school, as well as any changes in career goals since the intervention. In order to measure the effects of the intervention program, it was necessary to form control groups of equally gifted girls and boys so that course-taking behavior and career interests could be compared with what they presumably would have been without the intervention.

Selection of the Control Groups. Two control groups were formed, one of girls and one of boys. For each experimental girl who enrolled in the course, a control boy and a control girl were selected from among the other seventh-grade participants in the 1973 contests. The control students were matched with the experimental subjects on the basis of scores on the mathematical and verbal subtests of the SAT, education and occupation of father, and education of mother.

Although the matching was not perfect, the general pattern was to match within plus or minus twenty points on the SAT-M and the SAT-V while controling for the educational and occupational levels of parents. The mean scores for the experimental girls on the SAT-M and the SAT-V were 436 and 399, respectively. The mean scores for the control girls on the SAT-M and the SAT-V were 433 and 390, respectively, and the control boys, 443 and 393, respectively. The details for the matching variables for the three groups are reported elsewhere (Fox 1976a) and are summarized in table 10.1.

Pretest measures. Prior to the course, the experimental and control groups were tested on knowledge of algebra, values, and career interests. There were no significant differences in knowledge of algebra. Control boys did differ significantly from the experimental and control girls with respect to values and one measure of career interests: The control boys were more interested in investigative careers, which include mathematical

TABLE 10.1. Mean Scores on the SAT-M and the SAT-V and educational level of parents

Group	N	Mean		Mean educational level[a]	
		SAT-M	SAT-V	Mother	Father
Experimental girls	26	436	399	2.9	3.3
Control girls	26	433	390	2.9	3.7
Control boys	26	443	393	2.7	3.5

[a]Scale:
   1 = less than high school
   2 = high-school diploma
   3 = some college
   4 = bachelor's degree
   5 = graduate study beyond the bachelor's degree

and scientific careers, and scored significantly higher on the theoretical scale of the Allport-Vernon-Lindzey Study of Values (SV). Thus, at the start of the program the boys and the girls were not very different with respect to achievement and aptitude in mathematics, but the boys were already slightly more predisposed toward the pursuit of mathematics in school and careers.

Evaluating the program. The program was evaluated following the completion of the course. Details of this evaluation are reported in another volume in this series (Fox 1976a). Of concern were (1) whether an emphasis upon social factors was effective in recruiting girls to participate in the program, (2) the degree to which the girls succeeded in mastering algebra I, and (3) whether the program resulted in the girls' accelerating themselves in mathematics in school the following year.

As mentioned above, of the thirty-four girls invited to participate in the class, twenty-six (76.5 percent) enrolled. This was considerably better than the enrollment rates of 58 percent and 26 percent, respectively, for the two summer, mixed-sex accelerated classes conducted by SMPY prior to the experimental girls' class (Fox 1974; George and Denham 1976). Thus, the emphasis on social factors was successful in recruiting girls for such an accelerated program.

The mathematics course for the experimental girls was not totally successful. Of the twenty-six girls who enrolled for the course, only eighteen actually attended the classes on a fairly regular basis and completed the course. The completion rate for the course was not significantly higher than the completion rate for girls in two other accelerated classes that were coeducational and taught by a male (see Fox 1974; and George and Denham 1976).

Of the eighteen girls who completed the course, only eleven actually enrolled in algebra II the following year. This was the result of several factors, mainly the reluctance of teachers or principals to allow the girls to study algebra II in the next school year.

Follow-up assessments of course-taking. Follow-up studies were conducted in 1974, 1975, 1976, and 1977 to assess course-taking behavior. Table 10.2 shows the number of students accelerated in mathematics at the time of each follow-up. Ten girls successfully completed algebra II and were accelerated one year at the end of the 1973-74 school year. None of the control boys and girls was accelerated at this time.

The 1975 follow-up study was conducted when the students had completed the ninth grade. At that time, twelve of the twenty-four experimental girls who responded (50 percent) had completed algebra I, algebra II, and plane geometry and thus were accelerated a full year in mathematics. Only four control girls out of twenty-five (16 percent) and five control boys out of twenty-five (20 percent) were accelerated. Thus two years following the intervention, considerably more experimental girls than either control boys or control girls were accelerated in mathematics as a result of the special class.

By the end of the 1975-76 school year (at the end of tenth grade), twelve out of twenty-five experimental girls (48 percent), two out of twenty-three control girls (9 percent), and eight out of twenty-six control boys (31 percent) were accelerated at least one full year in mathematics. Thus after three years, still more experimental girls than students in the control groups were accelerated in mathematics. The number of boys had increased, however. In addition, one experimental girl, two control girls, and five control boys were accelerated one-half year in mathematics. The gap in terms of mathematics acceleration between the experimental girls and the control boys appeared to be narrowing. By this time, at the end of tenth grade, twelve experimental girls, two control girls, and eight control boys had completed all of the courses that typically precede the study of calculus.

By the end of the 1976-77 school year, the students were completing the eleventh grade. Following a normal sequence, bright students in Baltimore who had begun algebra I in the eighth grade would be completing a year of trigonometry and analytic geometry or elementary functions in eleventh grade. Anyone who had completed a full year of mathematics beyond this was considered accelerated for the purposes of the 1977 follow-up. Eleven out of twenty-six experimental girls (42 percent), two out of twenty-five control girls (8 percent), and twelve out of twenty-six control boys (46 percent) were accelerated one year or more in mathematics. Based on the chi-square test, the differences between the experimental girls and the control boys were not significant, but the differences between the experimental girls and the control girls and between the control boys and the control girls were significant ($p < .05$).

Over the four-year period following the intervention (shown in table 10.2), the number of experimental girls accelerated remained fairly constant.

TABLE 10.2. Students accelerated at least one year in mathematics in 1974, 1975, 1976, and 1977

Group	Number responding	Number accelerated	Percentage accelerated
		1974	
Experimental girls	26	10	39
Control girls	26	0	0
Control boys	26	0	0
		1975	
Experimental girls	24	12	50
Control girls	25	4	16
Control boys	25	5	20
		1976	
Experimental girls	25	12	48
Control girls	23	2	9
Control boys	26	8	31
		1977	
Experimental girls	26	11	42
Control girls	25	2	8
Control boys	26	12	46

The number of control girls accelerated a full year in mathematics dropped from four girls in 1975 to only two in 1976, and that number remained the same in 1977. The number of control boys accelerated in mathematics, on the other hand, increased fairly dramatically over the four-year period, from zero to five to eight to twelve.

The boys accelerated in mathematics on their own, without the special class. Most of the control girls failed to accelerate. The experimental girls kept pace with the control boys in terms of number accelerated in mathematics, but the special class appears to have been an important factor in making that possible. Nine of the eleven experimental girls accelerated in mathematics in 1977 became accelerated by virtue of not repeating algebra I at the end of the summer course. The evidence strongly suggests, therefore, that some type of intervention is necessary to ensure that girls will persist in mathematics at the same rate that boys do.

Follow-up studies of career interest. In 1973, prior to the start of the special class, all three groups were tested on two measures of vocational interest. On an abbreviated form of the Vocational Preference Inventory (VPI), the boys showed significantly more interest in investigative careers than did either group of girls. On a questionnaire item, however, while

TABLE 10.3. Career interests of experimental and control groups

Group	N	Number science/math	Number non-science	Percentage science/math
			Career interest	
			1973 pre-test	
Experimental girls	26	10	16	39
Accelerated experimental girls [a]	11	6	5	55
Control girls	25	8	17	32
Control boys	25	15	10	60
			1974 post-test	
Experimental girls	24	14	10	58
Accelerated experimental girls [a]	11	8	3	73
Control girls	24	9	15	38
Control boys	21	14	7	67
			1975 follow-up	
Experimental girls	21	13	8	62
Accelerated experimental girls [a]	10	8	2	80
Control girls	25	10	15	40
Control boys	21	15	6	71
			1976 follow-up	
Experimental girls	23	12	11	52
Accelerated experimental girls [a]	10	7	3	70
Control girls	23	14	9	61
Control boys	23	17	6	74

[a] Girls who accelerated immediately following intervention.

more boys than girls in either group stated a career preference in a mathematical or scientific area, the differences were not significant (Fox 1974).

Follow-up assessments of career interest were conducted in 1974, 1975, and 1976. The results of these follow-ups, as well as the results from the 1973 questionnaire, are summarized in table 10.3. By the end of the 1975-76 school year, there were no significant differences among the three groups. It does not seem that the intervention caused more girls to become interested in careers in mathematics and science. It appears, however, that experimental girls became interested in mathematics or science careers at an earlier age than the control girls. This early interest might affect course-taking and make the girls more willing to accelerate in mathematics in high school.

Conclusion. A comparison of the course-taking behavior of the control boys and of the control girls through 1977 supports the first hypothesis— that gifted boys and girls of equal ability in mathematics at grade seven and from similar home backgrounds will differ in the high-school years in terms of advanced courses in mathematics. Without any specific intervention designed to stimulate course-taking in mathematics, a greater percentage of control boys (46 percent) than control girls (8 percent) had accelerated themselves in mathematics.

The second hypothesis was that girls who received special encouragement and facilitation in mathematics vis-à-vis an accelerated algebra program would keep pace with or surpass their male and female cohorts with respect to course-taking. The experimental girls who participated in the special algebra class kept pace with the control boys in terms of acceleration (42 percent of the experimental girls and 46 percent of the control boys accelerated in 1977) and surpassed the number of control girls who accelerated (8 percent).

SOME VARIABLES CONTRIBUTING
TO DIFFERENTIAL COURSE-TAKING

What accounts for sex differences in mathematics course-taking? For the students in this study, mathematical ability was not a factor, since students were selected for the three groups on the basis of equal ability as measured by their SAT scores. An attempt was also made to control home variables by matching students on the basis of their father's education and occupation and their mother's education. In spite of this, sex differences were clearly evident in the course-taking behavior of the gifted students who were not in the intervention program. These sex differences in mathematics course-taking appear to be the result of different interests and differential encouragement by others.

Values

One factor contributing to sex differences in mathematics course-taking may be that mathematically gifted boys and girls have different values. Studies have found high theoretical scores on the SV to be characteristic of mathematically precocious adolescent males, while mathematically gifted girls are more likely than boys to have high social or aesthetic value scores (Fox 1976*b*; Fox and Denham 1974). High scores on the theoretical scale are associated with interests in science and mathematics.

An analysis of the experimental and control groups in the intervention study revealed that on the SV, the experimental and control girls scored significantly higher than the control boys on the social scale (p $<$ .005) and significantly lower on the theoretical scale (p $<$ .005) (Fox 1976*b*).

Since mathematics courses generally do not emphasize the applied aspects of mathematics and thus its social relevance, gifted girls may find the courses less interesting and less relevant to their interests than gifted boys. This may discourage the girls from electing to take mathematics courses. Perhaps some of the many social applications of mathematics should be included in mathematics courses to encourage girls whose interests are primarily social but who have a high aptitude for mathematics to take advanced courses in mathematics.

Career Interests and the Perceived Usefulness of Mathematics

Another factor contributing to differential mathematics course-taking may be the degree to which mathematics is perceived as useful for future career goals. A study of 67 girls and 104 boys selected from SMPY's 1974 mathematics talent search found girls to be significantly less likely than boys to report that mathematics would be very important to their future goals, and the girls were also less likely than the boys to name as career goals occupations of the type that require the most mathematical and scientific training (Fox 1975).

The Strong-Campbell Vocational Interest Inventory, when administered to the experimental and control groups in 1973, revealed sex differences. Control girls scored significantly higher than the control boys on the following scales: art, domestic arts, music/dramatics, nature, office practice, social service, teaching, writing (p $<$ .005); religious activities (p $<$ .01); and medical service (p $<$ .05). The boys scored higher on mechanical activities and science (p $<$ .005). The gifted girls scored higher in the mathematics and science areas than a comparison group of average girls, but not as high as the gifted boys (Fox, Pasternak, and Peiser 1976).

The results of following up career interest in the three groups in the intervention study have been summarized above and are shown in table 10.3. Included in table 10.3, as well, are the career interests of the eleven girls who accelerated immediately following the intervention by enrolling in algebra II. Eight of these girls (73 percent) expressed interest in a mathematical or scientific career in the 1974 post-test assessment of career interest. This suggests a possible relationship between interest in mathematical and scientific careers and willingness to accelerate in mathematics. A comparison of these eleven accelerated experimental girls with the control girls showed the accelerated experimental girls to be significantly more interested in mathematical and scientific careers than the control girls in 1974 and 1975. By 1976 this difference was no longer significant. Possibly the lack of interest early in the high-school years, however, was a factor in discouraging the control girls from accelerating in mathematics.

Other studies confirm a relationship between mathematics course-taking and the perceived career relevance of mathematics. Haven (1972) found that the two most significant predictors of mathematics course-taking in high school for girls of above-average ability were the perception of the usefulness of mathematics for future educational and career goals and greater interest in the natural sciences than in the social sciences. Sherman and Fennema (1977) also found that course-taking in high school was related to the perception of the usefulness of mathematics.

Differential Encouragement by Significant Others

Another factor that may contribute to sex differences in mathematics course-taking is differential encouragement by significant others. Because of a perception that mathematics is a domain more appropriate for men than for women, girls receive less encouragement than boys do to take advanced mathematics courses and to consider careers in mathematical and scientific fields. The significant others include parents, counselors, teachers, and peers. Books and the media also contribute to the perception of mathematics as a male domain and thereby discourage girls from entering it.

Numerous studies suggest that girls receive little encouragement from counselors to pursue mathematics. For example, Haven (1972) found that 42 percent of the girls who were interested in careers in mathematics or science reported being discouraged by counselors from taking courses in advanced mathematics. In chapter 9 of this volume Patricia Casserly also reports that counselors admitted discouraging girls from taking advanced mathematics courses. Their reasons reflected their stereotype of mathematics as a male domain.

Teachers' stereotypes may also discourage girls. Solano (1977) found that teachers' perceptions of mathematically gifted girls are more negative than their perceptions of mathematically gifted boys. Studies of student-teacher interaction suggest that teachers interact more with boys than with girls, particularly in mathematics and science classes (Bean 1976; Good, Sikes, and Brophy 1973). Yet Casserly found that when teachers do take an interest and actively recruit girls for mathematics programs and expect them to perform as well as boys, the results are significantly positive (see chapter 9).

Another source of influence to consider is the peer group. If the perception of mathematics as a male domain is common in the peer group, girls may fear peer rejection for accelerating too much in mathematics. One study of adolescents found that they hold a more negative stereotype of mathematically gifted girls than they do of mathematically gifted boys (Solano 1977). Thus girls may be perceiving real peer pressure against high mathematics achievement; boys do not seem to feel this same pressure.

Girls are reluctant to skip a grade, take college courses early, or in any way separate themselves from their peer group. One girl was ready to abandon a grade skip in the first week of school and return to the lower grade because she had no friends with whom to eat lunch. Another mathematically gifted girl dropped out of an accelerated mathematics program only because her best friend did (Angel 1974).

Perhaps the most powerful influence on children comes from their parents. In one study, mathematically gifted boys were significantly more likely to perceive their parents as favorable toward acceleration in mathematics than were gifted girls (Fox 1975). Parents of mathematically gifted boys are more likely to report having bought scientific and mathematical games and toys for their sons than are parents of gifted girls; they are also more likely to have noticed their child's ability at an early age and to have discussed college and career plans with him (Astin 1974).

A questionnaire was administered to the parents of the students in the experimental and control groups of the intervention study in 1973, prior to the treatment, to assess the parents' feelings about careers and the usefulness of mathematics for their child's future. The parents were asked how important a knowledge of mathematics would be for the child's future career. Responses were received from forty-five parents (mothers and fathers) in each of the control groups and from forty-seven parents in the experimental group. These responses are summarized in table 10.4. Chi-square tests of significance revealed significant differences between the responses of the parents of the experimental girls and those of the parents of the control boys (p < .001) and between the responses of the parents of the control girls and those of the parents of the control boys (p < .01). There were no significant differences between the responses of the parents of the two groups of girls. The boys' parents seem, therefore, to perceive mathematics as more important for their child's future career than do the girls' parents, and this may result in differential encouragement to take advanced mathematics courses.

The parents were also asked to list careers that they would most like to see their child pursue. By dividing the first-choice responses into mathematical/scientific and nonmathematical/nonscientific groups, sex differences became apparent. Sixty-three percent of the boys' parents who responded listed a mathematical or scientific career as first choice, while only 39 percent and 33 percent of the parents of the experimental girls and the control girls, respectively, listed a mathematical or scientific career as first choice. The ratio between the groups of parents is similar to the ratio obtained between the boys and girls themselves when their own career interests were assessed in 1973, so the parents may be reflecting their children's true interests. Nonetheless, differential encouragement regarding advanced mathematics course-taking may result.

The girls' parents were also asked to state the amount of time they expected their daughter to devote to her career (see table 10.5). Only one

TABLE 10.4. Parents' opinion of importance of mathematics for their child's future career

Parents of	Importance of mathematics				
	Very important	Fairly important	Slightly important	Not very important	Not at all important
Experimental girls	36	49	13	2	0
Control girls	38	53	7	2	0
Control boys	58	40	2	0	0

TABLE 10.5. Parents' expectations of the amount of time they expect their daughter to devote to a career

Expectation	Parents of experimental girls		Parents of control girls	
	Number	Percentage	Number	Percentage
Daughter will not work after she marries	1	2	1	2
Daughter will probably work only until she has children	5	11	8	17
Daughter will probably have a full-time career, except while her children are preschool age	22	47	14	30
Daughter will probably have a full-time career even while her children are young	5	11	12	26
Daughter will probably have only a part-time career until her children are grown	9	19	8	17
Other	5	11	3	7
Total	47	101[a]	46	99[a]

[a]Percentages do not total 100 because of rounding off.

parent of an experimental girl and one parent of a control girl did not expect their daughter to work at all after marrying. However, 11 percent of the experimental parents and 17 percent of the control parents expected their daughter to work only until she and her husband decided to have children. Forty-seven percent of the experimental parents and 30 percent of the control parents thought their daughter would have a full-time career except for the time when her children were of preschool age; 19 percent of the experimental parents and 17 percent of the control parents thought their daughter would have only a part-time career until her children were grown; and 11 percent of the experimental parents and 7 percent of the control parents did not want to predict what their daughter would do. Only 11 percent of the experimental girls' parents and 26 percent of the control girls' parents expected their daughter to have a full-time career even while her children were young, while presumably all the parents of the boys expect their sons to work full-time. This factor may contribute to differential encouragement. Although one father reported that he did not expect his daughter to work after she married, his aspiration was for her to become a doctor. This type of conflicting aspiration is presumably being transmitted to the child and surely must confuse her.

CONCLUSIONS AND RECOMMENDATIONS

Competence in mathematics is an important prerequisite for a wide variety of careers, particularly those of a professional nature. In addition to careers in mathematics and the natural sciences, careers in business and the social sciences are requiring a strong background in mathematics because of their increasing use of statistics and computer technology. For this reason, it is important to encourage students to take advanced mathematics courses in high school so that any college or career option will be open to them.

The study described in this chapter suggests that gifted girls may need more encouragement to study advanced mathematics than do gifted boys. The gifted boys in this study were accelerating themselves in mathematics and electing advanced mathematics courses at a faster rate than were the control girls, who were not given special encouragement. The intervention program, however, appeared to make a difference. The girls in the treatment group kept pace with the boys in terms of mathematical acceleration.

Although the intervention was apparently successful, it is difficult to determine which element was the most important in contributing to that success: the all-girl nature of the class, the female role models, the career-education aspect, the emphasis on the social relevance of mathematics, the accelerative component, the individualized instruction, or a combination of some or all of the above. The research suggests that girls' values, interests, and career goals may differ from those of boys and that girls may receive less encouragement from significant others to take advanced mathematics courses and to consider careers in mathematics and science. The intervention was designed to counteract as many of these negative influences as possible simultaneously, and it appears to have been successful in this respect. Possibly it would be enough, however, to concentrate on heightening career interest or to provide a role model who could give continued encouragement. More research is needed. Under Title IX same-sex classes will be difficult to arrange under most situations. A study is underway comparing the intervention study described in this chapter with mixed-sex accelerated classes and with an all-girl career-education class that has no accelerative component to determine the effect of these programs on course-taking behavior. (The career-education class is described in chapter 11.)

Although an all-female environment may not be necessary, one thing to consider in setting up special mathematics classes for the gifted may be the need for a minimum number of girls in the program so that girls will continue and succeed. Sometimes when the number of girls is small, girls begin to drop out, presumably because the class has become too much of a "male domain."

Educators should be encouraged to counteract the perception of mathematics as a male domain and to encourage mathematically talented girls to take courses in advanced mathematics. In-service programs for teachers, counselors, and parents are needed to explain the effects of sex-typing mathematics and to show the relevance of mathematics to a wide variety of careers, including those in the social sciences. At the same time, educators should explore changes in educational policies so as to foster an atmosphere that encourages talented young women to take advanced mathematics courses. Some approaches might include: (1) requiring four years of high-school mathematics for everyone (thus eliminating negative peer pressure against taking mathematics); (2) sponsoring career-education classes for both boys and girls to alert them to the relevance of mathematics to so many careers in our increasingly technical society; (3) selecting textbooks that are non-sexist in their portrayal of roles in our society; (4) increasing the emphasis in mathematics classes on the social applications of mathematics; and (5) sponsoring fast-paced accelerated classes for gifted students in order to provide challenging mathematics instruction and a strongly supportive peer group for the girls in the class.

All mathematically gifted girls need not aspire to become mathematicians or physicists. On the other hand, girls who avoid advanced mathematics courses in high school eliminate a wide variety of college and career options for themselves because they lack the high-school prerequisites. These gifted girls need special encouragement and programs to counteract the image of mathematics as more relevant for men than for women and to show them how the study of mathematics may be relevant to a wide variety of college majors and careers.

REFERENCES

Angel, M.F. 1974. Wolfson I: A study in precocious mathematical ability and education. Master's thesis, The Johns Hopkins University.

Astin, H. S. 1974. Sex differences in mathematical and scientific precocity. In *Mathematical talent: Discovery, description and development,* ed. J. C. Stanley; D. P. Keating; and L. H. Fox, pp. 70-86. Baltimore: Johns Hopkins University Press.

Bean, J. P. 1976. What's happening in mathematics and science classrooms: Student-teacher interactions. Paper presented at the meeting of the American Educational Research Association, San Francisco, April 1976.

Fox, L. H. 1974. Facilitating the development of mathematical talent in young women: Ph.D. diss., The Johns Hopkins University.

————. 1975. Career interests and mathematical acceleration for girls. Paper presented at the meeting of the American Psychological Association, Chicago, September 1975.

————. 1976a. Sex differences in mathematical precocity: Bridging the gap. In *Intellectual talent: Research and development,* ed. D. P. Keating, pp. 183-214. Baltimore: Johns Hopkins University Press.

————. 1976b. The values of gifted youth. In *Intellectual talent: Research and development,* ed. D. P. Keating, pp. 273-84. Baltimore: Johns Hopkins University Press.

Fox, L. H., and Denham, S. A. 1974. Values and career interests of mathematically and scientifically precocious youth. In *Mathematical talent: Discovery, description, and development,* ed. J. C. Stanley; D. P. Keating; and L. H. Fox, pp. 140-75. Baltimore: Johns Hopkins University Press.

Fox, L. H.; Pasternak, S. R.; and Peiser, N. L. 1976. Career related interests of adolescent boys and girls. In *Intellectual talent: Research and development,* ed. D. P. Keating, pp. 242-61. Baltimore: Johns Hopkins University Press.

George, W. C., and Denham, S. A. 1976. Curriculum experimentation for the mathematically talented. In *Intellectual talent: Research and development,* ed. D. P. Keating, pp. 103-31. Baltimore: Johns Hopkins University Press.

Good, T. L.; Sikes, J. N.; and Brophy, J. E. 1973. Effects of teacher sex and student sex on classroom interaction. *Journal of Educational Psychology* 65: 74-87.

Haven, E. W. 1972. Factors associated with the selection of advanced academic mathematics courses by girls in high school. Research bulletin 72-12. Princeton: Educational Testing Service.

Sherman, J. A., and Fennema, E. 1977. The study of mathematics among high school girls and boys: Related factors. *American Educational Research Journal* 14(2): 159-68.

Solano, C. H. 1977. Teacher and pupil stereotypes of gifted boys and girls. *Talents and Gifts* 19(4): 4.

11

CAREER INTERESTS
AND CAREER EDUCATION:
A KEY TO CHANGE

Dianne Tobin and Lynn H. Fox

ABSTRACT

Sex differences in career goals and the relationship between those goals and the study of mathematics are reviewed in this chapter about two intervention programs related to career awareness and mathematics.[1] The first program was developed for a mixed-sex group of mathematically able youngsters between ten and thirteen years of age. Topics included the relationship of mathematical concepts studied in school to skills required in certain jobs, as well as a broad overview of the world of work and an understanding of different occupations. The second program was designed specifically to encourage mathematically gifted girls to continue to study mathematics and to understand the uses of mathematics in a wide range of career fields. Recommendations are given for increasing female interest in mathematics-related subjects and careers.

The traditional role pattern for men and women in our society has been one in which men provide economic and financial support and women maintain the home and provide emotional support for the family structure. Although the pattern is changing, a 1972 study indicated that even among very young children, the traditional pattern was the one that was accepted. When asked to describe a day in their adult life, kindergarten boys were likely to tell about leaving the house to engage in some kind of productive, wage-producing activity. Girls, on the other hand, even those who had

[1] We would like to extend special thanks to Virginia Campbell, Phyllis Chinn, Gwendolyn Cooke, Maryellen Cunnion, Karen Douglas, Patricia Gucer, Allyson Handley, Susan Horn, Stephen Karon, Martin Levin, and Joyce Steeves, who helped develop and teach the classes described in this chapter, and to Mary Crovo, who helped with the evaluation of the career awareness class.

initially responded with a career choice to the question, What do you want to be when you grow up? were more likely to describe a typical day in their adult life in terms of homemaking and childcaring (Iglitzen 1973). These answers reflect a sex difference in attitude about careers and in perceptions of future roles. The differential study of mathematics by females and males is inexorably tied up with their different perceptions of the need for careers in general and of the usefulness of mathematics for achieving career goals.

In analyzing data from Project talent, Wise (1978) found that the single best predictor of mathematics course-taking for girls was their career interests in ninth grade. Similarly, Astin (1974a) found a strong relationship between career interests and mathematical aptitude in young women. Haven (1971) found that the two most significant predictors of mathematics course-taking were the perceived usefulness of mathematics for future studies and careers and greater interest in the natural sciences than in social studies. Girls who elected to take advanced courses in mathematics did so because they saw the courses as directly relevant to their career goals.

Girls, however, are less oriented to careers (other than homemaking), than are boys. Even those girls who consider careers seem to feel that marriage and child-rearing may be incompatible with a career (Rossi 1965). Women who anticipate a conflict between the homemaking role and a career are likely to forgo the career (Astin 1974b). It is not surprising that women who do not accent traditional sex-role stereotypes are more likely to desire professional careers than those who hold traditional views of sex roles (Ory and Helfrich 1976). Even women at the highest level of intelligence have not pursued careers at the same rate as their male counterparts, at least in part because women are less likely to be encouraged to pursue professional and high-level careers than are their equally able male cohorts. Of the women in Terman's gifted population, less than half had a career, and for most of them their career was secondary to their homemaking role (Sears and Barbee 1977). Even today society's expectations are more likely to limit the choices and put a ceiling on the aspirations of gifted girls than they are those of gifted boys. In fact, girls may be the most deprived subgroup within the population of gifted youngsters.

One might hope that the pattern is changing. In a 1965 follow-up study of National Merit Scholarship finalists from 1956 through 1960, 85 percent of the girls polled definitely planned a career (Watley 1969). (These students were polled, however, before most had completed their education and thus were indicating only their future expectations.) Yet a more recent study of data collected from a stratified random sample of 2,495 eleventh-grade students in Pennsylvania (1,226 boys and 1,269 girls) indicates that high-ability girls are still not accepting their potential (Marini and Greenberger 1978). Boys aspired to and expected higher levels of educational attainment than did the girls. Although in terms of educational aspirations and expectations sex differences were generally small, they were great among those who aspired to more than a college degree. Among those students with high aspirations, 72 percent of the boys, but only 58 percent of the girls, actually expected to attain their goals. Thus, at the highest level of aspiration, girls differed considerably from boys in their actual expectations for educational achievement.

Sex differences in career interests and aspirations are found among the academically gifted as early as grade seven. Even gifted girls who are oriented toward careers are less likely than boys of similar ability to be interested in careers of a scientific or mathematical nature; they are more likely than the boys to aspire to careers of a social or artistic nature (Fox and Denham 1974; Fox, Pasternak, and Peiser 1976).

The differences in career interests may result from the fact that the underlying values of gifted girls are somewhat different from those of gifted boys. Theoretical value orientations have been shown to be significantly related to creative achievement in mathematics (MacKinnon 1962). On the Allport-Vernon-Lindzey Study of Values the majority of women in any sample tend to score higher on measures of social values and lower on theoretical values and this is true of gifted girls as well (Fox 1978). Gifted seventh-grade boys generally score high on theoretical values and therefore have a well-developed interest and value pattern consistent with academic pursuits in science and mathematics and with their own high aptitude in those areas. Gifted girls, on the other hand, are faced with conflict and ambiguity because their interest and value patterns do not necessarily coincide with their mathematical potential (Fox 1978). Since more boys than girls aspire to scientific careers, it is not surprising that boys also perceive the study of mathematics as more relevant to their future goals than do girls (Fox 1975; Haven 1971).

Girls seem to be less aware that because of recent technological changes, careers that in the past did not require mathematical expertise now require more sophisticated knowledge of mathematics. Thus, high-level careers in business, nursing, education, and the social sciences sometimes require a knowledge of mathematics beyond the required mathematics taught in high school (Fox 1977; Fox, Tobin, and Brody 1979). In fact, almost all career objectives today undoubtedly involve some mathematics (Peterson and Peterson 1975). Girls who do not continue the study of mathematics beyond the required high-school courses may be seriously limiting their future career options. Yet these intellectually gifted adolescent students, many of whom score well above average on measures of aptitude for mathematics, appear to be unaware of all the career areas that require this talent.

One approach, therefore, to encourage the study of mathematics by able girls would seem to be to acquaint them with a wide variety of careers, including those that appear to be solely social or artistic but in fact require math reasoning to do well. Once students become more knowledgeable about career requirements, they may be more willing to take the advanced mathematics courses that will better prepare them for the career of their choice.

THE FIRST CAREER CLASS

A model for a career awareness program for mathematically gifted students aged ten through thirteen was developed by the Intellectually Gifted Child Study Group (IGCSG) in the fall of 1974 (Fox 1976). The model was designed for both males and females who exhibited academic potential, particularly in the area of mathematics, and who were presumed to be naive about careers, open and enthusiastic about learning, and at a level of cognitive development that would enable them to deal with abstract ideas.

The program was directed toward what Hoyt and Hebeler (1974) call the first stage of career awareness, an introduction to the concept of work and a broad overview of different occupations and the tasks they involve. In addition, the relationship of subjects studied in school to skills required for various professions was included. The goal of the model was to present mathematics as a tool for solving a wide range of problems. The program brought professional men and women and college students into contact with the younger students to serve as role models.

The model was first implemented and tested in the spring of 1975 on a group of twelve boys and twelve girls aged ten through thirteen who were enrolled in public schools in Baltimore City and had been identified as gifted. Four exploratory mini-courses were initiated that year, in: probability, computer science, statistics, and geometric drawing. The probability course included principles of probability theory and involved many activities in the testing of "fair" and "unfair" strategies for decision-making. The course in computer science, adapted from a basic course developed for older students by the Maryland Academy of Sciences, included the binary number system, the construction of a computer game, and work with a computer terminal and an audio oscillator. The statistics course introduced students to basic concepts of hypothesis testing and prediction. Students learned to interpret statistical graphs and information of the type reported in news articles on population statistics and the economy. The course in geometric drawing focused on imaginative, artistic, and creative applications of mathematics. Students compared their own geometric constructions and drawings to patterns found in nature and in art.

Three measures were used to evaluate the program: a pre-test and a post-test on the content of the courses, a pre-measure and a post-measure of attitudes and career interests, and a parent questionnaire. The results suggested that the model had potential but needed some modifications (Fox 1976). Students appeared to become more favorably disposed toward careers in mathematics; they learned the content of the courses and, according to their parents, became more knowledgeable about and interested in mathematics. Unfortunately they did not seem to become more knowledgeable about careers per se, except about that of the statistician. These courses were designed for a mixed-sex group, and no special attempt (other than including women as well as men as role models) was made to interest the girls in mathematical careers more than the boys. Research into the reasons why more girls did not pursue mathematics to a high level led to the belief that a career awareness program could be one approach to help reverse the tendency of girls to avoid mathematics courses. The program could generate interest in mathematics and mathematics-related areas by demonstrating and teaching mathematical skills necessary in social and esthetically oriented careers that superficially may appear to require limited mathematical background. If the wide variety of careers with mathematical components were emphasized, the girls might be made to understand the value of continuing the study of mathematics and thus keeping their future career options open.

CAREER AWARENESS MODEL FOR GIRLS

In 1977 the model was revised; it was designed more specifically to encourage girls with ability and potential in mathematics to continue their study of mathematics beyond the level required in high school. The hope was that the girls would be encouraged to ultimately pursue mathematical or mathematically-related majors in college and possibly careers in this area.

The focus of the revised model was slightly different from that of the earlier model in three ways. The course emphasized the importance of mathematics in occupations concerned with solving problems of a social nature. Fox (1974, 1978) reports that among the mathematically able students identified by the Study of Mathematically Precocious Youth (SMPY) at The Johns Hopkins University more girls than boys checked artistic and social occupations on the Vocational Preference Inventory (VPI) (Holland 1958). The boys preferred the investigative occupations, which would indicate a scientific and/or mathematical inclination (Fox and Denham 1974; MacKinnon 1962). Similarly, an analysis of scores on the Study of Values indicates that one difference between girls and boys with aptitude in mathematics is that the boys score high on the theoretical values, while the girls generally score high on social values (Fox 1978). Using the research evidence that girls seem to have preference for social occupations and social values, one objective of the course was to show that meaningful relationships between mathematics and humanity's ability to solve its social problems, as well as its theoretical problems, do exist.

It was an all-girl class. An all-girl special algebra class had been taught before at Johns Hopkins (see chapter 10 in this volume by Brody and Fox). Its success gave further credence to the hypothesis that an all-girl class tends to lessen girls' possible concerns about appearing unfeminine in front of their male peers by seeming too bright or ambitious. It was hoped that without the distraction of boys, interactions would develop more easily among the girls, encouraging the establishment of a peer support system of able girls. Casserly (in chapter 9 in this volume) has shown this to be a very important ingredient in encouraging girls to take mathematics courses.

Special efforts were made to use female role models as teachers, tutors, and guest speakers throughout the program. All seven instructors, the aide, and most of the guest speakers were female. It was hoped that showing that there really are female engineers, architects, physicists, and mathematicians would dispel the myth that mathematics is a masculine domain. The fact that some of the role models were married and had children of their own showed that marriage and a rewarding career do not have to be conflicting lifestyles and that it is realistic to aspire to both.

This revised program was conducted by the Intellectually Gifted Child Study Group at the Evening College and Summer Sessions of The Johns Hopkins University.[2] The girls, chosen from among the top scorers in a mathematics talent search among seventh graders in Maryland,[3] sponsored by the Study of Mathematically Precocious Youth, were invited to participate in a special summer course. Twenty-four elected to come.

The Courses

The class was divided into four units over a five-week period during the summer of 1977. Classes were held at The Johns Hopkins University on Tuesdays, Wednesdays, and Thursdays from 9:00 A.M. to 3:00 P.M. The morning session was devoted to one of four units: statistics and computers, aging, our man-made environment, and women and science. During the afternoons, the girls were taught critical reading and study skills, using articles suggested by the instructors on topics relevant to the morning instruction program. It was believed that learning to read and interpret scientific papers would alleviate possible future anxiety about similar assignments in advanced science and/or mathematics classes. The instructors were practicing professionals in the fields about which they were teaching. They and guest lecturers provided the girls with in-depth knowledge concerning their own careers and the applications of mathematics in solving human problems in their fields. A brief description of each course follows.

The first unit was an integrated course on statistics and computers that lasted for two weeks. It was taught by an associate professor of mathematical sciences at the Johns Hopkins University. At the first session she

---

[2] In the summer of 1977, under a grant from the Robert Sterling Clark Foundation.

[3] The girls were chosen on the basis of their scores on the Scholastic Aptitude Test (SAT), normally given to twelfth graders as a college-entrance examination: The sum of twice their score on the SAT-Mathematics plus their SAT-Verbal score had to be at least 1,330.

told the girls how she had become interested in statistics and eventually earned a Ph.D. in that subject. During the two-week period of the course, the rationale behind parametric and nonparametric statistical tests, concepts in probability, and hypothesis testing were discussed. Skills taught included basic statistical and graphing techniques and understanding of terminology. Learning to use the computer was a central feature of the session. The girls solved problems and performed data analysis and learned to use statistical packages already programmed into the computer. Whenever possible, instruction was designed to actively involve the girls. To illustrate the Rank Sum Test, the girls were asked to run a three-legged race and then to compute the various possible outcomes of the race using this nonparametric test. The girls were particularly enthusiastic about collecting and interpreting their own data and solving problems on the computer terminal.

The second unit, concerned with architectural planning for human needs, was taught by a woman who had both architectural and teaching experience. In order to encourage an understanding of how architecture can serve to merge esthetic and mathematical concerns, mathematical topics connected with architecture, such as the coordinate system for three-dimensional blueprints, and architectural concepts, such as scale, man-made and natural environments, and the design process, were taught with emphasis on problem-solving through practical exercises. The ways in which planners and architects must confront and solve human biological and environmental needs were presented and discussed through architectural drawings, city plans, and even computer-drawn designs. Students were encouraged to think about possible future environments and to take risks in making judgments. Discussion about the wide range of architectural experiences, from interior, landscape, and building design to the planning of entire cities, was enhanced by a visit from a city planner, who discussed his work with the class.

The third unit, on aging, was conducted by a psychological researcher at the National Institute of Health's Gerontology Research Center. The classes were designed to provide an example of a complex problem that is studied from psychological, medical, sociological, and statistical perspectives; to illustrate the importance of mathematics as a research tool; and to demonstrate the logic of scientific research and analysis of research findings. As an application of mathematics, especially of the statistical concepts they had recently learned, the girls did preliminary analysis on a questionnaire they had previously taken on attitudes toward the aged, and they were each given a computer print-out with more complicated data analysis of the same questionnaire as an aid in class discussion and interpretation of the data. Further applications of mathematics to the study of aging was provided by analyzing data on mortality rates and the development of formulas to predict life expectancies.

As part of this unit, the girls took a field trip to the Gerontology Research Center in Baltimore, where they watched their attitude questionnaire being run on the computer and learned how the computer had been programmed for this. At the center, several staff members spoke to the girls about topics ranging from research on biorhythms and aging to sex differences in aging, and they heard a general talk in which history of research on aging was used to show that quantification was the basis of all scientific endeavor. A tour of the research facilities was included to illustrate the nature of a longitudinal study, using the Baltimore longitudinal study of aging as an example. The girls particularly enjoyed taking some of the strength and breathing tests given to the participants in this study.

The final week was devoted to exploration of a wide variety of careers in medicine and science. The goals were to introduce role models of women in various fields of science and to illustrate how these women applied the skills they had acquired in their respective careers. The women talked about their educational and personal backgrounds and how these factors pertained to their choice of and satisfaction with their current occupation or field of study. Then each speaker presented a forty-to-fifty-minute discussion/demonstration on some aspect of her job, such as a current project or current research she was conducting.

The backgrounds of the women varied greatly. Two of the women who spoke to the girls were still in training for their intended careers. One had quit her job as head nurse at the Johns Hopkins neurosurgical operating room at age twenty-one because she felt that it did not offer enough future and challenge and now plans to enter medical school. The other is an accelerate majoring in electrical engineering at The Johns Hopkins University who plans to graduate in three years and continue in graduate school in business and engineering.

Three of the speakers were practicing engineers or physicists presently employed by NASA. One tests thermal-control systems for spacecraft; another conducts research on the ozone layer and has designed spacecraft orbits; and the third plans and manages image-processing equipment.

The biological sciences were represented by three speakers: two associate professors at the Johns Hopkins Medical School and the project director of a large cancer research center. Their topics included a discussion of the controversial drug Laetrile and its chemical analysis; viruses and antiviral drugs; and the transformation of cells.

The courses culminated with a field trip to introduce the students to the resources available at the Maryland Academy of Sciences in Baltimore in order to encourage their future use of that facility.

The four topics studied during the morning sessions were directly related to different careers and the uses of mathematics for those careers. The afternoon sessions were intended to provide some of the critical reading skills necessary for reading and understanding articles reporting scientific studies that the girls had not yet acquired. Although the girls admitted into the class had high scores on the verbal portion of the Scholastic Aptitude Test, a pretest on critical-reading skills had revealed that there were certain areas that needed to be taught before the girls could be comfortable reading scientific articles. A special unit, designed by graduate students in reading and the gifted, was developed. A visit to the university library, to familiarize the girls with methods of seeking information, was the first activity in this unit. Most of the afternoon sessions centered around articles that had been suggested by the course instructor of each topic. These articles served as a basis for reading instruction as well as to teach the girls some of the content that would be assumed in morning discussions. The girls were taught to critically evaluate the author's purpose and to differentiate between research evidence and fiction, fact and inference, statements and opinions. In addition, there was instruction in extending generalizations and suggesting other hypotheses. By the end of the program, the girls had learned to develop criteria for critical review of materials and to apply the skills they had learned to the content-oriented material provided by the morning-session instructors to extend their knowledge of the subject taught. It was felt that if scientific- and research-oriented articles were made more familiar to the girls, they would then be less apprehensive about reading them in the future.

EVALUATION

Immediate evaluation of the program was carried out through four different methods: (1) The parents were asked to complete a questionnaire on their perceptions of their daughter's experience in the program; (2) the students themselves were asked to complete a questionnaire about their opinions of the program; (3) the staff conducted a special seminar in which each member discussed the strengths and weaknesses of their part of the program and the group discussed possible alternate strategies for the future; (4) A pre-test and a post-test were given on the subject matter taught in the four morning units and on critical-reading skills.

Certain aspects of the program were considered to be extremely valuable. The all-girl nature of the class was especially appreciated by both the girls and their parents. There was increased interest in mathematics and in job and educational planning. A wider range of career expectations resulted. One parent summarized this feeling particularly well. "I think the signficance of this class has been the emphasis of girls entering any occupation or career—not to think in terms of a woman's job and men having specific careers in scientific fields."

The immediate evaluation indicated that the program was worthwhile for the girls, as evidenced by their own feelings and those of their parents and the staff and by the pre-test and post-test measures. The importance of this program is not assessable on a short term; however, what is really needed is to find out whether this type of program had any effect on the girls' future participation in mathematics classes and, ultimately, in mathematics-related careers.[4]

RECOMMENDATIONS

In view of the reluctance of most girls to pursue careers in general and in mathematics in particular and their lack of information on the uses of mathematics in many career fields, career awareness programs are particularly important for girls with potential in mathematics. Courses that aim to encourage girls to study advanced mathematics and to attract them into mathematically related fields should (*a*) reduce anticipated role conflict between marriage and career; (*b*) erase the stigma that mathematical study is unfeminine; (*c*) create an awareness of the broad spectrum of mathematically oriented careers that are also socially useful; and (*d*) provide information on how gifted girls should adequately prepare for a full range of careers by taking a complete program of mathematical studies in high school.

Although the model described was developed at a university and not by a school system, these programs would be best incorporated into school systems and developed naturally out of the basic curriculum to illustrate the applications of skills being learned in school and should not be isolated as a separate subject independent of what is learned in regular school.

Ideally, classes that aim specifically to encourage girls' mathematical interests should be all-girl classes, since some of the elements needed to encourage girls would not be justified in a mixed-sex class. For example, using exclusively female instructors to serve as role models would probably not be fair to the boys in the class. If classes must be coeducational, special attention should be paid to ensuring an appropriate number of female role models and having a sufficient number of girls in the class for a peer support system to be able to develop. In addition, the teacher should be particularly aware of the stereotypes that may be in the minds of both the boys and girls and actively work to change those images. Wherever possible, efforts should be made to present a view of careers and those who are in certain professions that is not stereotypic in regard to sex. Using women, wherever possible, as role models for careers not normally thought of as avenues open to women can help reduce both girls' and boys' perceptions of mathematically related careers as male domains. In those school systems that do not have ready access to role models in all occupational areas, video tapes or films might be substituted for live models. Educational television can be in the forefront of developing such programs. So long as most classes in regular school systems must be coeducational, teachers

[4] A follow-up study to discover the success of the program is presently being conducted under funding from the National Institute of Education, and future follow-ups are planned.

should actively work to change boys' attitudes. In the long run, this may be just as important as changing those of the girls because active support from male peers to seriously pursue mathematical interests may be very helpful to gifted girls.

Classes that aim to encourage girls to study mathematical subjects should emphasize not only the theoretical aspects of mathematics but the social aspects as well. The relationship of mathematics to the arts and music and its use as a tool to help humanity should be integrated into the program. The concept of the usefulness of mathematics can be broadened to include possible future uses of mathematics as well, since the careers students prepare to enter may be different by the time they are actually ready for them.

CONCLUSION

Women avoid mathematics courses and careers for numerous reasons. Numerous strategies may be required to combat the situation. One of these strategies may strike a responsive chord in one girl, while another girl may be more impressed by something else. A career awareness model is one possible approach. Unlike the humanities and the arts, which are considered suitable for study for their own sake, in order to make one a well-rounded individual, mathematics is usually valued in relation to its utility. Mathematicians speak of the beauty of mathematics, but its beauty may not be evident to the average high-school mathematics student. Although the practical use of eighteenth-century English literature may be no more apparent to a gifted girl than that of algebra, women are more willing, even today, to agree to its intrinsic worth to their intellectual development than they are to that of mathematics. Enjoyment of mathematics is ultimately crucial if girls are to desire advancement to higher levels of mathematics study, but it may be that emphasizing its value as a tool for future career possibilities will keep the girls in the courses long enough to begin to see its beauty. When girls, especially mathematically able ones, become aware that mathematics may be the key to their future, a future which can and should include a responsible and rewarding job, the number of girls participating in mathematics-related courses may increase.

REFERENCES

Allport, G. W.; Vernon, P. E.; and Lindzey, G. 1970. *Manual, study of values: A scale for measuring the dominant interests in personality.* Boston: Houghton Mifflin Co.

Astin, H. S. 1947*a*. Sex differences in mathematical and scientific precocity. In *Mathematical talent: Discovery, description and development,* ed. J. C. Stanley; D. P. Keating; and L. H. Fox, pp. 70-86. Baltimore: Johns Hopkins University Press.

————. 1974*b*. Overview of the findings. In *Women: A bibliography on their education and careers,* by H. Astin; H. Suniewick; and S. Dweck, pp. 1-10. New York: Behavioral Publications.

Fox, L. H. 1974. Facilitating the development of mathematical talent in young women. Ph.D. diss., The Johns Hopkins University.

————. 1975. Career interests and mathematical acceleration for girls. Paper presented at the meeting of the American Psychological Association, Chicago, Septermber 1975.

————. 1976. Women and the career relevance of mathematics and science. *School Science and Mathematics* 76: 347-53.

————. 1977. The effects of sex role socialization on mathematics participation and achievement. In *Women and mathematics: Research perspectives for change,* ed. J. Shoemaker, pp. 1-77. Papers in Education and Work, no. 8. Washington, D.C.: National Institute of Education U.S. Department of Health, Education and Welfare.

————. 1978. Interest correlates to differential achievement of gifted students. *Talents and gifts* 1(2): 24-36.

Fox, L. H., and Denham, S. A. 1974. Values and career interests of mathematically and scientifically precocious youth. In *Mathematical talent: Discovery, description and development,* ed. J. C. Stanley; D. P. Keating; and L. H. Fox, pp. 140-75. Baltimore: Johns Hopkins University Press.

Fox, L. H.; Pasternak, S. R.; and Peiser, N. L. 1976. Career related interests of adolescent boys and girls. In *Intellectual talent: Research and development,* ed. D. P. Keating, pp. 242-61. Baltimore: Johns Hopkins University Press.

Fox, L. H.; Tobin, D.; and Brody, L. 1979. Sex role socialization and achievement in mathematics. In *Determinants of sex related differences in cognitive functioning,* ed. M. Wittig and A. C. Petersen, pp. 303-32. New York: Academic Press.

Haven, E. W. 1971. Factors associated with the selection of advanced academic mathematics courses by girls in high school. Ph.D. diss., University of Pennsylvania.

Holland, J. L. 1958. A personality inventory employing occupation titles. *Journal of Applied Psychology* 42: 336-42.

Hoyt, K. B., and Hebeler, J. R., eds. 1974. *Career education for gifted and talented students.* Salt Lake City: Olympus Publishing Co.

Iglitzen, L. B. 1973. A child's eye view of sex roles. In *Sex role stereotyping in the schools,* ed. National Education Association, pp. 23-30. Washington, D.C.: National Education Association.

MacKinnon, D. W. 1962. The nature and nurture of creative talent. *American Psychologist* 17(7): 484-95.

Marini, M. M., and Greenberger, E. 1978. Sex differences in educational aspirations and expectations. *American Educational Research Journal* 15(2): 67-79.

Ory, J. C., and Helfrich, L. M. 1976. A study of individual characteristics and career aspirations. Paper presented at the meeting of the American Educational Research Association, San Francisco. April 1976.

Peterson, J. C., and Peterson, M. P. 1975. *Career education and mathematics.* Boston: Houghton Mifflin.

Rossi, A. 1965. Women in science: Why so few? *Science* 148 (3674): 1196-1202. Also in *Toward a sociology of women,* ed. C. Safilios-Rothschild, pp. 141-53. Lexington, Mass.: Xerox College Publishing, 1972.

Sears, P. S., and Barbee, A. H. 1977. Career and life satisfactions among Terman's gifted women. In *The gifted and the creative: A fifty-year perspective,* ed. J. C. Stanley; W. C. George; and C. H. Solano, pp. 28-65. Baltimore: Johns Hopkins University Press.

Watley, D. J. 1969. Career or marriage? A longitudinal study of able young women. National Merit Scholarship Corporation Research Reports vol. 5, no. 7. Evanston, Ill.

Wise, L. 1978. The role of mathematics in women's career development. Paper presented at the 86th annual meeting of the American Psychological Association, Toronto, August 29, 1978.

IV

Summary

12

Conclusions:
What Do We Know
and Where Should We Go?

Lynn H. Fox

Far fewer women than men pursue careers as mathematicians, and those who do not achieve equally with men in terms of employment status. Even among the highly creative female mathematicians studied by Helson, about a third were not professionally employed. Luchins and Luchins reported that female mathematicians feel that they are treated somewhat differently than men and that they received more discouragement from teachers and colleagues during the process of their development than was typical of successful male mathematicians.

Sells and others point to the sex differences in course-taking in the high-school years, which delimits women's career possibilities in a variety of areas, not just in pure or applied mathematics. Ernest points out the differential attrition rates in college courses for men and women. Even among the mathematically precocious there are differences between boys and girls with respect to acceleration and course-taking in mathematics that can not be explained by differences in ability. Fennema also reports that differential course-taking can occur in high schools where no ability differences are found.

None of the chapters in this volume deals directly with the question of whether there is a biological basis for sex differences in mathematical ability; they have focused, instead, on the socioenvironmental dimensions of the problem. The explanation for this is twofold. First, a discussion of an innate basis for observed sex differences with respect to mathematics learning and ability can only be highly speculative at this point in time. There is evidence suggesting that differences in the endocrine systems of males and females are related to differential sensitivity to and processing of sensory information (Reinisch, Gandelman, and Spiegel 1979). As yet, however, we do not know how these differences directly affect the learning of mathematics. There is also a possibility that the cerebral organization of men and women is somewhat different (Bryden 1979), but, again, we do not understand the relationship between cerebral organization and mathematics learning. Even if mathematical ability were someday proven to be a sex-linked, recessive inherited trait, socio-environmental factors would not be irrelevant, since heredity and environment are interactive (Wittig 1979). The second reason this volume focuses on social processes and intervention is because of several important differences between men and women in terms of mathematics course-taking and the pursuit of careers in mathematical and scientific fields appear unrelated to or go beyond ability differences. Far more boys than girls appear to be mathematically precocious in grade seven, but as described in chapters 7 and 9, girls of high ability differ from boys of high ability with respect to mathematical interests, course-taking, and career interests. Not all boys are better than all girls on measures of aptitude and achievement; indeed, in several studies of general school populations, as reported by Fennema, the differences on test performance are much smaller than those found for the precocious. Course-taking differences, however, are sizable, as noted by Sells and Ernest.

The thrust of this volume is to identify those sex differences with respect to mathematics that appear to be a result of social learning and to consider ways in which such behaviors and attitudes can be changed or prevented. The goal of this chapter is to integrate common themes and findings from the previous chapters and to suggest directions for research and strategies for change.

GENERAL THEMES

Although boys and girls do not differ with respect to achievement as measured by arithmetic tests in elementary school or on reported enjoyment of mathematics as a school subject, by the seventh grade striking sex differences emerge, most noticeably among the gifted; and by tenth or eleventh grade, when mathematics course-taking becomes optional, boys persist in the study of mathematics more than girls do. These differences seem to be accompanied by differences in reported self-confidence about learning mathematics and in the belief in the relevance of the study of mathematics for future career goals. It appears that the general societal message that mathematics is a male domain is conveyed to little girls in the home and throughout their schooling. Parents, teachers, peers, and the general school program or organization all influence the young girl's view of herself relative to mathematics.

Parents

Maccoby and Jacklin (1974) reviewed the literature on childhood socialization experiences and concluded that there is a great deal of similarity in the early socialization experiences of boys and girls. Subtle differences exist, however, in that parents often have lower educational expectations for daughters than for sons and reinforce sex-role stereotypes in their choice of toys or by their greater acceptance of low levels of achievement in mathematics for girls than for boys. In the study of mathematically gifted reported by Brody and Fox, parents of gifted girls were less likely to view a career in mathematics or science as appropriate for their child than were parents of gifted boys. Ernest points out that both boys and girls are more likely to seek help with mathematics homework from their father than from their mother, which says something about the probable lack of mathematically strong female role models in the home.

On the other hand, several women who are mathematicians and most of the girls taking advanced-placement courses in the Casserly study felt that parental or family support had been favorable. It seems likely that early and sustained support and encouragement in the home can be very potent. Alas, too little is known about the dynamics of the home environment relative to mathematical interest and achievement.

Teachers

The impact of teacher encouragement was seen as important by almost two thirds of the female mathematicians studied by Luchins and by many girls in the Casserly study. Yet, both groups also mentioned negative teacher behavior or attitudes. The adult group most frequently recalled discouragement in graduate school, while they remembered more encouragement as undergraduates and in high school. Ernest's findings suggest that many teachers may have stereotypic views of mathematics as a masculine domain, and Casserly's extremely supportive teachers come from only thirteen high schools in the nation in which girls are enrolled in relatively large numbers in the advanced courses. Such teachers may be very atypical.

Whether the sex of the teacher is important is not totally clear. Several of the successful intervention programs were taught by women, as was the remediation program described by MacDonald. Supportive teachers of both sexes were identified by Casserly. It seems likely that the attitudes and behaviors of teachers, not their sex per se, are critical.

Peers

Ernest reports that more high-school students believe boys are better than girls at mathematics than believe the converse. Fennema notes that high-school boys are more likely than the girls to agree with stereotyped statements about mathematics as a male domain.

Helson found a great deal of variability among creative female mathematicians, but two factors seemed to be common to all: (a) they were feminine, not masculine, in personality orientation, and (b) they were introverted rather than extroverted. One might speculate that introverted women are less vulnerable to peer pressure against intellectual attainment, especially if they are comfortable with their own sense of femininity.

The importance of the female peer group to support achievement and course-taking is suggested in the anecdotal reports of girls in the Casserly study and in the studies of intervention programs for the mathematically gifted. MacDonald's successful program for adult women in college also utilized all-female groups. Although Fennema cautions against all-girl classes, it may be important to have large numbers of girls involved in programs that are accelerative or lead to taking advanced courses in mathematics. Indeed, the early identification and "tracking" of the mathematically gifted may be very crucial to their later willingness to continue the study of mathematics. Perhaps there is a need for occasional groupings of girls only in order to explore feelings and reassure girls that they are not unfeminine or odd because they like mathematics.

School Practices and Policies

Brody and Fox, and Sells suggest that a major cause of sex differences in mathematics course-taking is the mere fact that advanced mathematics courses, unlike English courses, are optional in high school. Thus, the message conveyed is that mathematics is not equally necessary for everyone, and, unfortunately, far more girls interpret the message to mean it is not important for them. They are sometimes, of course, helped to reach this conclusion by the type of advice they receive from parents or counselors, as described by Casserly and by Luchins and Luchins.

Studies by Fennema, as well as the studies of the mathematically precocious, suggest that girls do not perceive the usefulness of mathematics for their future as clearly as boys do. This may be because girls are somewhat less career-oriented or because girls who have career goals are considering only stereotypically feminine career areas; and these stereotyped views may be reinforced by counselors, as found in the study by Casserly, or by parents, as found by Brody and Fox. Better counseling services for students and, perhaps, for their parents and integration of career awareness activities into the mathematics curriculum would seem desirable. The importance of exposure to female role models was mentioned by Ernest and by Tobin and Fox. The need for better counseling, role models, and career education was stressed by mathematicians in the Luchins and Luchins study.

At present, there are very few programs designed for the academically talented, especially in mathematics, at the elementary- and junior-high-school levels. Studies of the mathematically gifted and of young women in Advanced Placement calculus suggest that such programs could do a great deal to foster more achievement among girls, especially if the programs were begun in elementary school, involved sizable numbers of girls, and led gradually but forcibly to the study of calculus, physics, statistics, computer science, and so forth, in the high-school years.

DIRECTIONS FOR RESEARCH

There can be several interesting directions for new research efforts. Four broad areas of research might be examined. First, more research is needed to identify precisely any real cognitive-processing differences between the sexes that have implications for the teaching and learning of mathematics. Second, in applied settings, attempts to remediate or intervene could be conducted in accordance with principles of experimental or quasi-experimental design so that not only could the program impact be evaluated, but such studies could shed light on other basic research issues. Third, longitudinal descriptive studies and naturalistic observation could look at the dynamics and social processes within schools and homes that promote or inhibit achievement in mathematics. Fourth, intensive case studies of mathematically gifted students, their parents, and their teachers should be conducted. Some of these studies might be longitudinal, focusing on students before, during, and after special facilitation.

Cognitive Studies

Although it seems clear that sex-role socialization and the perception of mathematics as a male domain account for some of the observed sex differences in course-taking and career pursuits, evidence has not yet totally eliminated the possibility of basic sex differences in aptitude or learning styles with respect to mathematics. Fennema finds that sex differences in mathematical achievement are small in large, heterogeneous samples when differential course-taking is controlled, but differences among the mathematically precocious are large and can not be accounted for by differential course-taking alone. What we need to know is whether or not there are any real differences in mathematical reasoning ability that are not a result of differential learning. Some questions of concern are:

1. Do sex differences among the mathematically precocious exist prior to grade seven?

2. Do mathematically precocious males learn more mathematics outside of school than mathematically precocious females do? Is this the cause or effect of ability differences?

3. Is there a true sex difference in spatial ability, independent of early learning experiences, that would account for differential interest and study of topological or geometric topics in mathematics?

4. Are sex differences in mathematics the same in all cultures or ethnic groups?

5. Is it possible to disprove the notion that mathematical ability is a sex-linked inherited trait?

6. Do girls and boys use the same or different strategies to solve mathematical problems?

Experiments in Change

Although this volume presents several different types of intervention and remediation studies, there is much that is not known, such as which strategies are best at which points in time and, for each strategy, what the most salient features are. Some examples of specific research questions are as follows:

1. How lasting are the effects of exposure to a few role models for a short period of time? Must the role model be present as a continuing influence?

2. If brief exposure to a role model is effective, would video-taped or filmed presentation work as well as contact and interaction with live role models?

3. How are teacher attitudes about women and mathematics related to their behavior in the classroom? What changes, if any, would occur in teacher-pupil interactions in a classroom after teachers experienced training to raise their awareness of the problems?

4. Are mixed-sex and same-sex mathematics programs differentially effective for boys and girls if level of content and student abilities are controlled? Is there a critical number of girls needed to prevent attrition in accelerated or optional mathematics courses?

5. What is the most effective way to teach the applications of mathematics to a variety of career areas? Should career education be separate from the regular mathematics program or integrated with it?

6. Would it be more effective to change course-taking behavior directly by requiring four years of high-school mathematics than to try to change teacher, counselor, and student attitudes about the importance of studying mathematics?

7. If advanced mathematics courses were taught with greater emphasis on applications to problems in the social sciences and economics, would they be more appealing to girls than current courses?

8. Should the intervention take place as early as possible, or are there crucial times when it must take place in order for it to be most effective?

Longitudinal and Observational Studies

There are many general questions about the process of sex-role socialization, the dynamics of family environments, and the social environments
of schools and classrooms—all of which are of general interest in developmental, social, and educational psychology—that are appropriate to study,
keeping their relationship to mathematics learning in mind. Some examples
are:

1. What child-rearing philosophies and practices promote mathematical
and general intellectual interest, competencies, and achievement motivation
in boys and girls?

2. To what extent are sex differences in play in the preschool years
related to later abilities and interests? Are these activities encouraged or
reinforced for boys and girls?

3. How do differential values and interests develop from childhood to
adolescence? How are these values and interests shaped by significant
others?

4. What are the dynamics of the adolescent peer culture that promote or
inhibit the intellectual risk-taking and mathematical and scientific interests
and experiences of girls?

5. In what ways do teachers selectively reinforce different behaviors
with respect to academic achievement in girls and boys?

6. Are general societal attitudes about appropriate careers for women,
especially mathematical and scientific ones, changing? Are there fewer
overt and covert barriers to women's success in professional careers now
than ten or twenty years ago?

7. Are expectations of parents more or less potent than expectations of
teachers or peers in promoting self-confidence with respect to mathematics?

The Mathematically Gifted

A prime group of interest are those boys and girls who exhibit superior
mathematical reasoning ability as early as grade seven. Such students are
the most likely candidates for high-level professional careers. Research is
needed to explore the family backgrounds and educational experiences of
these students, as well as the amount of support and encouragement they
receive, in order to help explain sex differences in achievement and
participation in mathematics and careers. Some examples of specific
research questions follow:

1. In what ways are mathematically able boys and girls alike and different
with respect to variables assumed to be relevant to the study of advanced

mathematics and career choices (that is, self-confidence as a learner of mathematics; willingness to take educational and intellectual risks; perception of usefulness of studying mathematics; enjoyment of mathematical activities; career interests; and access to role models)? What are the inter-relationships among these variables for girls? for boys?

2. What relationships, if any, exist between socioeconomic variables and family-constellation variables—such as education of parents, occupation of parents, birth order, and sex of siblings—and mathematical abilities and interests? Are these relationships the same or different for boys and girls? for girls with high levels of confidence and enjoyment of mathematics and girls with low levels?

3. How do mathematically able youths perceive the support or lack of support for self-confidence, enjoyment of mathematics, intellectual risk-taking, and career choices from significant others in their lives (parents, teachers, peers)? Are perceptions of support independent of socioeconomic and family-constellation variables? Are they different for boys and girls?

4. What are the attitudes and behaviors of parents that foster or inhibit the development of self-confidence and enjoyment of mathematics among mathematically able boys and girls? How do parents encourage learning, self-confidence, intellectual risk-taking, and career choices in mathematics and science? Do they stereotype mathematics as more appropriate for men than for women?

5. Do mathematically able boys and girls learn mathematical and related skills at home before entering school or before topics or skills are taught in school? Who teaches them? Are there differences between boys and girls or between girls high on measures of self-confidence and enjoyment and girls low on these measures? Is the learning of mathematics in the home related to measures of self-confidence, enjoyment, and career interests or to socioeconomic and family-constellation variables?

6. What are the characteristics, attitudes, and behaviors of teachers who are perceived by highly able girls as having had a positive influence on the development of their self-confidence and interest in the study of mathematics and/or related careers?

DIRECTIONS FOR CHANGE

If we believe that sex differences in mathematics course-taking in high school, college, and graduate training and the pursuit of careers in fields that require high-level mathematical skills are at least partially caused by socio-environmental and educational factors, then strategies for change must seek to reduce or eliminate the sex-typing of mathematics and related careers as masculine domains and to provide more encouragement and support for women's achievement in the classroom and on the job. It appears that such support must begin early in the home and be reinforced in the schools and by society at large. At present, there is a need for three different approaches: (1) remediation for past victims of the mathematical mystique, (2) intervention for those young women caught in the period of transition from sexist to androgynous conceptions of intellectual abilities and mathematical competence, and (3) the prevention of future inequities in the lives and mathematics education of young women.

Remediation

How might one remediate women who have fallen under the spell of the mathematical mystique and thus have avoided studying advanced mathematics when they were indeed actually capable of mastering such material? Two populations of adult women seem the most likely candidates for remedial programs: (1) women who are considering entering the labor force after a period of unemployment outside the home and are seeking some post-secondary training to prepare them for a career and (2) women who are currently employed but who aspire to advancement within their career field or a shift to another career field and for whom new mathematical skills and competence would facilitate advancement.

The program described by MacDonald in chapter 8 of this volume is an excellent model for programs for such women, regardless of the level of skills to be mastered. The MacDonald model employs sympathetic female teachers as role models, female-peer-group reinforcement and camaraderie, and diagnostic testing and sequential training of basic skills to enhance feelings of competence before the student ventures into more traditional and advanced mathematics courses. It is interesting to note that for some of the students in her classes career aspirations were raised after a successful mathematical learning experience. On the other hand, the initial entry into the program was typically motivated by students' needs to prepare for a career.

MacDonald's model is not, however, the only prototype currently being advocated for remedial purposes. An internship-mentor model for professional women and minority males has been developed to increase the mathematical/statistical research skills of educators and social scientists (Epstein 1979). Tobias (1978) advocates a counseling approach to reduce "math anxiety" for adult "avoiders" or "phobics" before or in conjunction with mathematics courses.

To date, too little experimental research has been done to determine precisely what program dimensions are most salient for specific populations of adult women. The best guess might be that mathematics training that is conducted in a nurturing environment, such as the MacDonald program, and combines career counseling with sound principles of diagnostic-prescriptive teaching to close the "gaps" in a person's mathematical background before launching him or her into the "mainstream" of college mathematics courses would be the ideal.

Intervention

The target population for intervention attempts would be young women and girls who have not yet completed high school or college, for whom the choices of careers and course-taking are still open or reversible. A key group within this population would be mathematically talented adolescents, as described in this volume by Fox and Cohn and by Brody and Fox in chapters 7 and 10, respectively, and in previous volumes of this series. Intervention can have one or more of three goals: It can be aimed at influencing girls' attitudes and behaviors directly; it can seek to make changes in the standard learning environments; and/or it can try to influence attitudes and behaviors of the significant others in a girl's life, such as parents and teachers.

Attempts to change girls' attitudes and behaviors directly by means of special extracurricular activities include career-education classes, counseling sessions, and other types of experimental programs aimed at broadening girls' career horizons and/or impacting their course-taking plans and/or increasing their self-confidence as students of mathematics. One-day career workshops designed to expose high-school and college students to female role models employed in business, government, industry, and academia have been funded by the National Science Foundation for several years. A good example of this type of program is the series of workshops conducted by the Lawrence Hall of Science in Berkeley, California. A more intensive career awareness experience, including some instruction in statistics and computer science, is described by Tobin and Fox in chapter 11 of this volume. Another approach recommended for high-school students is an internship-mentor program, in which students are assigned to a laboratory or other work setting under the direction of an interested female scientist or other professional.

It is not yet clear whether direct intervention of this type is best for groups of girls only or for mixed-sex groups. There appear to be some advantages to having an all-girl program; for example, girls may be more willing to take intellectual risks or explore feelings and concerns more openly when there are no boys in the group. On the other hand, male peers' sexist attitudes or beliefs also need to be changed so that they can accept and support changes in attitudes and behaviors of the girls. Most girls will still want to date and marry. It may be futile to raise or change women's career aspirations and commitment if their future boyfriends and husbands will not support and encourage their career and educational activities. The two-career family can only be successful if both partners agree on the values and goals for each family member. Perhaps career education and counseling should utilize both mixed-sex and same-sex groups.

Although direct intervention as described above can be highly success-ful in heightening girls' perception of the value of the study of mathematics and raising or expanding career aspirations, such programs may not have lasting effects if there are no concomitant changes in their mathematics learning environments or the home. While girls may sign up for more mathematics and science courses, they may not continue in them or enjoy them if the climate of the classes or the behaviors and attitudes of the teachers are negative or nonsupportive. If the new values of the girls conflict with those of their parents, the girls may not have the ego-strength or the desire to oppose their parents' views. Thus, direct-intervention programs may be most potent if they are accompanied by changes in the school setting and the home.

Changes in the school setting, and in the mathematics classroom in particular, could involve a number of administrative and curriculum changes, such as simply requiring all students to take four years of mathematics and science in high school. If advanced mathematics, like senior-year English, were perceived as equally necessary for all students, achievement dif-ferences between the sexes might be greatly reduced. This might be the easiest way to increase the numbers of girls in advanced classes. Also, early identification of the mathematically able student, accompanied by long-range planning to ensure that such students, male and female, are en-couraged to take advanced courses in high school, as described by Casserly in chapter 9, seems to be desirable.

If advanced mathematics is to remain optional, perhaps some courses could be designed to appeal more to those girls who have strong social and esthetic interests. At the high-school and college levels, advanced mathe-matics courses are typically designed with a theoretical rather than an applied focus. There is no reason why much of "good mathematics" can't be taught within the context of the uses of mathematics in the social sciences or in architecture and urban planning. Some efforts to rename and "humanize" mathematics courses have been made at the college level in such schools as Wellesley.

If research efforts reveal any basic information-processing or cognitive style differences between the sexes that can be translated into changes in teaching and learning approaches to mathematical concepts, some more basic changes might be made in mathematics instruction in the future. If many females do indeed have a spatial deficit that is not a function of early learning experiences (that is, differential play with manipulative space in the preschool years), then perhaps the current approach to calculus is not as appropriate for these women as some other approaches might be. At present, we know too little about sex differences in the organization and operations of the brain to do more than speculate about these matters.

Several of the research studies reported in this volume suggest that attitudes and behaviors of parents and teachers are important to the development of female mathematicians and girls who elect to take Advanced Placement courses in calculus and the physical sciences. Therefore, the development of training and counseling programs for parents and teachers may be very critical. Indeed, if all parents, teachers, and the general public were sensitized to their sexist beliefs and changed their attitudes and behaviors, the mathematical mystique might vanish into the air without any other intervention being necessary. It may very well be that training for parents and teachers is the key to eventual prevention of mathematics avoidance and/or feelings of low confidence and ignorance of the value of the study of mathematics.

Prevention

Although the process by which one might construct a world in which mathematical competence were valued equally for all and in which achievement differences on tests, in course-taking, and in careers at every level and area were not related to sex is unclear, we can identify conditions in the home, the school, and the society that might give rise to an androgynous view of mathematics and related careers. Thus, we can speculate as to what life and school would be like in a world where boys and girls were similarly encouraged to develop interest and competence in mathematics and all career areas were considered equally acceptable or possible for women and men.

In an ideal home of the future (that is, ideal with respect to mathematics learning), parents would have expectations and aspirations for their children with respect to mathematics learning and careers that would not be a function of their sex. College and career plans would be discussed with girls as often as with boys. Thus, boys *and* girls would have access to toys involving spatial or mechanical manipulation (such as blocks, dump trucks, and so on) and would receive the same positive reinforcement for playing with such toys as they would for play with dolls or coloring books. In such a home, intellectual achievements for both sexes would be valued equally with social and physical achievements. Household chores would not be assigned on the basis of sex-role stereotypes. Perhaps in this wonderful "brave new world" mothers would not be heard to utter a discouraging word such as "Ask your father—I was always poor at math"; nor would fathers say, "Boys don't make passes at girls who can calculate better than they can."

Would it not be marvelous if children left the above-described ideal home for a school in which textbooks and tests did not reflect sex-role stereotypes; mathematics was required for everyone; career counseling and career education was part of the basic school program and stressed nonstereotyped views of women and men in the world of work. In such a school mathematically gifted boys and girls would receive similar, good treatment, and none would be viewed as odd or misfit by teachers or peers. Indeed, in such a school mathematical competence, intellectual risk-taking, curiosity, and high levels of achievement would be expected and respected equally in boys and in girls.

Such nurturing conditions in the home and school would need to be reinforced in the society as a whole. Thus, advertising, comic strips, television, and so forth, would not carry sexist images such as the stereotyped picture of a mathematically inept female seeking help from a logical, competent male. If stupidity can not be erased as a source of humor, at least let it be equally probable for men and women to be equally stupid about mathematics. More important, perhaps, than the messages of the media may be the messages to women about their true place in the world of work. If sex discrimination exists in hiring, promotion, and salary, and if society seeks to "punish," or at least burden, the working mother with extra responsibilities and guilt, then we must expect the story told in school or at mother's knee of equality, of "being anything you want to be," to be as harmful and cruel a myth as the other, older myth of the mathematical mystique.

In our modern technological society, an understanding and appreciation of mathematics is becoming more and more important in almost every aspect of human endeavor. If women are to participate equally with men in solving life's day-to-day problems and in designing the shape of the future, then they should not be encouraged or allowed to avoid the study of mathematics. It is hoped that the research studies and ideas discussed in this volume will stimulate each reader to examine his or her own ideas and behaviors with respect to women and the mathematical mystique.

REFERENCES

Bryden, M. P. 1979. Evidence for sex-related differences in cerebral organization. In *Sex-related differences in cognitive functioning: Developmental issues,* ed. M. A. Wittig and A. C. Petersen, pp. 121-43. New York: Academic Press.

Epstein, J. L. 1979. *An opportunity structures model for postdoctoral programs in educational research.* Center for Social Organization of Schools, report no. 272. Baltimore: The Johns Hopkins University.

Maccoby, E. E., and Jacklin, C. N. 1974. *The psychology of sex differences.* Stanford: Stanford University Press.

Reinisch, J. M.; Gandelman, R.; and Spiegel, F. S. 1979. Prenatal influences on cognitive abilities: Data from experimental animals and human and endocrine syndromes. In *Sex-related differences in cognitive functioning: De-*

velopmental issues, ed. M. A. Wittig and A. C. Petersen, pp. 215-39. New York: Academic Press.

Tobias, S. 1978. *Overcoming math anxiety.* New York: W. W. Norton.

Wittig, M. A. 1979. Genetic influences on sex-related differences in intellectual performance: Theoretical and methodological issues. In *Sex-related differences in cognitive functioning: Developmental issues,* ed. M. A. Wittig and A. C. Petersen, pp. 21-65. New York: Academic Press.

Name Index

Italic numbers indicate sections of the book written by the person indexed.

Ackerman, M., 92
Aiken, L. R., 77, 85, 90, 91, 100, 110
Alexandroff, P. S., 61
Allport, G. W., 181, 189
Alspektor, R. A., 69, 74
Angel, M. F., 174, 177
Astin, H. S., 99, 100, 107, 110, 174, 177, 180, 190

Bachman, A. M., 86, 90
Bailey, D. E., 32, 54
Barbee, A. H., 180, 191
Barron, F. X., 23, 25, 52, 53
Bean, J. P., 173, 177
Beckman, L., 53
Bell, E. T., 20, 21, 94, 110
Bem, S. L., 104, 110
Berglund, G. W., 67, 74, 87, 92, 100, 110
Bergman, H. G., 21
Berman, E., 119
Bers, L., 19
Bisconti, A. S., 107, 110
Bittinger, M. L., 119, 120, 135, 137
Black, J. D., 25
Block, J., 25, 51, 52
Blum, L., 73, 74
Blumberg, H., iii, xi
Bobbe, C. N., 87, 91
Boring, P. Z., 15, 21
Brody, L. E., ii, iii, vi, ix, 3, *164-78*, 181, 183, 190, 197, 198, 204
Bronowski, J., 84, 91
Brookover, W. B., 86, 91
Brophy, J. E., 88, 89, 92, 173, 178
Bryden, M. P., 195, 207

Callahan, L. G., 76, 77, 86, 91, 92
Campbell, D. P., 34, 52
Campbell, V., 179
Carey, G. L., 87, 91
Casserly, P. L., vi, ix, 2, 3, 89, *138-63*, 139, 163, 173, 184, 197, 198, 205
Centra, J. A., 8, 21
Chinn, P., 179
Christensen, P. R., 85, 92
Clark, R. S., xi, 3, 184
Clements, M. A., 81, 82, 91
Cohn, S. J., ii, v, ix, 2, 67, 82, *94-111*, 104, 105, 204
Colangelo, N., 111
Coleman, J. S., 68, 71, 74
Conway, J. K., 89, 91
Cooke, G., 179
Courant, R., 20, 21

Cox, C. M., 94, 110
Crandall, V. J., 86, 91
Crosswhite, F. J., 86, 91
Crovo, M., 179
Crutchfield, R. S., 24, 29, 34, 53
Cuca, J., 8, 21
Cunnion, M., 179
Currier, B., 118

Datta, L., 38, 53
Denham, S. A., 100, 106, 110, 167, 171, 178, 181, 183, 190
Denmark, F., 53
Dornbusch, S. M., 62, 65, 67, 74
Douglas, K., 179
Dubreil-Jacotin, M.-L., 14, 21
Dweck, S., 190

Eiduson, B. T., 53
Epstein, J. L., 203, 207
Erdmann, R., x
Erdmann, W., x
Erikson, E., 39, 41, 53
Ernest, J., v, ix, 2, *57-65,* 58, 62, 65, 67, 82, 120, 137, 196, 197, 198
Espinosa, R. W., 67, 74

Feldman, D. H., 88, 93
Fennema, E., v, ix, 2, 62, 65, *76-93,* 77, 80, 83, 85, 86, 87, 91, 93, 99, 173, 178, 197, 199
Fernandez, C., 67, 74
Fink, M. B., 86, 91
Flanagan, J. C., 77, 78, 91
Foster, J., 82, 91
Fox, L. H., ii, iii, v, vi, ix, xi, *1-3,* 67, 82, *94-111,* 91, 95, 100, 106, 110, 111, *164-78,* 165, 166, 167, 170, 171, 172, 174, 177, 178, *179-91,* 181, 182, 183, 190, *195-208,* 197, 198, 204
French, J. W., 85, 91
Fruchter, B., 84, 92
Fry, D. E., 139, 163

Gandelman, R., 195, 207
Gauss, C. F., 94
George, W. C., ii, 106, 107, 110, 111, 167, 178, 191
Glennon, V. J., 76, 77, 86, 91, 92
Good, T. L., 88, 89, 92, 173, 178
Gough, H. G., 25, 26, 27, 44, 53
Green, R. F., 85, 92
Greenberger, E., 180, 190
Gruber, H. E., 53

209

The Johns Hopkins University Press

This book was set in Alphatype Times Roman text and
display by David Lorton from a design by Charles West. It
was printed on 50-lb. #66 Eggshell Offset Wove and bound
by The Maple Press Company.